PRO L. MURENA
ORATIO

CICERO
PRO MURENA

Edited with Introduction,
Notes and Vocabulary by

C. Macdonald, M.A.

Bristol Classical Press
(by arrangement with Macmillan Education Ltd)

Cover illustration: Cicero, from a portrait bust,
Vatican Museums, Rome

First published by Macmillan & Co. Ltd in 1969

Reprinted, with permission, in 1982, 1983, 1988, 1995 by
Bristol Classical Press
an imprint of
Gerald Duckworth & Co. Ltd
The Old Piano Factory
48 Hoxton Square, London N1 6PB

A catalogue record for this book is available
from the British Library

ISBN 0-86292-010-8

Available in USA and Canada from:
Focus Information Group
PO Box 369
Newburyport
MA 01950

Printed in Great Britain by
Booksprint, Bristol

CONTENTS

PREFACE

THE purpose of this edition is to provide for members of Sixth Forms and for Students who do not have to make a specialist study of this speech the material necessary for an intelligent reading of the *pro Murena*. The introduction and notes seek to strike a balance between linguistic and historical material. Their aim is three-fold: to help the reader to translate the Latin accurately; to appreciate Cicero's literary and rhetorical powers; and to follow the argument with an adequate understanding of the historical, constitutional, and legal issues involved. It is assumed that the reader is not meeting Cicero for the first time; but even so, at the beginning of the notes in particular, detailed assistance is given. It was thought better to be too liberal rather than too sparing with help and thus ensure that the reader gets quickly under way.

The text is that of the Oxford Classical Texts edited by A. C. Clark, and reference is made to textual problems only when they have to be introduced in order to explain a passage satisfactorily.

It did not seem appropriate, in view of the reader for whom this book is intended, to make detailed references in the notes to ancient sources and modern works of scholarship. There are instead a Select Bibliography containing a list of books which can be conveniently consulted for further information, and a limited number of references in the notes to books or journals which are likely to be accessible.

This practice has the defect of failing to acknowledge my indebtedness to many whose names do not appear but whose work I have consulted. I therefore welcome this opportunity of declaring my heavy debt to them, but for the defects of this volume I alone am responsible.

C. M.

INTRODUCTION

1. CHRONOLOGICAL TABLE 70–63 B.C.

	Rome and Italy	**Abroad**
70	First consulship of Pompey and Crassus *Lex Aurelia* Verrine Orations Restoration of the powers of the tribunate	
69	Cicero plebeian aedile[1]	Lucullus invades Armenia
68		Mithridates returns to Pontus
67	*Lex Gabinia* *Lex Calpurnia*	Pompey's campaign against the pirates Victory of Mithridates at Zela
66	Cicero praetor *Lex Manilia*	Pompey supersedes Lucullus and defeats Mithridates
65	Crassus censor	
63	Cicero consul Catilinarian conspiracy *Pro Murena* between 8 November and 5 December	Death of Mithridates. Pompey organises his conquests

[1] See Broughton, *The Magistrates of the Roman Republic*, vol. II, p. 132.

2. LIFE OF CICERO

MARCUS TULLIUS CICERO was born at Arpinum, a Volscian hill-town, on 3 January 106 B.C. and was killed on 7 December 43 B.C. on the instructions of M. Antonius. His family was well-to-do and had links with senatorial circles at Rome. His father, a member of the Equestrian Order, was a man of literary tastes and took Marcus and Quintus, his younger brother, to Rome where they were given a good schooling by the leading philosophers and orators of the day. In 90 or 91 he assumed the *toga virilis*, came into contact with Q. Mucius Scaevola the Augur and, on his death, with Q. Scaevola the Pontifex Maximus. Here, amongst others who were to be his lifelong friends, he met Sulpicius. This was an important stage in his life because it saw the start of his legal career and brought him into contact with many members of the governing class.

During the Social War he served in 89 with Sulla's army but took no part in the subsequent civil wars. Soon after Sulla's victory he accepted his first brief when he defended P. Quinctius in a civil case and had to face two of the most powerful nobles of the time, Q. Hortensius and L. Marcius Philippus. In the following year he was involved in his first criminal case and defended Sextus Roscius, a victim of one of Sulla's men in the civil war. He had to tread carefully, and the success of his speech helped both to establish his professional standing and to confirm his political position as a supporter of the nobility.

For the next two years (79–77), the victim of ill health, he was in the East pursuing his study of

rhetoric in Greece and Asia Minor. On his return to
Rome he resumed his activity in the courts, particularly
on behalf of the equestrian *publicani*. Attention is
drawn in the notes to Cicero's skill at riding two horses –
the nobility and *Equites*.[1] He was a candidate for the
quaestorship of 76 and was elected, thanks to the
political support which he had won by his work in court
and his success in avoiding the antagonism of either
Senate or *Equites*. Under one of the provisions of
Sulla's constitution he was now automatically a member
of the Senate, and all the time his court work was
enlarging his *clientela*. His great triumph came in 70
when he secured the condemnation of Verres in the face
of Hortensius and three members of one of the most
powerful families in Rome, the Metelli.

His legal success was enhanced in the same year by
his election as aedile in spite of attempted bribery by
Verres. This was an important office because it gave a
man, if he could lay his hands on the necessary money.
the chance to win easy popularity with the people by
putting on lavish public games. An effective show of
this sort could be of great assistance in attaining the
next step in the *cursus honorum*, the praetorship.
Cicero was not extravagant in his games but this
moderation did not act to his detriment, because not
only was he elected praetor in 67 but he headed the poll,
and in his year of office presided over the *quaestio de
repetundis*. In this year he made his first speech on a
question of public policy, the speech *pro lege Manilia*,
in which he strongly supported the proposal of Manilius
in the face of bitter opposition from the extreme

[1] See pp. 60 and 97.

Optimates.[1] While laying him open to the charge of trying to be all things to all men, this speech which pleased many nobles, *Equites*, and the people, may also be seen as containing the seeds of the wish to establish a *concordia ordinum*.

Another speech in the same year, on behalf of Cluentius, saw Cicero again take up a position acceptable to both *Equites* and Senate. Even though arguments in forensic speeches do not always, owing to the exigencies of the case, reflect his genuine political feelings, this speech can probably be held to show what Cicero really thought.

Cicero's speech in support of Pompey had not endeared him to Crassus, and the next few years saw Cicero and Crassus move further apart as Cicero, although a supporter of Pompey whom the Optimates feared, became steadily more conservative. He played his part in thwarting Crassus' schemes and the story of events leading up to his consulship and of his consulship itself is told elsewhere.[2]

Cicero, impressed by the way in which moderate men from all backgrounds had rallied under his leadership against the extremists, now hoped to establish a lasting *concordia ordinum*. There was, however, one important obstacle to be surmounted – Pompey. He had cast himself in the role of Saviour of his Fatherland and did not care to see the mantle that he coveted sitting so easily upon the shoulders of the *novus homo* who had forestalled him.

In the event, when Pompey returned, the relationship between the two men, in spite of Crassus' attempt

[1] See p. xvii.   [2] See p. xviii f.

to make bad blood between them by eulogising Cicero in the Senate, was friendlier than it might have been. Cicero's hopes, however, were not to last long. The *concordia ordinum* was soon shaken by the Clodius scandal, by the weakness of the equestrian order, and by the stupidity of some of the Optimates in their extreme antipathy towards Pompey. And, although Cicero had ' arrived ' politically, the boasting of a *novus homo* about his achievement in 63, his execution of nobles without trial, and his financial difficulties caused by his new status were weakening the strength of his position in aristocratic circles.

In 61, realising that his ideal was collapsing about his ears, Cicero turned more and more towards Pompey, but rejected the overtures of the ' First Triumvirate ' in loyalty to the ideal of constitutional government. He did not have to wait long to pay the penalty for his choice. Increasing disillusionment with Pompey soon grew into fears for his own safety. When Clodius as tribune in 58 set about securing Cicero's exile for executing the Catilinarian conspirators without trial, a request to Pompey for help was met by nothing more than bland assurances. Caesar offered ways of escape which Cicero was too honourable to accept. As a result he was driven into exile in March 58.

Clodius and his roughs now turned their attention on Pompey who in his own self-interest supported Cicero's friends in their efforts to secure his return. This they finally secured, after a long struggle, on 4 September 57.

Having on his return thanked Pompey and the Senate, supported the proposal for fifteen days' thanksgiving for Caesar's victories in Gaul, and proposed that Pompey be appointed commissioner in charge of the city's corn-supply, he then in his defence of P. Sestius, who had been accused *de vi*, called for all moderates to support the Senate and the republican constitution. A union of all loyal citizens drawn from a wider spectrum of the community than hitherto, resisting the pressure of Populares and would-be autocrats, and ensuring *cum dignitate otium*, internal tranquillity for the people of Rome in which political power would lie in the hands of the 'Best Man'. was to be the new body of Optimates,

These men were to replace the 'Triumvirate' which he mistakenly thought was beginning to fall apart. He attacked Caesar's agrarian legislation, hoping to force Pompey and Caesar further apart, but all that he and his political colleagues achieved was a swift reaction from the threatened partner. The 'Triumvirate' was patched up at the Conference of Luca in 56 and Cicero was given the choice of doing the Triumvirs' will or taking the consequences of his disobedience. He chose subservience, and his speech *de provinciis consularibus*, urging that Caesar should retain his Gallic command, was one of the fruits of his choice.

For the remainder of the decade until the outbreak of the Civil War Cicero remained on reasonably friendly terms with both Caesar and Pompey. This dual allegiance, however, became increasingly difficult. The death of Crassus in the Battle of Carrhae in 53 and the death of Caesar's daughter Julia, who was married to Pompey, removed two of the links holding Caesar and Pompey together and as they drew apart Cicero inclined more and more to Pompey.

During the years between 52 and 46 Cicero made few speeches in either courts or Senate, and in 51 was the unwilling proconsul of Cilicia, an office forced upon him by the temporary shortage of eligible ex-magistrates caused by Pompey's legislation aimed at discouraging extortion in the provinces. From his year's absence he hurried back to a city facing inevitable civil war. After hesitation he joined the Pompeian forces, but when the fighting was over made his peace with the victorious Caesar. Though severely disapproving of Caesar's unconstitutional rule, he had no part in the dictator's murder.

In February 45 he had suffered the bitter blow of his beloved Tullia's death and consoled himself with an intense literary activity in which he was immersed when Caesar died. He now became bitterly opposed to Caesar's successor, Antony, and in the autumn of 44 delivered the first of the violent attacks upon him which, in imitation of Demosthenes's attacks upon Philip of Macedon, he called *Philippics*. The last of this series was delivered in April 43, and of the remaining months of his life we know little. Livy tells us that he faced death bravely and his estimate of the man, preserved for us by Seneca, is as just as any: ' si quis tamen virtutibus vitia pensaret, vir magnus et memorabilis fuit, et in cuius laudes exsequendas Cicerone laudatore opus fuerit.'

3. The Historical Background

The consulship of Pompey and Crassus in 70 saw the final disappearance of the contentious elements of

Sulla's constitution. The tribunate received back the powers which Sulla had taken away, the censorship was revived, the two consuls of 72 were elected censors, and sixty-four members were expelled from the Senate.

An event of the year, however, which had other far-reaching results was the prosecution of Verres by Cicero, who had been retained by the Sicilian provincials whom Verres had plundered during his praetorship. The case not only provided a bitter indictment of senatorial government in the provinces but ended the senatorial monopoly of the law-courts and established Cicero as the leading advocate at Rome.

At the end of the year neither consul received a pro-consular command and both retired into private life, leaving the field clear for Optimate candidates to be elected to the senior magistracies. In 67, however, the tribunes, once more men of spirit and talent now that the political restrictions upon holders of the office had been removed, were active. C. Cornelius sought to improve the administration of justice, while A. Gabinius proposed that a consular – Pompey was clearly in his mind – should be appointed to combat the menace of the pirates with an *imperium* of three years' duration and various other provisions to ensure that he had the authority and the resources adequate for his task. The *lex Gabinia* was only finally passed amid disorder after it had been denounced by the Optimate leaders, Catulus and Hortensius, and Gabinius resisted by two other tribunes, Roscius Otho and Trebellius.

Pompey departed for his brief and successful campaign, but in his absence from Rome Lucullus' conduct of the war against Mithridates came under increasing criticism in the capital. He was accused by his political enemies, the *Equites*, of prolonging the war for his own glory. These enemies he had acquired by his just settlement of the finances of the province of Asia to the detriment of their financial interests. Each year his command was reduced: in 69 the province of Asia was taken from him; in 68, Cilicia; in 67 Gabinius passed a law which assigned Bithynia and Pontus to the consul of that year, M'. Acilius Glabrio. Then in the following year, the tribune C. Manilius proposed that Cilicia, Bithynia and Pontus, and the command against Mithridates should be entrusted to Pompey who was to retain the forces allotted to him for his campaign against the pirates. Caesar was again a supporter of a bill to give Pompey a command and Cicero in his praetorship spoke in its favour.

Pompey was in Cilicia when he heard of the unprecedented powers given him under the *lex Manilia* for the struggle with Mithridates. By 63 he had succeeded where so many other Roman generals had failed; Mithridates was dead, and he now devoted his attention to the settlement of the East. He returned to Rome at the end of 62 to celebrate in the following year a triumph of outstanding magnificence for his victories over the pirates and over Mithridates.

In Rome Crassus must during the years after the passing of the *lex Gabinia* have become increasingly envious of Pompey's success and power. He had the foresight to realise that much though his wealth could achieve for him in the world of Roman politics, it could not withstand Pompey's army should he care to use it on his return from the East. The shadow of Sulla continued to lie heavy upon men's minds for many years after the sixties.

Although the Optimate leaders, including Hortensius, must have been just as – if not more – fearful of Pompey's return, no political alliance between them and Crassus was formed.

The so-called First Catilinarian Conspiracy was the occasion for the start of the political struggle in Rome itself. P. Autronius Paetus and P. Cornelius Sulla were elected consuls for 65 but under the *lex Calpurnia* of 67 were condemned for *ambitus*. A second election had to be held in which one of the potential candidates was L. Sergius Catilina, an impoverished patrician who had served with Sulla in the Civil Wars but who had been accused of extortion while propraetor in Africa in 67–6. The presiding consul refused to accept Catiline as a candidate and L. Aurelius Cotta and L. Manlius Torquatus were elected consuls. A plot appears to have been formed to murder the consuls on 1 January 65 and replace them by Autronius and either Sulla or Catiline. The scheme failed and the details of what exactly was planned and what actually happened are obscure as is the part played by Crassus in it.

Catiline was duly brought to trial for extortion but secured an acquittal, and now prepared with the backing of Crassus to stand at the consular elections in the summer of 64 with C. Antonius. These candidates were unacceptable to the Optimates and in the absence of any strong candidate of their own, despite the fact that he was a *novus homo*, a supporter of Pompey, and the recipient of equestrian support, Cicero was accepted as a man more likely to support the aims of the *nobiles* than the other candidates. In the elections Cicero in his *Oratio in Toga Candida* gave dark hints of sinister backers behind Catiline and secured his own election to the consulship of 63 with Antonius as his colleague.

Nothing daunted, Catiline stood again as a candidate for the consulship of 62 and since he needed wider support proposed a cancellation of all debts which would appeal to those in financial difficulties – and there must have been many in Italy at the time – but he would be opposed by all who had an interest in financial stability, whether senators, equestrians, or small tradesmen and workers. He also made imprudent threats and gave Cicero the chance to make good propaganda out of them on the day of the elections by means of an ostentatious appearance with a bodyguard and breast-plate theatrically revealed for all to see. Catiline was again an unsuccessful candidate and L. Licinius Murena and D. Iunius Silanus were elected consuls for 62. With his hopes of power gained by constitutional means shattered he now turned to plans for revolution.

Time was needed to put these plans into operation and although Cicero learnt from Fulvia, an intimate of one of the conspirators, what preparations were under way he had no evidence to lay before the Senate. On the night of 20–21 October Crassus with M. Marcellus and Metellus Scipio laid before Cicero at his home anonymous warnings of a massacre intended by Catiline. The next day in the Senate the letters were produced and Cicero reported the news that Manlius was to start a revolt in Etruria on the twenty-seventh and that on the next day there was to be a massacre of nobles in Rome. The Senate finally agreed to take action, and passed the *senatus consultum ultimum* instructing the consuls to take such action as they saw fit to protect the state. Cicero raised a body of volunteers in the city and thanks to his precautions the day passed so uneventfully that not until news came from Faesulae that Manlius was under arms and that slave revolts had broken out in Capua and Apulia did the Senate take any active steps.

Catiline still remained in Rome and on the night of 5 November met his fellow conspirators at the house of M. Porcius Laeca where he issed his instructions. He was himself going to join Manlius, others were to go to Etruria and Cisalpine Gaul, and others to await the rising in Rome itself. Cicero was to be eliminated but, warned by Fulvia of what was afoot, he barricaded his house and thwarted their designs upon him.

Cicero now called the Senate to a meeting in the temple of Jupiter Stator where to his amazement he found Catiline in his place. In order to convince the Senate of the danger of civil war he now delivered the speech known as the First Catilinarian Oration, published in the form in which we have it three years later. By this speech he forced Catiline's hand and compelled him to leave Rome and join his confederates without endangering Cicero's position. But since there was still no clear evidence of Catiline's guilt and his financial proposals were popular with some of the people Cicero on the next day in a *contio* justified his action in the Senate.

A few days later Q. Catulus read in the Senate a letter from Catiline attempting to justify his actions and leaving no doubt that he meant to use force against the

state. The Senate declared Catiline and Manlius *hostes*
and ordered Antonius to pursue Catiline, and Cicero
to protect Rome. Once again because nothing untoward
happened some thought that Cicero had been exaggerating the danger and that any danger that there might
have been had now passed with Catiline's departure
from the city.

This complacent view seems to have been shared by
some at least of the Optimates because Cato and
Sulpicius now prosecuted Murena for *ambitus*, a piece
of political revenge by one of the rejected candidates.
They could hardly have chosen a worse moment because
if they were successful there would only be one consul
to meet the crisis in the New Year and the only person
to benefit from this dissension among the *boni* would be
Catiline. In addition, therefore, to all his cares of state,
Cicero had to undertake the defence. Murena was
acquitted and thereafter events moved quickly to their
close.

The co-operation of the embassy from the Gallic
tribe, the Allobroges, which was in Rome at the time,
enabled Cicero to acquire the concrete evidence of the
conspirators' guilt which he had so far lacked. The
Senate was summoned to the Temple of Concord.
Hailed as the saviour of his country, Cicero addressed
the people in a *contio* on the same evening and justified
all that he had done. The Senate met again on 4
December and then on the fifth, when Cicero asked what
was to be the prisoners' fate. Murena was among those
who supported the extreme penalty which was opposed
by Caesar, who sowed seeds of doubt in the minds of
many of his audience. Cicero then sought to clarify the

issues in the speech which we now know as the Fourth
Catilinarian Oration and was followed by Cato who
strongly supported Cicero's exposure of the inconsis-
tencies of Caesar's proposals. This speech stiffened the
Senate's resolve, and Cato's motion that the conspirators be put to death was passed by an overwhelming
majority.

4. THE TRIAL

The Court. Murena was tried before one of the standing courts, the *quaestio de ambitu.* These standing
courts, the *iudicia publica* or *quaestiones perpetuae*, were
in origin one of the results of Rome's growth into an
imperial power. There was at first no court before
which Rome's subjects could complain of the mis-
behaviour of their governors, and their complaints came
in the first instance before the Senate, which adopted
the remedy of instructing a praetor to hear the action
with a bench empanelled from the Senate itself. This
procedure was perpetuated by the earliest law to found
a *quaestio perpetua*, the *lex Calpurnia repetundarum*
passed by L. Calpurnius Piso Frugi, a tribune of 149.
It was twice reconstituted: firstly, by a *lex Iunia* of the
tribune M. Iunius to be dated between 149 and 123; and
secondly, by the *lex Acilia* of 123.

There then follows the Gracchan legislation of 123
which may have set up a separate *quaestio* to deal with
judicial corruption. Whether or no this *quaestio* ever
existed, Sulla's re-enactment of this legislation made no
similar provision.

Another old-established court also to be dated to

the middle of the second century was the *quaestio inter sicarios*. A *quaestio de ambitu* seems to have existed by 116 when Marius was accused as a result of his candidature for the praetorship.

These and a number of other measures dealt with public or semi-political offences but certain state offences (e.g. treason) and private wrong-doing were handled in a variety of ways until Sulla in 81 undertook his work of codification. Each group of offences now became the subject of a separate *lex Cornelia* and these laws defined seven types of crime, some by re-enactment and some by the introduction of new measures. Four dealt with offences in public life:

1. Extortion (*repetundarum*).
2. Treason (*maiestas*).
3. Peculation (*peculatus*).
4. Electoral corruption (*ambitus*).

and three with the more serious crimes of private life:

1. Assassination, poisoning, and arson (*de sicariis et veneficis*).
2. Breach of trust (*de falsis*).
3. Personal violence (*de vi*).

The crime. Electoral corruption formed, together with extortion and judicial corruption, the great evil of Roman public life. It was a scandal as early as the first half of the second century but it reached its height with the restoration of the democracy after the collapse of the Sullan constitution when it became the accepted practice for the voters to support the candidate who paid them the most handsomely.

Three laws attempting to deal with this crime followed each other in quick succession and each tried to remedy the failure of its predecessor by providing more severe penalties. The *lex Calpurnia* of 67, a law of the consul C. Calpurnius Piso, expelled the guilty man from the Senate, permanently excluded him from holding further office and imposed a fine. Cicero's own *lex Tullia* of 63 provided banishment from Rome, and probably from Italy, for ten years. The *lex Licinia de sodaliciis* passed subsequently in 55 by the consul M. Licinius Crassus Dives had interdiction as its penalty. Pompey in 52 and Caesar in 49 had to pass further measures.

The jury. It followed naturally from the early development of the *quaestiones perpetuae* that the *iudices* should be senators. The Gracchi, as part of their efforts to diminish the authority of the Senate, transferred jurisdiction in the existing *quaestiones* to the *Equites*, i.e. all those who possessed the equestrian census and who were not past or present members of the Senate. Thus was set in train the struggle for the juries as an adjunct to political power which caused further changes at the end of the century, the details of which are uncertain and which do not effect the constitution of the juries in the sixties.

In 81 Sulla enacted that the *iudices* were to be drawn from the Senate, restored by the addition of some three hundred *Equites* to a strength of about six hundred and ensured of an annual influx of new blood from the quaestorship. Of this number, after all otherwise engaged in the service of the state have been eliminated, only about four hundred would be available each year for jury service. To find out who was able to sit in the courts a register (*album iudicum*) was drawn up.

The whole body of *iudices* was divided into a number of artificial groups known as *decuriae*, in each of which senators of all grades were included. The praetor assigned the decury for each case according to its position on the list, and then the *iudices* for the case were selected by lot. A number exceeding the total required was always chosen to allow for challenging (*reiectio*) by accuser and accused.

These senatorial juries quickly discredited themselves by repeatedly acquitting guilty members of their own order. The result was that the leaders of the reaction against Sulla's provisions yet again transferred the juries from the Senate, but this time instead of handing them over in their entirety to the *Equites*, the law of L. Aurelius Cotta, praetor in 70, provided that senators, *equites*, and *tribuni aerarii* should form juries in equal numbers. The inclusion of the *tribuni aerarii* can scarcely be regarded as an attempt to introduce a popular element. It is often difficult to distinguish them from the *Equites* and as moderately wealthy men they would only in their means be the inferior of the *ordo equester* and then only by a small margin. The list of *iudices* was prepared annually by the *praetor urbanus* and each of the three parts of the *album* seems to have been divided into decuries.

Procedure. It was first necessary to request the praetor or the *iudex quaestionis* for permission to bring the charge (*postulatio*). When this had been granted, if more than one man wished to prosecute, a *praeiudicium* was necessary to decide who it was to be since there could only be one accuser for a single offence. This was known as the *divinatio*. Thereafter came a more specific statement of the charge (*nominis* or *criminis delatio*) before the president sitting alone, at which the accused was required to be present. Questions were put to him by the accuser (*interrogatio*) in order to satisfy the president that there was a *prima facie* case. If the president was satisfied that there was, he drew up a statement of the charge (*inscriptio*) which was signed by the prosecutor, the accused now became technically a *reus*, and a date was fixed for his appearance before the full court.

If at this stage the prosecutor withdrew, the case was immediately dismissed. The State thus relied upon the *bona fides* of the accuser for the punishment of crimes dealt with by these *quaestiones*, and rules of conduct which could be enforced by law were developed for the accuser. Malpractice by the prosecution came under three headings:

1. *Calumnia*. Prosecution knowingly undertaken on false grounds, prompted by malice and conducted by fraud.
2. *Praevaricatio*. Collusion with the defendant to secure his acquittal.
3. *Tergiversatio*. Abandonment of the prosecution for private and improper reasons.

The parties and the jury were cited to appear by the herald, and the presence of the jury could be enforced by *coercitio*. The excusable absence of the defendant led to the adjournment of the case. The chief grounds were the tenure of a magistracy, *absentia rei publicae causa*, presence in another court, or illness. The jury was then empanelled and sworn.

In the main trial the prosecutor had to conduct his case in person with the aid of assistants (*subscriptores*) who remedied any rhetorical or legal deficiencies in the main accuser and prevented collusion or abandonment of the case. They could be up to three in number.

The accused could have *patroni* or pleaders to help him, all nominally equal, but counsels' speeches were limited in length by the special laws of the *quaestiones*. The case was opened by the prosecutor who was answered by the counsel for the accused and after the pleadings the evidence was taken. The prosecutor and defendant then replied in the form of brief questions and answers by their respective *patroni* (*altercatio*).

The *iudices* then gave their judgement by ballot and could give one of three verdicts: *absolvo*, *condemno*, and *non liquet*. The majority of votes decided the verdict. An absolute majority was required for condemnation and if this was not secured the defendant was acquitted, even though some of the votes might have been *non liquet*. For this verdict too an absolute majority was required. The votes were counted by the president who then announced the verdict.

In trials for extortion and peculation conviction was followed by an assessment of damages (*litis aestimatio*). This assessment was conducted by the trial jury which had a wide discretion and tended to be generous to plaintiffs. Once a conviction had been secured, their sympathy for the accused seems to have disappeared.

5. THE PARTIES TO THE TRIAL

The defendant. L. Licinius Murena, the son of a
homonymous father, was a member of a family of the
gens Licinia which came originally from the old Latin
town of Lanuvium. The family name is said to
have been acquired as the result of an ancestor's
liking for lampreys (*murenae*) and building tanks for
them.

He served under his father who as propraetor of Asia
in 84 had provoked the Second Mithridatic War and at
some uncertain date before 74 was *praefectus fabrum*.
He was elected quaestor in that year with Ser. Sulpicius
Ruufs, his fellow-candidate for the consulship of 62.

In the following year he served as a legate under
Lucullus in Asia, Bithynia and Pontus and in 72 was
placed by him in charge of the siege of Amisus while
Lucullus advanced against Mithridates. Some time
before 66, probably in 70, ten commissioners were
elected and sent to assist Lucullus in the organisation
of the territory formerly belonging to Mithridates. The
identification of the defendant as one of these commissioners must remain uncertain. The man is either he or
his father but the relevant passage in this speech[1] makes
no reference to his holding such a special position when
describing the son's services in Pontus and Armenia.
We know that the father was dead before 63 but nowhere do we learn the exact date.

In 65 he was elected *praetor urbanus* and in 64 and 63
was proconsul in command of Transalpine and Cisalpine
Gaul. In the latter year he left his brother, C. Murena,

[1] 20.

as temporary governor of both provinces when he returned to Rome for the elections.

He secured election to the consulship in company with D. Iunius Silanus but only after surviving the prosecution which is the subject of this speech did he take office on 1 January 62.

His consulship was a stormy one, largely owing to the agitation of the tribune, Q. Caecilius Metellus Nepos, who attacked Cicero's execution of the Catilinarian conspirators and vetoed his final speech at the end of the year. He protected one of his accusers, Cato, who had successfully sought election as tribune in order to oppose Nepos. Among the other measures of this consulship was the passage of the *lex Licinia Iunia* which required copies of all legislation to be deposited in the treasury.

After his consulship he passes into oblivion. He does not appear to have held any further proconsular command or office and the date of his death is not known.

For the defence. 1. M. Tullius Cicero. See p. x ff.

2. Q. Hortensius Hortalus (114–50) won fame as an advocate at an early age and was for many years the great forensic rival of Cicero. He first opposed him in the trial of P. Quinctius in 81 and his pre-eminence in the courts continued until 70 when he was retained to defend Verres.

He was active in politics, probably quaestor in about 80, aedile in 75, *praetor de repetundis* in 72 and consul in 69. As a supporter of the supremacy of the Senate he opposed the tribunician legislation of Gabinius and Manilius in 67 and 66.

Subsequently he co-operated with Cicero and acted with him for the defence in a number of cases: in 65 for the senator C. Rabirius, who had been indicted for the murder of the tribune Saturninus in 100; in 63 for Murena; in 62 for P. Sulla, accused as an accomplice of Catiline; in 59 for L. Flaccus, accused of extortion in Asia; and in 56 for P. Sestius. His standing is shown by the order in which M. Piso, the consul of 61, called upon senators to speak. Cicero ranked second and Hortensius fourth; and in the cases which they jointly undertook he ceded to Cicero the right to speak last.

He was the leader of the florid or ' Asianic ' school of rhetoric which indulged in an excess of ornament and verbal conceit. His interpretation of this style of speaking was clearly very effective but the style itself could easily degenerate into mere bombast.

3. M. Licinius Crassus Dives (c. 112–53) was largely responsible for Sulla's victory at the Colline Gate. His speculation in real estate soon marked him out as the leader of the financial interests at Rome. Praetor in 72, he defeated the slave revolt under Spartacus when the consuls had failed, saw Pompey arrive at the last minute to usurp the major share of the laurels, but then in 70 joined with him as consul in dismantling what remained of Sulla's constitution. Throughout the middle sixties he devoted his energies to strengthening his position at Rome against Pompey's return from the East. His efforts to this end were largely unsuccessful. He failed to achieve the annexation of Egypt in 65 which he could turn to his own advantage and his attempt to win support as censor by enfranchising the Transpadane Gauls left him with little tangible gain.

He attached Caesar to himself by assisting him with his heavy debts, and although he supported Catiline at the consular elections of 64 he played no part in the conspiracy this year; indeed the information that he passed to Cicero and his assistance in the defence of Murena show where his sympathies lay as the crisis progressed.

Pompey returned to Italy in 62, and in 60 Caesar brought the two together as members of the ' First Triumvirate '. In the first half of the next decade his relationship with Pompey became increasingly strained but at the Conference of Luca Caesar prevented a split, and in 55 he and Pompey once again shared the consulship. Together they passed a number of constitutional reforms and he obtained through the *lex Trebonia* the military command for which he had been waiting. After some difficulty in raising troops he left at the end of 55 for his Parthian campaign and met his end in battle against the Parthians at Carrhae in 53.

For the prosecution. 1. Ser. Sulpicius Rufus. The son of an *eques*, he was almost an exact contemporary of Cicero. He studied rhetoric with him at Rhodes but later turned his attention to the study of the law at which he excelled. His fame rested upon his upright character and his ability both as orator and as jurisconsult.

He became quaestor in 74 and was allotted Ostia as his *provincia*; *praetor de peculatu* in 65; *interrex* in 52, naming Pompey as sole consul; consul in the following year with M. Claudius Marcellus and subsequently a legate or proconsul under Caesar in Greece. His position in the Civil War was that of a moderate and after his death on the embassy to Antony in January 43 he was honoured with a public funeral.

He remained throught his life a close friend of Cicero who eulogises him in the Ninth Philippic and in the *Brutus* attributes his success as an orator to his extreme clarity of thought and exposition. The collection of Cicero's letters to and from his friends contains two from him, one of which is the famous letter of consolation on the death of his daughter, Tullia.

2. M. Porcius Cato Uticensis (95–46) was the great-grandson of M. Porcius Cato Censorius. He lost both parents in childhood and was brought up by his maternal uncle, M. Livius Drusus. In 67 he was elected military tribune and served under Rubrius in Macedonia, returning to Rome to become praetor, probably in 64.

As tribune designate he joined in the accusation of Murena and in that office, apart from conciliating the mob by increasing the distribution of cheap corn, refused to compromise. He blocked the revision of the Asian tax contracts in 61 and by his attitude helped throw the members of the ' First Triumvirate ' together. He was subsequently a bitter opponent of Caesar and was removed from the political scene by the tribune Clodius who forced him to undertake the annexation of Cyprus. He became *praetor de repetundis* in 54 after being defeated by Vatinius who had employed bribery extensively to secure his own election.

In the Civil War he was a resolute supporter of Pompey and after Pompey's defeat joined the Pompeians in Africa and governed Utica until his famous self-inflicted death after the Battle of Thapsus.

He was unpleasant in character, but his adherence to a mixture of Stoic and old Roman principles was genuine. He had by the time of this speech already won his reputation for moral rectitude, a reputation strong enough to survive the loss of his accounts on his voyage back from Cyprus.

3. Ser. Sulpicius. Nothing more is known about him than can be learnt from this speech.[1] It has sometimes been assumed that he was the son of the accuser but this relationship cannot be substantiated.

4. C. Postumus. Similarly, nothing more is known of him than can be learnt from this speech.[2]

6. Pro L. Murena Oratio

Roman Oratory. The Romans were, as in almost every sphere of intellectual activity, deeply indebted to the Greeks for their development of oratory as a literary genre. The idea of oratory as an art was well established in Rome by the beginning of the first century and the Roman pupils of the Greek rhetoricians followed their masters in adopting the threefold classification of *eloquentia* into the simple, ornate, and middle styles (*tenuis* or *exilis, grandis* or *ornata*, and *media*).

The simple or Attic style was descended from Lysias, who composed his speeches in a form which paid particular attention to brevity, directness, and clarity. All verbal extravagance and any over-elaborate phraseology were carefully avoided. There were some orators, known as the *novi Attici*, following these precepts during

[1] 56–57.　　　[2] 54, 56, 57, 69.

this period, and the leading exponents of this group were C. Licinius Calvus and M. Brutus. Their speeches, however, do not seem to have aroused the enthusiasm of their audiences and did not long hold their place in men's memories. Their style, indeed, must have lacked warmth and inspiration. Latin would prove a less apt medium for its exponents than Attic Greek, although Caesar, a master of his language, has shown us in the *Commentaries* how effective a simple style can be.

In contrast with this extreme simplicity there also at this time flourished an Asiatic school. Hortensius was its leader, but no examples of his work, nor of that of any Asianist, survives. We can, however, learn much about it from Cicero's criticisms. He distinguishes two styles, one *sententiosum et argutum* and the other *verbis volucre atque incitatum*. The chief characteristics of the first were an emphasis on antithesis and as many ingenious turns of thought or phrase, called by the Romans *sententiae*, as possible. The language was high-flown and the vocabulary that of poetry rather than everyday speech. There was also a straining after rhythmical effects. It is easy to understand how readily so extravagant a style could degenerate into utter artificiality and a mere cleverness often quite inappropriate to the matter in hand.

Cicero steered a middle course between the two extremes. He took as his model Demosthenes, but his was no slavish imitation. He well knew how far apart in character stood Athenian and Roman and how different were the Greek and Latin languages. He insisted upon the accurate use of vocabulary and idiom, carefully avoiding all that was unusual. His style was

plain and unadorned when this was appropriate, but
in his view it was essential for a good orator at times
to attempt something more, and then ornament was
certainly required.

This speech has its fair share of such ornament. The
following is a representative, but not complete, list
included as a guide to the type of figure employed.
Other instances are indicated in the Notes.

1. **Allegoria.** A series of metaphors.
    3. Quodsi . . . obligavit, . . .
    4. Quodsi . . . subeundas.
    6. Ego autem . . . postulabat.

2. **Antithesis.** The contrast of opposites.
    9. . . . inimicis . . . amicis[1] . . .
    11. . . . gravissima . . . levis[1] . . .
    20. . . . imperatore . . . imperator.[1]

3. **Asyndeton.** The omission of conjunctions.
    19. . . . didicit . . . exsorbuit; . . .
    79. . . . reieci . . . compressi . . .

4. **Chiasmus.** The a:b, b:a order of contrasting words.
    29. . . . eos . . . qui . . . qui . . . eos . . .

5. **Expolitio.** The expression of the same idea in different
ways.
    12. . . . laus . . . memoria . . . honos et gloria . . .

6. **Gradatio.** A series of words each of which is stronger than
the last.
    10. . . . officio, fidei, religioni, . . .

7. **Metaphora.** The use of words to describe others to which
they are not strictly applicable.
    66. . . . asperseris . . . condita . . .

8. **Paronomasia.** A play upon words.
    8. . . . peteres . . . petas, . . .
    22. . . . capiantur . . . arceantur; . . .
    30. . . . manum consertum, . . .

[1] See notes *ad loc.*, p. 64, p. 66 and 79.

Cicero's greatest achievements, however, were the development of the ' period ', and the adoption and extension of one of the Asiatic school's most important adornments, the use of a clearly defined rhythm before a break in the sense.

The German scholar Zielinski has analysed these endings and found the commonest to be a cretic and trochee or spondee (– ∪ – – ⌣). Other final rhythms are a cretic or molossus followed by a trochee and doubtful syllable (– ⌣ – – ∪ ⌣), a cretic and a double trochee (– ⌣ – – ∪ – ∪). Long syllables may be resolved (e.g. – ∪ ⌣⌣ – ∪ gives the famous *esse videatur*) and sometimes the cretic is followed by spondees to give a solemn effect (– ⌣ – – – – –). It will not require any detailed study of this speech to gauge the extent to which Cicero, probably only half consciously, employed these rhythms.

Outline of the Speech

    Exordium.   The introduction: 1–10.

    Confutatio. 1. *de vita Murenae:* 11–14.

                2. *contentio dignitatis:* 15–53

                3. *de ambitus criminibus:* 54–83

    Peroratio.   The conclusion: 83–90

A running synopsis of the subject-matter is provided in the text.

The Speech

This is one of the most moderately written of Cicero's speeches and its moderation combines with its good humour to make it one of the most enjoyable to read. The violent personal abuse which for modern readers detracts much from ancient forensic oratory is entirely absent; the points at issue can be seen against a background of which we have a detailed knowledge; and the situation was such as to call forth from Cicero a wide variety of his skills as orator and advocate.

The complexity of Cicero's position makes the argument difficult to follow at times but, considering the problems which faced him, the speech is a remarkable achievement. A lesser man would have been daunted by a task which had to be undertaken in addition to the calls upon his time and energy made by the Catilinarian Conspiracy. Even if we make allowance for a certain amount of subsequent editing, Murena's acquittal is sufficient indication of the speed and skill with which Cicero marshalled his arguments and presented them without giving offence to those whose political support he could not afford to forfeit.

Cicero had been the returning officer of the consular elections, had himself declared Murena elected, they were friends, and both were *novi homines*. His support of Murena might therefore seem natural, but unfortunately the prosecution was led by Sulpicius whom Cicero had supported as a consular candidate against Murena and he was therefore liable to a charge of inconsistency. Furthermore, Cicero was himself the author of the *lex Tullia* under which Murena was being charged and he thus laid himself open to further attack for defending acts which his own law declared to be illegal. Murena was in all likelihood guilty and the prosecution had clearly sought to strengthen their position by painting Murena's earlier life in lurid colours in their attempt to show that he was an unworthy candidate for the consulship in ways other than that stated formally in the accusation. Sulpicius on the other hand was, they declared, a wholly worthy candidate, very properly supported by Cicero, and one who would have been elected had it not been for Murena's corrupt practices.

We may assume that the other speeches for the defence had dealt with the details of the charge. There remained a number of other lines which Cicero could pursue. The imputation of a lack of consistency on his own part had to be rebutted but this required the greatest tact and it would not have been a topic on which Cicero would have wished to dwell longer than necessary. More hopeful prospects lay in taking advantage of the false move made by Sulpicius when he denigrated Murena's capacity as a military commander and in ridiculing Cato's unwise extension of the charge against Murena to make it include the violation of Stoic moral principles. He could deal with these attacks upon Murena without impugning the characters or motives of the prosecutors, yet would raise doubts in the jury's minds about the validity of the central charge as well as rehabilitating Murena's past.

We must always remember that Roman juries were not expected to – and did not – ignore material irrelevant to a charge. The nature of Cicero's reply to the prosecutors, moreover, did not make any difference to their feelings for Cicero. Only shortly afterwards Cato's speech in support of the punishment advocated by Cicero for the Catilinarian prisoners was to decide the day and Sulpicius remained a life-long friend.

The heart of Cicero's defence, however, lay in the political situation. He may have laughed Sulpicius and Cato out of court, but the vital arguments were more serious. They were three in number. Firstly, the state needed all its magistrates at this time of crisis, but if the jury condemned Murena they might not have two consuls on 1 January, at a time when the crisis could be expected to be at its height. They should therefore keep the consuls they had. Secondly, the times needed a man of action such as Murena, not a legal quibbler like Sulpicius. They should, therefore, not condemn Murena to make way for Sulpicius. Thirdly, even if Murena were to some degree guilty, the present crisis was more perilous than any dangers resulting from *ambitus*. They should therefore as patriots acquit Murena.

A number of passages is listed below to illustrate various aspects of Cicero's skill as an advocate:

1. 15. The comparison of the families of Sulpicius and Murena in which Cicero not only makes good his argument that any contempt for Murena's family is unjustified but does so without saying anything to which Sulpicius could take exception.

2. 18. In his discussion of the *dignitas* claimed for the praetor whose election was announced first, he makes the best of what was not a very strong position.

3. 29. By his introduction of the contrast between lawyers, whose concern is formulae and verbal quibbles, and orators, he makes a strong case for his own argument at the expense of Sulpicius – quite unfairly but in a way which would seem reasonable to the jury. Sulpicius was of course both jurisconsult and orator.

4. 34. In order to show how important was the war in which Murena fought Cicero introduces the service of Lucullus and of Pompey. Although several years have passed since his speech *pro lege Manilia* the supersession of Lucullus by Pompey is still dangerous ground and he has to tread warily to avoid offence to either party. Romans had long memories where affronts to their *dignitas* were concerned.

5. 58. What Cicero says is complimentary to the prosecutor, Cato, yet turned to his client's advantage.

The low key in which this speech is set apart from a comparatively few passages causes those parts which are more humorous or more serious than the remainder to stand out more than they would have done otherwise. Both in his treatment of the jurisconsult[1] and of the Stoic Wise Man[2] the light-hearted raillery is an effective device and the direct speech introduced in both passages makes them more vivid and telling.

There are a number of occasions in which the rhetoric becomes more powerful. There is, for example, a strong end to the *Exordium*,[3] another to the account of Murena's military service,[4] and another to complete the argument for the precedence to be accorded to the soldier over the jurisconsult.[5] The most rhetorical passages of all are naturally reserved for the peril of Catiline. From 75 to the end of the speech the language is highly rhetorical and reminiscent of the Catilinarian Orations, rising to a climax in the *commiseratio* or appeal to the feelings of the jury.[6]

---

[1] 23–26.   [2] 61–62.   [3] 10.   [4] 12.   [5] 22.   [6] 86 f.

M. TULLI CICERONIS

PRO L. MURENA ORATIO

*1–2. Cicero repeats on behalf of Murena the prayer that he offered
to the gods on the day of the consular elections.*

I. 1. Quae precatus a dis immortalibus sum, iudices,
more institutoque maiorum illo die quo auspicato
comitiis centuriatis L. Murenam consulem renuntiavi,
ut ea res mihi fidei magistratuique meo, populo plebique
Romanae bene atque feliciter eveniret, eadem precor ab 5
isdem dis immortalibus ob eiusdem hominis consulatum
una cum salute obtinendum, et ut vestrae mentes atque
sententiae cum populi Romani voluntatibus suffragiisque consentiant, eaque res vobis populoque Romano
pacem, tranquillitatem, otium concordiamque adferat. 10
Quod si illa sollemnis comitiorum precatio consularibus
auspiciis consecrata tantam habet in se vim et religionem
quantam rei publicae dignitas postulat, idem ego sum
precatus ut eis quoque hominibus quibus hic consulatus
me rogante datus esset ea res fauste feliciter prospereque 15
eveniret. 2. Quae cum ita sint, iudices, et cum omnis
deorum immortalium potestas aut translata sit ad vos
aut certe communicata vobiscum, idem consulem
vestrae fidei commendat qui antea dis immortalibus
commendavit, ut eiusdem hominis voce et declaratus 20
consul et defensus beneficium populi Romani cum
vestra atque omnium civium salute tueatur.

2. Cicero justifies his decision to defend Murena.

Et quoniam in hoc officio studium meae defensionis
ab accusatoribus atque etiam ipsa susceptio causae
reprensa est, ante quam pro L. Murena dicere instituo,
pro me ipso pauca dicam, non quo mihi potior hoc
5 quidem tempore sit offici mei quam huiusce salutis
defensio, sed ut meo facto vobis probato maiore auctoritate ab huius honore fama fortunisque omnibus inimicorum impetus propulsare possim.

*3-5. Cicero replies to Cato's criticism of his decision. Although
he has passed a law against bribery, it is appropriate for him, a
consul, to defend a consul-elect, and anyway Murena is innocent.*

II. 3. Et primum M. Catoni vitam ad certam rationis normam derigenti et diligentissime perpendenti momenta officiorum omnium de officio meo respondebo.
Negat fuisse rectum Cato me et consulem et legis am-
5 bitus latorem et tam severe gesto consulatu causam L.
Murenae attingere. Cuius reprehensio me vehementer
movet, non solum ut vobis, iudices, quibus maxime
debeo, verum etiam ut ipsi Catoni, gravissimo atque
integerrimo viro, rationem facti mei probem. A quo
10 tandem, M. Cato, est aequius consulem defendi quam a
consule? Quis mihi in re publica potest aut debet esse
coniunctior quam is cui res publica a me iam traditur
sustinenda magnis meis laboribus et periculis sustentata? Quod si in eis rebus repetendis quae mancipi
15 sunt is periculum iudici praestare debet qui se nexu
obligavit, profecto etiam rectius in iudicio consulis
designati is potissimum consul qui consulem declar-
avit auctor benefici populi Romani defensorque periculi esse debebit. 4. Ac si, ut non nullis in civitatibus

fieri solet, patronus huic causae publice constitueretur, 20
is potissimum summo honore adfecto defensor daretur
qui eodem honore praeditus non minus adferret ad
dicendum auctoritatis quam facultatis. Quod si e portu
solventibus ei qui iam in portum ex alto invehuntur
praecipere summo studio solent et tempestatum ratio- 25
nem et praedonum et locorum, quod natura adfert ut
eis faveamus qui eadem pericula quibus nos perfuncti
sumus ingrediantur, quo tandem me esse animo oportet
prope iam ex magna iactatione terram videntem in
hunc cui video maximas rei publicae tempestates esse 30
subeundas? Qua re si est boni consulis non solum videre
quid agatur verum etiam providere quid futurum sit,
ostendam alio loco quantum salutis communis intersit
duos consules in re publica Kalendis Ianuariis esse.
5. Quod si ita est, non tam me officium debuit ad homi- 35
nis amici fortunas quam res publica consulem ad
communem salutem defendendam vocare.

III. Nam quod legem de ambitu tuli, certe ita tuli
ut eam quam mihimet ipsi iam pridem tulerim de civium periculis defendendis non abrogarem. Etenim si 40
largitionem factam esse confiterer idque recte factum esse defenderem, facerem improbe, etiam si alius
legem tulisset; cum vero nihil commissum contra legem
esse defendam, quid est quod meam defensionem latio
legis impediat? 45

6. *For Cicero to undertake Murena's defence is not inconsistent
with his treatment of Catiline.*

6. Negat esse eiusdem severitatis Catilinam exitium
rei publicae intra moenia molientem verbis et paene
imperio ex urbe expulisse et nunc pro L. Murena dicere.

Ego autem has partis lenitatis et misericordiae quas me
5 natura ipsa docuit semper egi libenter, illam vero gravitatis severitatisque personam non appetivi, sed ab re
publica mihi impositam sustinui, sicut huius imperi
dignitas in summo periculo civium postulabat. Quod
si tum, cum res publica vim et severitatem desiderabat,
10 vici naturam et tam vehemens fui quam cogebar, non
quam volebam, nunc cum omnes me causae ad misericordiam atque ad humanitatem vocent, quanto tandem
studio debeo naturae meae consuetudinique servire?
Ac de officio defensionis meae ac de ratione accusationis
15 tuae fortasse etiam alia in parte orationis dicendum
nobis erit.

*7–10. Cicero replies to Sulpicius' complaint that his defence
of Murena is inconsistent with their friendship and his support
of Sulpicius in the elections.*

7. Sed me, iudices, non minus hominis sapientissimi
atque ornatissimi, Ser. Sulpici, conquestio quam Catonis
accusatio commovebat qui gravissime et acerbissime se
ferre dixit me familiaritatis necessitudinisque oblitum
5 causam L. Murenae contra se defendere. Huic ego,
iudices, satis facere cupio vosque adhibere arbitros.
Nam cum grave est vere accusari in amicitia, tum, etiam
si falso accuseris, non est neglegendum. Ego, Ser.
Sulpici, me in petitione tua tibi omnia studia atque
10 officia pro nostra necessitudine et debuisse confiteor et
praestitisse arbitror. Nihil tibi consulatum petenti a me
defuit quod esset aut ab amico aut a gratioso aut a
consule postulandum. Abiit illud tempus; mutata ratio
est. Sic existimo, sic mihi persuadeo, me tibi contra
15 honorem Murenae quantum tu a me postulare ausus sis,

tantum debuisse, contra salutem nihil debere. 8. Neque
enim, si tibi tum cum peteres consulatum studui, nunc
cum Murenam ipsum petas, adiutor eodem pacto esse
debeo. Atque hoc non modo non laudari sed ne concedi
quidem potest ut amicis nostris accusantibus non etiam 20
alienissimos defendamus. IV. Mihi autem cum Murena,
iudices, et magna et vetus amicitia est, quae in capitis
dimicatione a Ser. Sulpicio non idcirco obruetur quod
ab eodem in honoris contentione superata est. Quae si
causa non esset, tamen vel dignitas hominis vel honoris 25
eius quem adeptus est amplitudo summam mihi superbiae crudelitatisque infamiam inussisset, si hominis et
suis et populi Romani ornamentis amplissimi causam
tanti periculi repudiassem. Neque enim iam mihi licet
neque est integrum ut meum laborem hominum periculis 30
sublevandis non impertiam. Nam cum praemia mihi
tanta pro hac industria sint data quanta antea nemini,
sic existimo, labores quos in petitione exceperis, eos, cum
adeptus sis, deponere, esse hominis et astuti et ingrati.
9. Quod si licet desinere, si te auctore possum, si nulla 35
inertiae infamia, nulla superbiae turpitudo, nulla inhumanitatis culpa suscipitur, ego vero libenter desino.
Sin autem fuga laboris desidiam, repudiatio supplicum
superbiam, amicorum neglectio improbitatem coarguit,
nimirum haec causa est eius modi quam nec industrius 40
quisquam nec misericors nec officiosus deserere possit.
Atque huiusce rei coniecturam de tuo ipsius studio,
Servi, facillime ceperis. Nam si tibi necesse putas etiam
adversariis amicorum tuorum de iure consulentibus
respondere, et si turpe existimas te advocato illum 45
ipsum quem contra veneris causa cadere, noli tam esse
iniustus ut, cum tui fontes vel inimicis tuis pateant,

nostros etiam amicis putes clausos esse oportere. 10.
Etenim si me tua familiaritas ab hac causa removisset,
50 et si hoc idem Q. Hortensio, M. Crasso, clarissimis viris,
si item ceteris a quibus intellego tuam gratiam magni
aestimari accidisset, in ea civitate consul designatus
defensorem non haberet in qua nemini umquam infimo
maiores nostri patronum deesse voluerunt. Ego vero,
55 iudices, ipse me existimarem nefarium si amico, crudelem
si misero, superbum si consuli defuissem. Qua re quod
dandum est amicitiae, large dabitur a me, ut tecum
agam, Servi, non secus ac si meus esset frater, qui mihi
est carissimus, isto in loco; quod tribuendum est officio,
60 fidei, religioni, id ita moderabor ut meminerim me
contra amici studium pro amici periculo dicere.

11-12. *The reply to the prosecution's attack upon Murena's way*
of life. His service in Asia is defended.

V. 11. Intellego, iudices, tris totius accusationis
partis fuisse, et earum unam in reprehensione vitae,
alteram in contentione dignitatis, tertiam in criminibus
ambitus esse versatam. Atque harum trium partium
5 prima illa quae gravissima debebat esse ita fuit infirma
et levis ut illos lex magis quaedam accusatoria quam
vera male dicendi facultas de vita L. Murenae dicere
aliquid coegerit. Obiecta est enim Asia; quae ab hoc
non ad voluptatem et luxuriam expetita est sed in
10 militari labore peragrata. Qui si adulescens patre suo
imperatore non meruisset, aut hostem aut patris
imperium timuisse aut a parente repudiatus videretur.
An cum sedere in equis triumphantium praetextati
potissimum filii soleant, huic donis militaribus patris
15 triumphum decorare fugiendum fuit, ut rebus com-

muniter gestis paene simul cum patre triumpharet?
12. Hic vero, iudices, et fuit in Asia et viro fortissimo,
parenti suo, magno adiumento in periculis, solacio in
laboribus, gratulationi in victoria fuit. Et si habet
Asia suspicionem luxuriae quandam, non Asiam num- 20
quam vidisse sed in Asia continenter vixisse laudandum
est. Quam ob rem non Asiae nomen obiciendum
Murenae fuit ex qua laus familiae, memoria generi,
honos et gloria nomini constituta est, sed aliquod aut
in Asia susceptum aut ex Asia deportatum flagitium ac 25
dedecus. Meruisse vero stipendia in eo bello quod tum
populus Romanus non modo maximum sed etiam solum
gerebat virtutis, patre imperatore libentissime meruisse
pietatis, finem stipendiorum patris victoriam ac
triumphum fuisse felicitatis fuit. Maledicto quidem 30
idcirco nihil in hisce rebus loci est quod omnia laus
occupavit.

13-14. *The slanderous attack upon Murena's morals is refuted
and his life shown to be blameless.*

VI. 13. Saltatorem appellat L. Murenam Cato.
Maledictum est, si vere obicitur, vehementis accusatoris,
sin falso, maledici conviciatoris. Qua re cum ista sis
auctoritate, non debes, M. Cato, adripere maledictum
ex trivio aut ex scurrarum aliquo convicio neque temere 5
consulem populi Romani saltatorem vocare, sed circumspicere quibus praeterea vitiis adfectum esse necesse sit
eum cui vere istud obici possit. Nemo enim fere saltat
sobrius, nisi forte insanit, neque in solitudine neque in
convivio moderato atque honesto. Tempestivi convivi, 10
amoeni loci, multarum deliciarum comes est extrema
saltatio. Tu mihi adripis hoc quod necesse est omnium

vitiorum esse postremum, relinquis illa quibus remotis
hoc vitium omnino esse non potest? Nullum turpe
15 convivium, non amor, non comissatio, non libido, non
sumptus ostenditur, et, cum ea non reperiantur quae
voluptatis nomen habent quamquam vitiosa sunt, in
quo ipsam luxuriam reperire non potes, in eo te umbram
luxuriae reperturum putas? 14. Nihil igitur in vitam
20 L. Murenae dici potest, nihil, inquam, omnino, iudices.
Sic a me consul designatus defenditur ut eius nulla fraus,
nulla avaritia, nulla perfidia, nulla crudelitas, nullum
petulans dictum in vita proferatur. Bene habet; iacta
sunt fundamenta defensionis. Nondum enim nostris
25 laudibus, quibus utar postea, sed prope inimicorum confessione virum bonum atque integrum hominem defendimus. Quo constituto facilior est mihi aditus ad contentionem dignitatis, quae pars altera fuit accusationis.

15–18. *Cicero replies to the attack by Sulpicius on Murena's
birth and family and shows that in this respect there is nothing
to choose between them.*

VII. 15. Summam video esse in te, Ser. Sulpici,
dignitatem generis, integritatis, industriae ceterorum-
que ornamentorum omnium quibus fretum ad consulatus
petitionem adgredi par est. Paria cognosco esse ista in
5 L. Murena, atque ita paria ut neque ipse dignitate vinci
a te potuerit neque te dignitate superarit. Contempsisti
L. Murenae genus, extulisti tuum. Quo loco si tibi hoc
sumis, nisi qui patricius sit, neminem bono esse genere
natum, facis ut rursus plebes in Aventinum sevocanda
10 esse videatur. Sin autem sunt amplae et honestae
familiae plebeiae, et proavus L. Murenae et avus praetor
fuit, et pater, cum amplissime atque honestissime ex

praetura triumphasset, hoc faciliorem huic gradum
consulatus adipiscendi reliquit quod is iam patri debitus
a filio petebatur. 16. Tua vero nobilitas, Ser. Sulpici, 15
tametsi summa est, tamen hominibus litteratis et
historicis est notior, populo vero et suffragatoribus
obscurior. Pater enim fuit equestri loco, avus nulla
inlustri laude celebratus. Itaque non ex sermone
hominum recenti sed ex annalium vetustate eruenda 20
memoria est nobilitatis tuae. Qua re ego te semper in
nostrum numerum adgregare soleo, quod virtute indus-
triaque perfecisti ut, cum equitis Romani esses filius,
summa tamen amplitudine dignus putarere. Nec mihi
umquam minus in Q. Pompeio, novo homine et fortis- 25
simo viro, virtutis esse visum est quam in homine nobili-
ssimo, M. Aemilio. Etenim eiusdem animi atque ingeni
est posteris suis, quod Pompeius fecit, amplitudinem
nominis quam non acceperit tradere et, ut Scaurus,
memoriam prope intermortuam generis sua virtute 30
renovare. VIII. 17. Quamquam ego iam putabam,
iudices, multis viris fortibus ne ignobilitas generis obiceretur meo labore esse perfectum, qui non modo Curiis,
Catonibus, Pompeiis, antiquis illis fortissimis viris,
novis hominibus, sed his recentibus, Mariis et Didiis 35
et Caeliis, commemorandis id agebam. Cum vero ego
tanto intervallo claustra ista nobilitatis refregissem, ut
aditus ad consulatum posthac, sicut apud maiores
nostros fuit, non magis nobilitati quam virtuti pateret,
non arbitrabar, cum ex familia vetere et inlustri consul 40
designatus ab equitis Romani filio consule defendere-
tur, de generis novitate accusatores esse dicturos. Etenim mihi ipsi accidit ut cum duobus patriciis, altero
improbissimo atque audacissimo, altero modestissimo

45 atque optimo viro, peterem; superavi tamen dignitate
Catilinam, gratia Galbam. Quod si id crimen homini
novo esse deberet, profecto mihi neque inimici neque
invidi defuissent. 18. Omittamus igitur de genere dicere
cuius est magna in utroque dignitas; videamus cetera.

18. *Cicero replies to what Sulpicius has said concerning the merits
of their respective quaestorships.*

' Quaesturam una petiit et sum ego factus prior.'
Non est respondendum ad omnia. Neque enim vestrum
quemquam fugit, cum multi pares dignitate fiant, unus
autem primum solus possit obtinere, non eundem esse
5 ordinem dignitatis et renuntiationis, propterea quod
renuntiatio gradus habeat, dignitas autem sit persaepe
eadem omnium. Sed quaestura utriusque prope modum
pari momento sortis fuit. Habuit hic lege Titia provinciam tacitam et quietam, tu illam cui, cum quaestores
10 sortiuntur, etiam adclamari solet, Ostiensem, non tam
gratiosam et inlustrem quam negotiosam et molestam.
Consedit utriusque nomen in quaestura. Nullum enim
vobis sors campum dedit in quo excurrere virtus cog-
noscique posset.

19–22. *The subsequent careers of Murena and Sulpicius are now
compared. Sulpicius turned to the law while Murena became a
military commander. Military service takes precedence over all
other professions.*

19. Reliqui temporis spatium in contentionem
vocatur. Ab utroque dissimillima ratione tractatum
est. IX. Servius hic nobiscum hanc urbanam militiam
respondendi, scribendi, cavendi plenam sollicitudinis ac
5 stomachi secutus est; ius civile didicit, multum vigilavit,
laboravit, praesto multis fuit, multorum stultitiam

perpessus est, adrogantiam pertulit, difficultatem
exsorbuit; vixit ad aliorum arbitrium, non ad suum.
Magna laus et grata hominibus unum hominem elaborare in ea scientia quae sit multis profutura. 20. Quid 10
Murena interea? Fortissimo et sapientissimo viro,
summo imperatori legatus, L. Lucullo, fuit; qua in
legatione duxit exercitum, signa contulit, manum
conseruit, magnas copias hostium fudit, urbis partim
vi, partim obsidione cepit, Asiam istam refertam et 15
eandem delicatam sic obiit ut in ea neque avaritiae
neque luxuriae vestigium reliquerit, maximo in bello
sic est versatus ut hic multas res et magnas sine imperatore gesserit, nullam sine hoc imperator. Atque
haec quamquam praesente L. Lucullo loquor, tamen 20
ne ab ipso propter periculum nostrum concessam vide-
amur habere licentiam fingendi, publicis litteris testata
sunt omnia, quibus L. Lucullus tantum laudis impertiit
quantum neque ambitiosus imperator neque invidus
tribuere alteri in communicanda gloria debuit. 21. 25
Summa in utroque est honestas, summa dignitas;
quam ego, si mihi per Servium liceat, pari atque eadem
in laude ponam. Sed non licet; agitat rem militarem,
insectatur totam hanc legationem, adsiduitatis et
operarum harum cotidianarum putat esse consulatum. 30
'Apud exercitum mihi fueris' inquit; 'tot annos forum
non attigeris; afueris tam diu et, cum longo intervallo
veneris, cum his qui in foro habitarint de dignitate
contendas?' Primum ista nostra adsiduitas, Servi,
nescis quantum interdum adferat hominibus fastidi, 35
quantum satietatis. Mihi quidem vehementer expediit
positam in oculis esse gratiam; sed tamen ego mei
satietatem magno meo labore superavi et tu item

fortasse; verum tamen utrique nostrum desiderium
40 nihil obfuisset. 22. Sed ut hoc omisso ad studiorum
atque artium contentionem revertamur, qui potest
dubitari quin ad consulatum adipiscendum multo plus
adferat dignitatis rei militaris quam iuris civilis gloria?
Vigilas tu de nocte ut tuis consultoribus respondeas, ille
45 ut eo quo intendit mature cum exercitu perveniat; te
gallorum, illum bucinarum cantus exsuscitat; tu
actionem instituis, ille aciem instruit; tu caves ne tui
consultores, ille ne urbes aut castra capiantur; ille
tenet et scit ut hostium copiae, tu ut aquae pluviae
50 arceantur; ille exercitatus est in propagandis finibus,
tuque in regendis. X. Ac nimirum – dicendum est
enim quod sentio – rei militaris virtus praestat ceteris
omnibus. Haec nomen populo Romano, haec huic
urbi aeternam gloriam peperit, haec orbem terrarum
55 parere huic imperio coegit; omnes urbanae res, omnia
haec nostra praeclara studia et haec forensis laus et
industria latet in tutela ac praesidio bellicae virtutis.
Simul atque increpuit suspicio tumultus, artes ilico
nostrae conticiscunt

23–25. *The profession of jurisconsult does not lead to the consulship as do military and rhetorical distinction. It is
only concerned with unimportant quibbles. Lawyers are
derided for their invention of legal formulae to keep themselves in
business.*

23. Et quoniam mihi videris istam scientiam iuris
tamquam filiolam osculari tuam, non patiar te in tanto
errore versari ut istud nescio quid quod tanto opere
didicisti praeclarum aliquid esse arbitrere. Aliis ego
5 te virtutibus, continentiae, gravitatis, iustitiae, fidei,

ceteris omnibus, consulatu et omni honore semper
dignissimum iudicavi; quod quidem ius civile didicisti,
non dicam operam perdidisti, sed illud dicam, nullam
esse in ista disciplina munitam ad consulatum viam.
Omnes enim artes, quae nobis populi Romani studia 10
concilient, et admirabilem dignitatem et pergratam
utilitatem debent habere.   XI. 24. Summa dignitas
est in eis qui militari laude antecellunt; omnia enim
quae sunt in imperio et in statu civitatis ab his defendi
et firmari putantur; summa etiam utilitas, si quidem 15
eorum consilio et periculo cum re publica tum etiam
nostris rebus perfrui possumus.   Gravis etiam illa est
et plena dignitatis dicendi facultas quae saepe valuit
in consule deligendo, posse consilio atque oratione et
senatus et populi et eorum qui res iudicant mentis 20
permovere. Quaeritur consul qui dicendo non numquam
comprimat tribunicios furores, qui concitatum populum
flectat, qui largitioni resistat.   Non mirum, si ob hanc
facultatem homines saepe etiam non nobiles consulatum
consecuti sunt, praesertim cum haec eadem res plurimas 25
gratias, firmissimas amicitias, maxima studia pariat.
Quorum in isto vestro artificio, Sulpici, nihil est.   25.
Primum dignitas in tam tenui scientia non potest esse;
res enim sunt parvae, prope in singulis litteris atque
interpunctionibus verborum occupatae. Deinde, etiam 30
si quid apud maiores nostros fuit in isto studio admirationis, id enuntiatis vestris mysteriis totum est con-
temptum et abiectum.   Posset agi lege necne pauci
quondam sciebant; fastos enim volgo non habebant.
Erant in magna potentia qui consulebantur; a quibus 35
etiam dies tamquam a Chaldaeis petebatur.   Inventus
est scriba quidam, Cn. Flavius, qui cornicum oculos

confixerit et singulis diebus ediscendis fastos populo
proposuerit et ab ipsis his cautis iuris consultis eorum
40 sapientiam compilarit. Itaque irati illi, quod sunt
veriti ne dierum ratione pervolgata et cognita sine sua
opera lege agi posset, verba quaedam composuerunt ut
omnibus in rebus ipsi interessent.

26–27. *Examples of these legal formulae and the ways of lawyers
are mocked.*

XII. 26. Cum hoc fieri bellissime posset: ' Fundus
Sabinus meus est.' ' Immo meus.' deinde iudicium,
noluerunt. ' FUNDUS ' inquit ' QUI EST IN AGRO QUI
SABINUS VOCATUR.' Satis verbose; cedo quid postea?
5 ' EUM EGO EX IURE QUIRITIUM MEUM ESSE AIO.' Quid
tum? ' INDE IBI EGO TE EX IURE MANUM CONSERTUM
VOCO.' Quid huic tam loquaciter litigioso responderet
ille unde petebatur non habebat. Transit idem iuris
consultus tibicinis Latini modo. ' UNDE TU ME ' inquit
10 ' EX IURE MANUM CONSERTUM VOCASTI, INDE IBI EGO TE
REVOCO.' Praetor interea ne pulchrum se ac beatum
putaret atque aliquid ipse sua sponte loqueretur, ei quoque carmen compositum est cum ceteris rebus absur-
dum tum vero in illo: ' SUIS UTRISQUE SUPERSTITIBUS
15 PRAESENTIBUS ISTAM VIAM DICO; ITE VIAM.' Praesto
aderat sapiens ille qui inire viam doceret. ' REDITE
VIAM.' Eodem duce redibant. Haec iam tum apud illos
barbatos ridicula, credo, videbantur, homines, cum
recte atque in loco constitissent, iuberi abire ut, unde
20 abissent, eodem statim redirent. Isdem ineptiis fucata
sunt illa omnia: ' QUANDO TE IN IURE CONSPICIO ' et
haec: 'ANNE TU DICAS QUA EX CAUSA VINDICAVERIS? '
Quae dum erant occulta, necessario ab eis qui ea tene-

bant petebantur; postea vero pervolgata atque in manibus iactata et excussa, inanissima prudentiae reperta 25
sunt, fraudis autem et stultitiae plenissima. 27. Nam,
cum permulta praeclare legibus essent constituta, ea
iure consultorum ingeniis pleraque corrupta ac depra-
vata sunt. Mulieres omnis propter infirmitatem consili
maiores in tutorum potestate esse voluerunt; hi invene- 30
runt genera tutorum quae potestate mulierum continerentur. Sacra interire illi noluerunt; horum ingenio
senes ad coemptiones faciendas interimendorum sacrorum causa reperti sunt. In omni denique iure civili
aequitatem reliquerunt, verba ipsa tenuerunt, ut, quia 35
in alicuius libris exempli causa id nomen invenerant,
putarunt omnis mulieres quae coemptionem facerent
' Gaias ' vocari. Iam illud mihi quidem mirum videri
solet, tot homines, tam ingeniosos, post tot annos etiam
nunc statuere non potuisse utrum ' diem tertium ' an 40
' perendinum,' ' iudicem ' an ' arbitrum,' ' rem ' an
' litem ' dici oporteret.

*28. A profession engaged in petty details of its own devising does
not lead either to the consulship or to popularity with others.*

XIII. 28. Itaque, ut dixi, dignitas in ista scientia
consularis numquam fuit, quae tota ex rebus fictis
commenticiisque constaret, gratiae vero multo etiam
minus. Quod enim omnibus patet et aeque promptum
est mihi et adversario meo, id esse gratum nullo pacto 5
potest. Itaque non modo benefici conlocandi spem sed
etiam illud quod aliquamdiu fuit ' LICET CONSULERE? '
iam perdidistis. Sapiens existimari nemo potest in ea
prudentia quae neque extra Romam usquam neque
Romae rebus prolatis quicquam valet. Peritus ideo 10

haberi nemo potest quod in eo quod sciunt omnes nullo
modo possunt inter se discrepare. Difficilis autem res
ideo non putatur quod et perpaucis et minime obscuris
litteris continetur. Itaque si mihi, homini vehementer
15 occupato, stomachum moveritis, triduo me iuris consultum esse profitebor. Etenim quae de scripto aguntur,
scripta sunt omnia, neque tamen quicquam tam anguste
scriptum est quo ego non possim ' QUA DE RE AGITUR '
addere; quae consuluntur autem, minimo periculo
20 respondentur. Si id quod oportet responderis, idem
videare respondisse quod Servius; sin aliter, etiam
controversum ius nosse et tractare videare.

29. *Men who have sought to become orators but have failed often*
become jurisconsults.

29. Quapropter non solum illa gloria militaris vestris
formulis atque actionibus anteponenda est verum etiam
dicendi consuetudo longe et multum isti vestrae exercitationi ad honorem antecellit. Itaque mihi videntur
5 plerique initio multo hoc maluisse, post, cum id adsequi
non potuissent, istuc potissimum sunt delapsi. Ut aiunt
in Graecis artificibus eos auloedos esse qui citharoedi
fieri non potuerint, sic nos videmus, qui oratores evadere
non potuerint, eos ad iuris studium devenire. Magnus
10 dicendi labor, magna res, magna dignitas, summa autem
gratia. Etenim a vobis salubritas quaedam, ab eis qui
dicunt salus ipsa petitur. Deinde vestra responsa atque
decreta et evertuntur saepe dicendo et sine defensione
orationis firma esse non possunt. In qua si satis pro-
15 fecissem, parcius de eius laude dicerem; nunc nihil
de me dico, sed de eis qui in dicendo magni sunt aut
fuerunt.

30. *Of the two professions that lead to the consulship – that of the soldier and that of the orator – the soldier's takes first place.*

XIV. 30. Duae sint artes igitur quae possint locare homines in amplissimo gradu dignitatis, una imperatoris, altera oratoris boni. Ab hoc enim pacis ornamenta retinentur, ab illo belli pericula repelluntur. Ceterae tamen virtutes ipsae per se multum valent, iustitia, fides, 5 pudor, temperantia; quibus te, Servi, excellere omnes intellegunt. Sed nunc de studiis ad honorem appositis, non de insita cuiusque virtute disputo. Omnia ista nobis studia de manibus excutiuntur, simul atque aliqui motus novus bellicum canere coepit. Etenim, ut ait 10 ingeniosus poeta et auctor valde bonus, 'proeliis promulgatis pellitur e medio' non solum ista vestra verbosa simulatio prudentiae sed etiam ipsa illa domina rerum, 'sapientia; vi geritur res, spernitur orator' non solum odiosus in dicendo ac loquax verum etiam 'bonus; 15 horridus miles amatur,' vestrum vero studium totum iacet. 'Non ex iure manum consertum, sed mage ferro' inquit 'rem repetunt.' Quod si ita est, cedat, opinor, Sulpici, forum castris, otium militiae, stilus gladio, umbra soli; sit denique in civitate ea prima res propter 20 quam ipsa est civitas omnium princeps.

31–34. *Cicero rebuts Cato's argument that the war against Mithridates was a trivial affair by giving a detailed account of the campaigns which Rome has had to fight in the East against him and men like him.*

31. Verum haec Cato nimium nos nostris verbis magna facere demonstrat et oblitos esse bellum illud omne Mithridaticum cum mulierculis esse gestum. Quod ego longe secus existimo, iudices; deque eo pauca

5 disseram; neque enim causa in hoc continetur. Nam
si omnia bella quae cum Graecis gessimus contemnenda
sunt, derideatur de rege Pyrrho triumphus M'. Curi,
de Philippo T. Flaminini, de Aetolis M. Fulvi, de rege
Perse L. Pauli, de Pseudophilippo Q. Metelli, de
10 Corinthiis L. Mummi. Sin haec bella gravissima vic-
toriaeque eorum bellorum gratissimae fuerunt, cur
Asiaticae nationes atque ille a te hostis contemnitur?
Atqui ex veterum rerum monumentis vel maximum
bellum populum Romanum cum Antiocho gessisse
15 video; cuius belli victor L. Scipio aequa parta cum P.
fratre gloria, quam laudem ille Africa oppressa cognomine ipso prae se ferebat, eandem hic sibi ex Asiae
nomine adsumpsit. 32. Quo quidem in bello virtus
enituit egregia M. Catonis, proavi tui; quo ille, cum
20 esset, ut ego mihi statuo, talis qualem te esse video,
numquam cum Scipione esset profectus, si cum mulierculis bellandum arbitraretur. Neque vero cum P.
Africano senatus egisset ut legatus fratri proficisceretur,
cum ipse paulo ante Hannibale ex Italia expulso, ex
25 Africa eiecto, Carthagine oppressa maximis periculis
rem publicam liberasset, nisi illud grave bellum et
vehemens putaretur. XV. Atqui si diligenter quid
Mithridates potuerit et quid effecerit et qui vir fuerit
consideraris, omnibus quibuscum populus Romanus
30 bellum gessit hunc regem nimirum antepones. Quem
L. Sulla maximo et fortissimo exercitu, pugnax et acer
et non rudis imperator, ut aliud nihil dicam, cum bello
invectum totam in Asiam cum pace dimisit; quem L.
Murena, pater huiusce, vehementissime vigilantissime-
35 que vexatum repressum magna ex parte, non oppressum
reliquit; qui rex sibi aliquot annis sumptis ad confir-

mandas rationes et copias belli tantum spe conatuque
valuit ut se Oceanum cum Ponto, Sertori copias cum
suis coniuncturum putaret. 33. Ad quod bellum duobus
consulibus ita missis ut alter Mithridatem persequeretur, 40
alter Bithyniam tueretur, alterius res et terra et mari
calamitosae vehementer et opes regis et nomen auxe-
runt; L. Luculli vero res tantae exstiterunt ut neque
maius bellum commemorari possit neque maiore consilio
et virtute gestum. Nam cum totius impetus belli ad 45
Cyzicenorum moenia constitisset eamque urbem sibi
Mithridates Asiae ianuam fore putasset qua effracta
et revolsa tota pateret provincia, perfecta a Lucullo
haec sunt omnia ut urbs fidelissimorum sociorum defen-
deretur et omnes copiae regis diuturnitate obsessionis 50
consumerentur. Quid? illam pugnam navalem ad
Tenedum, cum contento cursu acerrimis ducibus hostium classis Italiam spe atque animis inflata peteret,
mediocri certamine et parva dimicatione commissam
arbitraris? Mitto proelia, praetereo oppugnationes 55
oppidorum; expulsus regno tandem aliquando tantum
tamen consilio atque auctoritate valuit ut se rege
Armeniorum adiuncto novis opibus copiisque renovarit.
XVI. Ac si mihi nunc de rebus gestis esset nostri exercitus imperatorisque dicendum, plurima et maxima 60
proelia commemorare possem; sed non id agimus.
34. Hoc dico: Si bellum hoc, si hic hostis, si ille rex
contemnendus fuisset, neque tanta cura senatus et
populus Romanus suscipiendum putasset neque tot
annos gessisset neque tanta gloria L. Lucullus, neque 65
vero eius belli conficiendum exitum tanto studio populus
Romanus ad Cn. Pompeium detulisset. Cuius ex omnibus pugnis, quae sunt innumerabiles, vel acerrima mihi

videtur illa quae cum rege commissa est et summa
70 contentione pugnata. Qua ex pugna cum se ille
eripuisset et Bosphorum confugisset quo exercitus adire
non posset, etiam in extrema fortuna et fuga nomen
tamen retinuit regium. Itaque ipse Pompeius regno
possesso ex omnibus oris ac notis sedibus hoste pulso
75 tamen tantum in unius anima posuit ut, cum ipse omnia
quae tenuerat, adierat, sperarat, victoria possideret,
tamen non ante quam illum vita expulit bellum confectum iudicarit. Hunc tu hostem, Cato, contemnis quo-
cum per tot annos tot proeliis tot imperatores bella
80 gesserunt, cuius expulsi et eiecti vita tanti aestimata
est ut morte eius nuntiata denique bellum confectum
arbitrarentur? Hoc igitur in bello L. Murenam legatum
fortissimi animi, summi consili, maximi laboris cogni-
tum esse defendimus, et hanc eius operam non minus
85 ad consulatum adipiscendum quam hanc nostram
forensem industriam dignitatis habuisse.

*35-36. That Sulpicius was declared elected first in the election
of praetors cannot be taken as precedent for subsequent elections.
Nothing is less predictable than the electorate, and elections
produce many surprises.*

XVII. 35. At enim in praeturae petitione prior
renuntiatus est Servius. Pergitisne vos tamquam ex
syngrapha agere cum populo ut, quem locum semel
honoris cuipiam dederit, eundem in reliquis honoribus
5 debeat? Quod enim fretum, quem Euripum tot motus,
tantas, tam varias habere putatis agitationes com-
mutationesque fluctuum, quantas perturbationes et
quantos aestus habet ratio comitiorum? Dies inter-
missus aut nox interposita saepe perturbat omnia, et

totam opinionem parva non numquam commutat aura 10
rumoris. Saepe etiam sine ulla aperta causa fit aliud
atque existimaris, ut non numquam ita factum esse
etiam populus admiretur, quasi vero non ipse fecerit.
36. Nihil est incertius volgo, nihil obscurius voluntate
hominum, nihil fallacius ratione tota comitiorum. Quis 15
L. Philippum summo ingenio, opera, gratia, nobilitate
a M. Herennio superari posse arbitratus est? quis Q.
Catulum humanitate, sapientia, integritate antecellen-
tem a Cn. Mallio? quis M. Scaurum, hominem gravissimum, civem egregium, fortissimum senatorem, a Q. 20
Maximo? Non modo horum nihil ita fore putatum est
sed, ne cum esset factum quidem, qua re ita factum
esset intellegi potuit. Nam, ut tempestates saepe
certo aliquo caeli signo commoventur, saepe improviso
nulla ex certa ratione obscura aliqua ex causa concit- 25
antur, sic in hac comitiorum tempestate populari saepe
intellegas quo signo commota sit, saepe ita obscura causa
est ut casu excitata esse videatur.

37. *Murena laboured under two disadvantages when a candidate
for the praetorship: the absence of soldiers to support him, and
the fact that he had not given any public shows. These disadvantages had both been removed when he was a consular candidate.*

XVIII. 37. Sed tamen si est reddenda ratio, duae res
vehementer in praetura desideratae sunt quae ambae
in consulatu multum Murenae profuerunt, una exspectatio muneris quae et rumore non nullo et studiis
sermonibusque competitorum creverat, altera quod ei 5
quos in provincia ac legatione omni et liberalitatis et
virtutis suae testis habuerat nondum decesserant.
Horum utrumque ei fortuna ad consulatus petitionem

reservavit. Nam et L. Luculli exercitus qui ad trium-
10 phum convenerat idem comitiis L. Murenae praesto fuit,
et munus amplissimum quod petitio praeturae desiderat
praetura restituit.

*38–40. The support of the soldiers was very important to Murena,
but if Sulpicius denies this he cannot deny that Murena won
popularity from his magnificent games. Since Sulpicius had
not given any, he was in this respect at a disadvantage.*

38. Num tibi haec parva videntur adiumenta et
subsidia consulatus, voluntas militum, quaeque cum per
se valet multitudine, cum apud suos gratia, tum vero
in consule declarando multum etiam apud universum
5 populum Romanum auctoritatis habet, suffragatio
militaris? Imperatores enim comitiis consularibus,
non verborum interpretes deliguntur. Qua re gravis
est illa oratio: 'Me saucium recreavit, me praeda
donavit; hoc duce castra cepimus, signa contulimus;
10 numquam iste plus militi laboris imposuit quam sibi
sumpsit, ipse cum fortis tum etiam felix.' Hoc quanti
putas esse ad famam hominum ac voluntatem? Etenim,
si tanta illis comitiis religio est ut adhuc semper omen
valuerit praerogativum, quid mirum est in hoc felicitatis
15 famam sermonemque valuisse?

XIX. Sed si haec leviora ducis quae sunt gravissima
et hanc urbanam suffragationem militari anteponis,
noli ludorum huius elegantiam et scaenae magnificentiam tam valde contemnere; quae huic admodum
20 profuerunt. Nam quid ego dicam populum ac volgus
imperitorum ludis magno opere delectari? Minus est
mirandum. Quamquam huic causae id satis est; sunt
enim populi ac multitudinis comitia. Qua re, si populo

ludorum magnificentia voluptati est, non est mirandum
eam L. Murenae apud populum profuisse. 39. Sed si 25
nosmet ipsi qui et ab delectatione communi negotiis
impedimur et in ipsa occupatione delectationes alias
multas habere possumus, ludis tamen oblectamur et
ducimur, quid tu admirere de multitudine indocta?
40. L. Otho, vir fortis, meus necessarius, equestri ordini 30
restituit non solum dignitatem sed etiam voluptatem.
Itaque lex haec quae ad ludos pertinet est omnium
gratissima, quod honestissimo ordini cum splendore
fructus quoque iucunditatis est restitutus. Qua re
delectant homines, mihi crede, ludi, etiam illos qui 35
dissimulant, non solum eos qui fatentur; quod ego in
mea petitione sensi. Nam nos quoque habuimus
scaenam competitricem. Quod si ego qui trinos ludos
aedilis feceram tamen Antoni ludis commovebar, tibi
qui casu nullos feceras nihil huius istam ipsam quam 40
inrides argenteam scaenam adversatam putas?

41–42. *If nevertheless Sulpicius does deny this, let him contrast
their respective praetorships. His own refusal of a province
cannot be criticised, but Murena gained much advantage from
accepting one.*

41. Sed haec sane sint paria omnia, sit par forensis
opera militari, militaris suffragatio urbanae, sit idem
magnificentissimos et nullos umquam fecisse ludos;
quid? in ipsa praetura nihilne existimas inter tuam et
huius sortem interfuisse? XX. Huius sors ea fuit quam 5
omnes tui necessarii tibi optabamus, iuris dicundi; in
qua gloriam conciliat magnitudo negoti, gratiam aequitatis largitio; qua in sorte sapiens praetor qualis hic fuit
offensionem vitat aequabilitate decernendi, benivolen-

10 tiam adiungit lenitate audiendi. Egregia et ad consulatum apta provincia in qua laus aequitatis, integritatis,
facilitatis ad extremum ludorum voluptate concluditur.
42. Quid tua sors? Tristis, atrox, quaestio peculatus
ex altera parte lacrimarum et squaloris, ex altera plena
15 accusatorum atque indicum; cogendi iudices inviti,
retinendi contra voluntatem; scriba damnatus, ordo
totus alienus; Sullana gratificatio reprehensa, multi
viri fortes et prope pars civitatis offensa est; lites severe
aestimatae; cui placet obliviscitur, cui dolet meminit.
20 Postremo tu in provinciam ire noluisti. Non possum id
in te reprehendere quod in me ipso et praetore et consule
probavi. Sed tamen L. Murenae provincia multas bonas
gratias cum optima existimatione attulit. Habuit
proficiscens dilectum in Umbria; dedit ei facultatem res
25 publica liberalitatis, qua usus multas sibi tribus quae
municipiis Umbriae conficiuntur adiunxit. Ipse autem
in Gallia ut nostri homines desperatas iam pecunias
exigerent aequitate diligentiaque perfecit. Tu interea
Romae scilicet amicis praesto fuisti; fateor; sed tamen
30 illud cogita non nullorum amicorum studia minui solere
in eos a quibus provincias contemni intellegunt.

*43–46. Murena and Sulpicius have equal claims to the consulship,
but the threats made by Sulpicius against Murena when they were
candidates weakened his own campaign. His supporters thought
that he was losing confidence in his chances of success and
that he could not both manage a campaign and prepare an indictment.*

XXI. 43. Et quoniam ostendi, iudices, parem dignitatem ad consulatus petitionem, disparem fortunam
provincialium negotiorum in Murena atque in Sulpicio
fuisse, dicam iam apertius in quo meus necessarius fuerit

inferior, Servius, et ea dicam vobis audientibus amisso 5
iam tempore quae ipsi soli re integra saepe dixi. Petere
consulatum nescire te, Servi, persaepe tibi dixi; et in
eis rebus ipsis quas te magno et forti animo et agere et
dicere videbam tibi solitus sum dicere magis te fortem
accusatorem mihi videri quam sapientem candidatum. 10
Primum accusandi terrores et minae quibus tu cotidie
uti solebas sunt fortis viri, sed et populi opinionem a spe
adipiscendi avertunt et amicorum studia debilitant.
Nescio quo pacto semper hoc fit – neque in uno aut
altero animadversum est sed iam in pluribus – simul 15
atque candidatus accusationem meditari visus est, ut
honorem desperasse videatur. 44. Quid ergo? acceptam iniuriam persequi non placet? Immo vehementer
placet; sed aliud tempus est petendi, aliud persequendi.
Petitorem ego, praesertim consulatus, magna spe, magno 20
animo, magnis copiis et in forum et in campum deduci
volo. Non placet mihi inquisitio candidati, praenuntia
repulsae, non testium potius quam suffragatorum
comparatio, non minae magis quam blanditiae, non
denuntiatio potius quam persalutatio, praesertim cum 25
iam hoc novo more omnes fere domos omnium con-
cursent et ex voltu candidatorum coniecturam faciant
quantum quisque animi et facultatis habere videatur.
45. ' Videsne tu illum tristem, demissum? iacet, diffidit,
abiecit hastas.' Serpit hic rumor. ' Scis tu illum accusa- 30
tionem cogitare, inquirere in competitores, testis
quaerere? Alium fac iam, quoniam sibi hic ipse
desperat.' Eius modi rumoribus candidatorum amici
intimi debilitantur, studia deponunt; aut certam rem
abiciunt aut suam operam et gratiam iudicio et accusa- 35
tioni reservant. XXII. Accedit eodem ut etiam ipse

candidatus totum animum atque omnem curam operam
diligentiamque suam in petitione non possit ponere.
Adiungitur enim accusationis cogitatio, non parva res
40 sed nimirum omnium maxima. Magnum est enim te
comparare ea quibus possis hominem e civitate, praesertim non inopem neque infirmum, exturbare, qui et
per se et per suos et vero etiam per alienos defendatur.
Omnes enim ad pericula propulsanda concurrimus et
45 qui non aperte inimici sumus etiam alienissimis in capitis periculis amicissimorum officia et studia praesta-
mus. 46. Qua re ego expertus et petendi et defendendi
et accusandi molestiam sic intellexi in petendo studium
esse acerrimum, in defendendo officium, in accusando
50 laborem. Itaque sic statuo fieri nullo modo posse ut
idem accusationem et petitionem consulatus diligenter
adornet atque instruat. Unum sustinere pauci possunt,
utrumque nemo. Tu cum te de curriculo petitionis
deflexisses animumque ad accusandum transtulisses,
55 existimasti te utrique negotio satis facere posse. Vehementer errasti. Quis enim dies fuit, postea quam in
istam accusandi denuntiationem ingressus es, quem tu
non totum in ista ratione consumpseris?

46–47. *Sulpicius' demand for harsher legislation damaged
further his chances of success.*

XXIII. Legem ambitus flagitasti, quae tibi non
deerat; erat enim severissime scripta Calpurnia. Gestus
est mos et voluntati et dignitati tuae. Sed tota illa lex
accusationem tuam, si haberes nocentem reum, fortasse
5 armasset; petitioni vero refragata est. 47. Poena
gravior in plebem tua voce efflagitata est; commoti
animi tenuiorum. Exsilium in nostrum ordinem;

concessit senatus postulationi tuae, sed non libenter duriorem fortunae communi condicionem te auctore constituit. Morbi excusationi poena addita est; 10 voluntas offensa multorum quibus aut contra valetudinis commodum laborandum est aut incommodo morbi etiam ceteri vitae fructus relinquendi. Quid ergo? haec quis tulit? Is qui auctoritati senatus, voluntati tuae paruit, denique is tulit cui minime proderant. Illa 15 quidem quae mea summa voluntate senatus frequens repudiavit mediocriter adversata tibi esse existimas? Confusionem suffragiorum flagitasti, perrogationem legis Maniliae, aequationem gratiae, dignitatis, suffragiorum. Graviter homines honesti atque in suis vicini- 20 tatibus et municipiis gratiosi tulerunt a tali viro esse pugnatum ut omnes et dignitatis et gratiae gradus tollerentur. Idem editicios iudices esse voluisti, ut odia occulta civium quae tacitis nunc discordiis continentur in fortunas optimi cuiusque erumperent. 25

48–53. *The greatest damage, however, was done to Sulpicius' candidature by his failure to realise where the public interest lay when Catiline was so confident of success. Thus men who feared that the failure of Sulpicius to press his own campaign might cause Catiline to be elected turned to Murena.*

48. Haec omnia tibi accusandi viam muniebant, adipiscendi obsaepiebant.

Atque ex omnibus illa plaga est iniecta petitioni tuae non tacente me maxima, de qua ab homine ingeniosissimo et copiosissimo, Q. Hortensio, multa gravissime 5 dicta sunt. Quo etiam mihi durior locus est dicendi datus ut, cum ante me et ille dixisset et vir summa dignitate et diligentia et facultate dicendi, M. Crassus, ego in extremo non partem aliquam agerem causae sed

10 de tota re dicerem quod mihi videretur. Itaque in
isdem rebus fere versor et quoad possum, iudices, occurro
vestrae satietati. XXIV. Sed tamen, Servi, quam te
securim putas iniecisse petitioni tuae, cum populum
Romanum in eum metum adduxisti ut pertimesceret
15 ne consul Catilina fieret, dum tu accusationem com-
parares deposita atque abiecta petitione? 49. Etenim
te inquirere videbant, tristem ipsum, maestos amicos;
observationes, testificationes, seductiones testium, secessiones subscriptorum animadvertebant, quibus rebus
20 certe ipsi candidatorum voltus obscuriores videri
solent; Catilinam interea alacrem atque laetum, stipa-
tum choro iuventutis, vallatum indicibus atque sicariis,
inflatum cum spe militum tum conlegae mei, quem ad
modum dicebat ipse, promissis, circumfluentem colono-
25 rum Arretinorum et Faesulanorum exercitu; quam
turbam dissimillimo ex genere distinguebant homines
perculsi Sullani temporis calamitate. Voltus erat
ipsius plenus furoris, oculi sceleris, sermo adrogantiae,
sic ut ei iam exploratus et domi conditus consulatus
30 videretur. Murenam contemnebat, Sulpicium accusatorem suum numerabat non competitorem; ei vim
denuntiabat, rei publicae minabatur. XXV. 50. Quibus rebus qui timor bonis omnibus iniectus sit quanta-
que desperatio rei publicae, si ille factus esset, nolite a
35 me commoneri velle; vosmet ipsi vobiscum recorda-
mini. Meministis enim, cum illius nefarii gladiatoris
voces percrebruissent quas habuisse in contione domestica dicebatur, cum miserorum fidelem defensorem
negasset inveniri posse nisi eum qui ipse miser esset;
40 integrorum et fortunatorum promissis saucios et miseros
credere non oportere; qua re qui consumpta replere,

erepta reciperare vellent, spectarent quid ipse deberet,
quid possideret, quid auderet; minime timidum et
valde calamitosum esse oportere eum qui esset futurus
dux et signifer calamitosorum. 51. Tum igitur, his rebus 45
auditis, meministis fieri senatus consultum referente me
ne postero die comitia haberentur, ut de his rebus in
senatu agere possemus. Itaque postridie frequenti
senatu Catilinam excitavi atque eum de his rebus iussi,
si quid vellet, quae ad me adlatae essent dicere. Atque 50
ille, ut semper fuit apertissimus, non se purgavit sed
indicavit atque induit. Tum enim dixit duo corpora
esse rei publicae, unum debile infirmo capite, alterum
firmum sine capite; huic, si ita de se meritum esset,
caput se vivo non defuturum. Congemuit senatus 55
frequens neque tamen satis severe pro rei indignitate
decrevit; nam partim ideo fortes in decernendo non
erant, quia nihil timebant, partim, quia omnia. Erupit
e senatu triumphans gaudio quem omnino vivum illinc
exire non oportuerat, praesertim cum idem ille in eodem 60
ordine paucis diebus ante Catoni, fortissimo viro,
iudicium minitanti ac denuntianti respondisset, si quod
esset in suas fortunas incendium excitatum, id se non
aqua sed ruina restincturum. XXVI. 52. His tum
rebus commotus et quod homines iam tum coniuratos 65
cum gladiis in campum deduci a Catilina sciebam,
descendi in campum cum firmissimo praesidio fortissi-
morum virorum et cum illa lata insignique lorica, non
quae me tegeret – etenim sciebam Catilinam non latus
aut ventrem sed caput et collum solere petere – verum 70
ut omnes boni animadverterent et, cum in metu et
periculo consulem viderent, id quod est factum, ad opem
praesidiumque concurrerent. Itaque cum te, Servi,

remissiorem in petendo putarent, Catilinam et spe et
75 cupiditate inflammatum viderent, omnes qui illam ab
re publica pestem depellere cupiebant ad Murenam se
statim contulerunt. 53. Magna est autem comitiis consularibus repentina voluntatum inclinatio, praesertim
cum incubuit ad virum bonum et multis aliis adiumentis
80 petitionis ornatum. Qui cum honestissimo patre atque
maioribus, modestissima adulescentia, clarissima legatione, praetura probata in iure, grata in munere, ornata
in provincia petisset diligenter, et ita petisset ut neque
minanti cederet neque cuiquam minaretur, huic miran-
85 dum est magno adiumento Catilinae subitam spem
consulatus adipiscendi fuisse?

*54–56. Cicero expresses his sorrow that Murena has been accused
by old friends who have no personal grudge against him.*

54. Nunc mihi tertius ille locus est relictus orationis,
de ambitus criminibus, perpurgatus ab eis qui ante me
dixerunt, a me, quoniam ita Murena voluit, retractan-
dus; quo in loco C. Postumo, familiari meo, ornatissimo
5 viro, de divisorum indiciis et de deprehensis pecuniis,
adulescenti ingenioso et bono, Ser. Sulpicio, de equitum
centuriis, M. Catoni, homini in omni virtute excellenti,
de ipsius accusatione, de senatus consulto, de re publica respondebo. XXVII. 55. Sed pauca quae meum
10 animum repente moverunt prius de L. Murenae fortuna
conquerar. Nam cum saepe antea, iudices, et ex aliorum
miseriis et ex meis curis laboribusque cotidianis fortu-
natos eos homines iudicarem qui remoti a studiis am-
bitionis otium ac tranquillitatem vitae secuti sunt, tum
15 vero in his L. Murenae tantis tamque improvisis
periculis ita sum animo adfectus ut non queam satis

neque communem omnium nostrum condicionem neque huius eventum fortunamque miserari. Qui primum, dum ex honoribus continuis familiae maiorumque suorum unum ascendere gradum dignitatis conatus est, ve- 20 nit in periculum ne et ea quae ei relicta, et haec quae ab ipso parta sunt amittat, deinde propter studium novae laudis etiam in veteris fortunae discrimen adducitur. 56. Quae cum sunt gravia, iudices, tum illud acerbissimum est quod habet eos accusatores, non qui odio inimici- 25 tiarum ad accusandum, sed qui studio accusandi ad inimicitias descenderint. Nam ut omittam Servium Sulpicium quem intellego non iniuria L. Murenae sed honoris contentione permotum, accusat paternus amicus, C. Postumus, vetus, ut ait ipse, vicinus ac necessarius, 30 qui necessitudinis causas compluris protulit, simultatis nullam commemorare potuit. Accusat Ser. Sulpicius, sodalis filius, cuius ingenio paterni omnes necessarii munitiores esse debebant. Accusat M. Cato qui cum a Murena nulla re umquam alienus fuit, tum ea condici- 35 one nobis erat in hac civitate natus ut eius opes, ut ingenium praesidio multis etiam alienis, exitio vix cuiquam inimico esse deberet.

57. *Cicero replies to Postumus.*

57. Respondebo igitur Postumo primum qui nescio quo pacto mihi videtur praetorius candidatus in consularem quasi desultorius in quadrigarum curriculum incurrere. Cuius competitores si nihil deliquerunt, dignitati eorum concessit, cum petere destitit; sin 5 autem eorum aliquis largitus est, expetendus amicus est qui alienam potius iniuriam quam suam persequatur.

DE POSTUMI CRIMINIBUS, DE SERVI ADULESCENTIS.

58–59. *Cicero replies to Cato whose influence he fears more than the strength of his case.*

XXVIII. 58. Venio nunc ad M. Catonem, quod est fundamentum ac robur totius accusationis; qui tamen ita gravis est accusator et vehemens ut multo magis eius auctoritatem quam criminationem pertimescam. 5 In quo ego accusatore, iudices, primum illud deprecabor ne quid L. Murenae dignitas illius, ne quid exspectatio tribunatus, ne quid totius vitae splendor et gravitas noceat, denique ne ea soli huic obsint bona M. Catonis quae ille adeptus est ut multis prodesse possit. Bis 10 consul fuerat P. Africanus et duos terrores huius imperi, Carthaginem Numantiamque, deleverat cum accusavit L. Cottam. Erat in eo summa eloquentia, summa fides, summa integritas, auctoritas tanta quanta in imperio populi Romani quod illius opera tenebatur. Saepe hoc 15 maiores natu dicere audivi, hanc accusatoris eximiam vim et dignitatem plurimum L. Cottae profuisse. Noluerunt sapientissimi homines qui tum rem illam iudicabant ita quemquam cadere in iudicio ut nimiis adversarii viribus abiectus videretur. 59. Quid? Ser. Galbam – 20 nam traditum memoriae est – nonne proavo tuo, fortissimo atque florentissimo viro, M. Catoni, incumbenti ad eius perniciem populus Romanus eripuit? Semper in hac civitate nimis magnis accusatorum opibus et populus universus et sapientes ac multum in posterum 25 prospicientes iudices restiterunt. Nolo accusator in iudicium potentiam adferat, non vim maiorem aliquam, non auctoritatem excellentem, non nimiam gratiam. Valeant haec omnia ad salutem innocentium, ad opem impotentium, ad auxilium calamitosorum, in periculo 30 vero et in pernicie civium repudientur.

60–66. *The jury must not assume that a defendant is guilty merely because Cato is a prosecutor. It is unfortunate that Cato has followed so unswervingly the rigid precepts of Zeno, the founder of the Stoic school. He would have done better to have been influenced by later Stoics who were kinder and more flexible.*

60. Nam si quis hoc forte dicet, Catonem descensurum ad accusandum non fuisse, nisi prius de causa iudicasset, iniquam legem, iudices, et miseram condicionem instituet periculis hominum, si existimabit iudicium accusatoris in reum pro aliquo praeiudicio valere oportere. 5

XXIX. Ego tuum consilium, Cato, propter singulare animi mei de tua virtute iudicium vituperare non possum; non nulla forsitan conformare et leviter emendare possim. 'Non multa peccas,' inquit ille fortissimo viro senior magister, 'sed peccas; te 10 regere possum.' At ego non te; verissime dixerim peccare te nihil neque ulla in re te esse huius modi ut corrigendus potius quam leviter inflectendus esse videare. Finxit enim te ipsa natura ad honestatem, gravitatem, temperantiam, magnitudinem animi, ius- 15 titiam, ad omnis denique virtutes magnum hominem et excelsum. Accessit istuc doctrina non moderata nec mitis sed, ut mihi videtur, paulo asperior et durior quam aut veritas aut natura patitur. 61. Et quoniam non est nobis haec oratio habenda aut in imperita multi- 20 tudine aut in aliquo conventu agrestium, audacius paulo de studiis humanitatis quae et mihi et vobis nota et iucunda sunt disputabo. In M. Catone, iudices, haec bona quae videmus divina et egregia ipsius scitote esse propria; quae non numquam requirimus, ea sunt 25 omnia non a natura verum a magistro. Fuit enim quidam summo ingenio vir, Zeno, cuius inventorum

aemuli Stoici nominantur. Huius sententiae sunt et
praecepta eius modi. Sapientem gratia numquam
30 moveri, numquam cuiusquam delicto ignoscere; neminem misericordem esse nisi stultum et levem; viri non
esse neque exorari neque placari; solos sapientes esse,
si distortissimi sint, formosos, si mendicissimi, divites,
si servitutem serviant, reges; nos autem qui sapientes
35 non sumus fugitivos, exsules, hostis, insanos denique
esse dicunt; omnia peccata esse paria; omne delictum
scelus esse nefarium, nec minus delinquere eum qui
gallum gallinaceum, cum opus non fuerit, quam eum
qui patrem suffocaverit; sapientem nihil opinari, nullius
40 rei paenitere, nulla in re falli, sententiam mutare numquam. XXX. 62. Hoc homo ingeniosissimus, M. Cato,
auctoribus eruditissimis inductus adripuit, neque dis-
putandi causa, ut magna pars, sed ita vivendi. Petunt
aliquid publicani; cave ne quicquam habeat momenti
45 gratia. Supplices aliqui veniunt miseri et calamitosi;
sceleratus et nefarius fueris, si quicquam misericordia
adductus feceris. Fatetur aliquis se peccasse et sui
delicti veniam petit; 'nefarium est facinus ignoscere.'
At leve delictum est. 'Omnia peccata sunt paria.'
50 Dixisti quippiam: 'fixum et statutum est.' Non re
ductus es sed opinione; 'sapiens nihil opinatur.' Errasti
aliqua in re; male dici putat. Hac ex disciplina nobis
illa sunt: 'Dixi in senatu me nomen consularis candidati delaturum.' Iratus dixisti. 'Numquam' inquit
55 'sapiens irascitur.' At temporis causa. 'Improbi'
inquit 'hominis est mendacio fallere; mutare sententiam turpe est, exorari scelus, misereri flagitium.' 63.
Nostri autem illi – fatebor enim, Cato, me quoque in
adulescentia diffisum ingenio meo quaesisse adiumenta

doctrinae – nostri, inquam, illi a Platone et Aristotele, 60
moderati homines et temperati, aiunt apud sapientem
valere aliquando gratiam; viri boni esse misereri;
distincta genera esse delictorum et disparis poenas;
esse apud hominem constantem ignoscendi locum;
ipsum sapientem saepe aliquid opinari quod nesciat, 65
irasci non numquam, exorari eundem et placari, quod
dixerit interdum, si ita rectius sit, mutare, de sententia
decedere aliquando; omnis virtutes mediocritate quadam esse moderatas. XXXI. 64. Hos ad magistros si
qua te fortuna, Cato, cum ista natura detulisset, non tu 70
quidem vir melior esses nec fortior nec temperantior
nec iustior – neque enim esse potes – sed paulo ad leni-
tatem propensior. Non accusares nullis adductus
inimicitiis, nulla lacessitus iniuria, pudentissimum
hominem summa dignitate atque honestate praeditum; 75
putares, cum in eiusdem anni custodia te atque L.
Murenam fortuna posuisset, aliquo te cum hoc rei
publicae vinculo esse coniunctum; quod atrociter in
senatu dixisti, aut non dixisses aut, si potuisses, mitiorem
in partem interpretarere. 65. Ac te ipsum, quantum 80
ego opinione auguror, nunc et animi quodam impetu
concitatum et vi naturae atque ingeni elatum et recentibus praeceptorum studiis flagrantem iam usus flectet,
dies leniet, aetas mitigabit. Etenim isti ipsi mihi
videntur vestri praeceptores et virtutis magistri finis 85
officiorum paulo longius quam natura vellet protulisse
ut, cum ad ultimum animo contendissemus, ibi tamen
ubi oporteret consisteremus. ' Nihil ignoveris.' Immo
aliquid, non omnia. ' Nihil gratiae causa feceris.'
Immo resistito gratiae, cum officium et fides postulabit. 90
' Misericordia commotus ne sis.' Etiam, in dissolvenda

severitate; sed tamen est laus aliqua humanitatis.
' In sententia permaneto.' Vero, nisi sententiam sententia alia vicerit melior. 66. Huiusce modi Scipio
95 ille fuit quem non paenitebat facere idem quod tu,
habere eruditissimum hominem Panaetium domi; cuius
oratione et praeceptis, quamquam erant eadem ista
quae te delectant, tamen asperior non est factus sed, ut
accepi a senibus, lenissimus. Quis vero C. Laelio
100 comior fuit, quis iucundior eodem ex studio isto, quis
illo gravior, sapientior? Possum de L. Philo, de C.
Gallo dicere haec eadem, sed te domum iam deducam
tuam. Quemquamne existimas Catone, proavo tuo,
commodiorem, communiorem, moderatiorem fuisse ad
105 omnem rationem humanitatis? De cuius praestanti
virtute cum vere graviterque diceres, domesticum te
habere dixisti exemplum ad imitandum. Est illud
quidem exemplum tibi propositum domi, sed tamen
naturae similitudo illius ad te magis qui ab illo ortus es
110 quam ad unum quemque nostrum pervenire potuit, ad
imitandum vero tam mihi propositum exemplar illud est
quam tibi. Sed si illius comitatem et facilitatem tuae
gravitati severitatique asperseris, non ista quidem
erunt meliora, quae nunc sunt optima, sed certe condita
115 iucundius.

67–68. Cato's name and influence must be disregarded.

XXXII. 67. Qua re, ut ad id quod institui revertar,
tolle mihi e causa nomen Catonis, remove vim, prae-
termitte auctoritatem quae in iudiciis aut nihil valere
aut ad salutem debet valere, congredere mecum crimini-
5 bus ipsis. Quid accusas, Cato, quid adfers ad iudicium,
quid arguis? Ambitum accusas; non defendo. Me

reprehendis, quod idem defendam quod lege punierim. Punivi ambitum, non innocentiam; ambitum vero ipsum vel tecum accusabo, si voles. Dixisti senatus consultum me referente esse factum, si mercede obviam 10 candidatis issent, si conducti sectarentur, si gladiatoribus volgo locus tributim et item prandia si volgo essent data, contra legem Calpurniam factum videri. Ergo ita senatus iudicat, contra legem facta haec videri, si facta sint; decernit quod nihil opus est, dum candi- 15 datis morem gerit. Nam factum sit necne vehementer quaeritur; sin factum sit, quin contra legem sit dubitare nemo potest. 68. Est igitur ridiculum, quod est dubium, id relinquere incertum, quod nemini dubium potest esse, id iudicare. Atque id decernitur omnibus postu- 20 lantibus candidatis, ut ex senatus consulto neque cuius intersit, neque contra quem sit intellegi possit. Qua re doce ab L. Murena illa esse commissa; tum egomet tibi contra legem commissa esse concedam.

68–73. *Murena's alleged crime is dealt with under three headings:*

(1) 68–69. *A crowd went to meet him on his return from his province. This was no more than what he deserved and it would have been more remarkable had it not happened.*

(2) 70–71. *Many people followed him about in public. Only if it can be proved they were* hired *to do so has any crime been committed.*

(3) 72–73. *It is alleged that free seats at games were given to* whole *tribes and free meals to the* whole *people. It cannot be proved that this was done. What he did was normal practice and did not break the law.*

XXXIII. 'Multi obviam prodierunt de provincia decedenti.' Consulatum petenti solet fieri; eccui autem non proditur revertenti? 'Quae fuit ista multi-

tudo? ' Primum, si tibi istam rationem non possim
5 reddere, quid habet admirationis tali viro advenienti,
candidato consulari, obviam prodisse multos? quod nisi
esset factum, magis mirandum videretur. 69. Quid?
si etiam illud addam quod a consuetudine non abhorret,
rogatos esse multos, num aut criminosum sit aut miran-
10 dum, qua in civitate rogati infimorum hominum filios
prope de nocte ex ultima saepe urbe deductum venire
soleamus, in ea non esse gravatos homines prodire hora
tertia in campum Martium, praesertim talis viri nomine
rogatos? Quid? si omnes societates venerunt quarum
15 ex numero multi sedent iudices; quid? si multi homines
nostri ordinis honestissimi; quid? si illa officiosissima
quae neminem patitur non honeste in urbem introire
tota natio candidatorum, si denique ipse accusator
noster Postumus obviam cum bene magna caterva sua
20 venit, quid habet ista multitudo admirationis? Omitto
clientis, vicinos, tribulis, exercitum totum Luculli
qui ad triumphum per eos dies venerat; hoc dico,
frequentiam in isto officio gratuitam non modo dignitati nullius umquam sed ne voluntati quidem
25 defuisse. 70. At sectabantur multi. Doce mercede;
concedam esse crimen. XXXIV. Hoc quidem remoto
quid reprendis? ' Quid opus est' inquit ' sectatoribus? '
A me tu id quaeris, quid opus sit eo quo semper
usi sumus? Homines tenues unum habent in nos-
30 trum ordinem aut promerendi aut referendi benefici
locum, hanc in nostris petitionibus operam atque adsectationem. Neque enim fieri potest neque postulandum est a nobis aut ab equitibus Romanis ut suos
necessarios candidatos adsectentur totos dies; a quibus
35 si domus nostra celebratur, si interdum ad forum

deducimur, si uno basilicae spatio honestamur, diligenter
observari videmur et coli; tenuiorum amicorum et non
occupatorum est ista adsiduitas, quorum copia bonis
viris et beneficis deesse non solet. 71. Noli igitur
eripere hunc inferiori generi hominum fructum offici, 40
Cato; sine eos qui omnia a nobis sperant habere ipsos
quoque aliquid quod nobis tribuere possint. Si nihil
erit praeter ipsorum suffragium, tenues, etsi suffra-
gantur, nil valent gratia. Ipsi denique, ut solent loqui,
non dicere pro nobis, non spondere, non vocare domum 45
suam possunt. Atque haec a nobis petunt omnia neque
ulla re alia quae a nobis consequuntur nisi opera sua
compensari putant posse. Itaque et legi Fabiae quae
est de numero sectatorum, et senatus consulto quod est
L. Caesare consule factum restiterunt. Nulla est enim 50
poena quae possit observantiam tenuiorum ab hoc
vetere instituto officiorum excludere. 72. At spectacula
sunt tributim data et ad prandium volgo vocati. Etsi
hoc factum a Murena omnino, iudices, non est, ab eius
amicis autem more et modo factum est, tamen admo- 55
nitus re ipsa recordor quantum hae conquestiones in
senatu habitae punctorum nobis, Servi, detraxerint.
Quod enim tempus fuit aut nostra aut patrum nostro-
rum memoria quo haec sive ambitio est sive liberalitas
non fuerit ut locus et in circo et in foro daretur amicis 60
et tribulibus? Haec homines tenuiores praemia com-
modaque a suis tribulibus vetere instituto adseque-
bantur***

[*Deest non nihil.*]

XXXV. 73. Praefectum fabrum semel locum tribu- 65
libus suis dedisse, quid statuent in viros primarios
qui in circo totas tabernas tribulium causa compara-

runt? Haec omnia sectatorum, spectaculorum, prandi-
orum item crimina a multitudine in tuam nimiam dili-
70 gentiam, Servi, coniecta sunt, in quibus tamen Murena
ab senatus auctoritate defenditur. Quid enim? senatus
num obviam prodire crimen putat? Non, sed mercede.
Convince. Num sectari multos? Non, sed conductos.
Doce. Num locum ad spectandum dare aut ad prandium
75 invitare? Minime, sed volgo, passim. Quid est volgo?
Universos. Non igitur, si L. Natta, summo loco
adulescens, qui et quo animo iam sit et qualis vir futurus
sit videmus, in equitum centuriis voluit esse et ad hoc
officium necessitudinis et ad reliquum tempus gratiosus,
80 id erit eius vitrico fraudi aut crimini, nec, si virgo
Vestalis, huius propinqua et necessaria, locum suum
gladiatorium concessit huic, non et illa pie fecit et hic
a culpa est remotus. Omnia haec sunt officia necessa-
riorum, commoda tenuiorum, munia candidatorum.

*74–77. Cato should not apply his Stoic principles too rigidly to
the institutions of Rome. The people should have the opportunity
of enjoying traditional pleasures, and the candidates that of
bestowing them.*

74. At enim agit mecum austere et Stoice Cato, negat
verum esse adlici benivolentiam cibo, negat iudicium
hominum in magistratibus mandandis corrumpi volup-
tatibus oportere. Ergo, ad cenam petitionis causa si
5 quis vocat, condemnetur? ' Quippe ' inquit ' tu mihi
summum imperium, tu summam auctoritatem, tu
gubernacula rei publicae petas fovendis hominum
sensibus et deleniendis animis et adhibendis voluptati-
bus? Utrum lenocinium ' inquit ' a grege delicatae
10 iuventutis, an orbis terrarum imperium a populo

Romano petebas? ' Horribilis oratio; sed eam usus,
vita, mores, civitas ipsa respuit. Neque tamen Lace-
daemonii, auctores istius vitae atque orationis, qui
cotidianis epulis in robore accumbunt, neque vero Cretes
quorum nemo gustavit umquam cubans, melius quam 15
Romani homines qui tempora voluptatis laborisque
dispertiunt res publicas suas retinuerunt; quorum
alteri uno adventu nostri exercitus deleti sunt, alteri
nostri imperi praesidio disciplinam suam legesque con-
servant. XXXVI. 75. Qua re noli, Cato, maiorum 20
instituta quae res ipsa, quae diuturnitas imperi comprobat nimium severa oratione reprehendere. Fuit
eodem ex studio vir eruditus apud patres nostros et
honestus homo et nobilis, Q. Tubero. Is, cum epulum
Q. Maximus P. Africani, patrui sui, nomine populo 25
Romano daret, rogatus est a Maximo ut triclinium
sterneret, cum esset Tubero eiusdem Africani sororis
filius. Atque ille, homo eruditissimus ac Stoicus, stravit
pelliculis haedinis lectulos Punicanos et exposuit vasa
Samia, quasi vero esset Diogenes Cynicus mortuus et 30
non divini hominis Africani mors honestaretur; quem
cum supremo eius die Maximus laudaret, gratias egit
dis immortalibus quod ille vir in hac re publica potissimum natus esset; necesse enim fuisse ibi esse terrarum
imperium ubi ille esset. Huius in morte celebranda 35
graviter tulit populus Romanus hanc perversam sapientiam Tuberonis, 76. itaque homo integerrimus, civis
optimus, cum esset L. Pauli nepos, P. Africani, ut
dixi, sororis filius, his haedinis pelliculis praetura deiectus est. Odit populus Romanus privatam luxuriam, 40
publicam magnificentiam diligit; non amat profusas
epulas, sordis et inhumanitatem multo minus; dis-

tinguit rationem officiorum ac temporum, vicissitudinem
laboris ac voluptatis. Nam quod ais nulla re adlici
45 hominum mentis oportere ad magistratum mandandum
nisi dignitate, hoc tu ipse in quo summa est dignitas
non servas. Cur enim quemquam ut studeat tibi, ut te
adiuvet rogas? Rogas tu me ut mihi praesis, ut com-
mittam ego me tibi. Quid tandem? istuc me rogari
50 oportet abs te, an te potius a me ut pro mea salute
laborem periculumque suscipias? 77. Quid quod habes
nomenclatorem? in eo quidem fallis et decipis. Nam,
si nomine apellari abs te civis tuos honestum est, turpe
est eos notiores esse servo tuo quam tibi. Sin iam noris,
55 tamenne per monitorem apellandi sunt cum petis, quasi
incertus sis? Quid quod, cum admoneris, tamen, quasi
tute noris, ita salutas? Quid, postea quam es designatus,
multo salutas neglegentius? Haec omnia ad rationem
civitatis si derigas, recta sunt; sin perpendere ad dis-
60 ciplinae praecepta velis, reperiantur pravissima. Qua
re nec plebi Romanae eripiendi fructus isti sunt ludorum, gladiatorum, conviviorum, quae omnia maiores
nostri comparaverunt, nec candidatis ista benignitas
adimenda est quae liberalitatem magis significat quam
65 largitionem.

78–83. *Cato maintains that he has brought the charge in the interests
of the state, but these in fact require the reverse of a successful
prosecution – that there should be two consuls in office on 1
January. The threat of Catiline makes it his duty to ensure
that a capable man like Murena is not deprived of the consulship.*

XXXVII. 78. At enim te ad accusandum res publica
adduxit. Credo, Cato, te isto animo atque ea opinione
venisse; sed tu imprudentia laberis. Ego quod facio,

iudices, cum amicitiae dignitatisque L. Murenae gratia
facio, tum me pacis, oti, concordiae, libertatis, salutis, 5
vitae denique omnium nostrum causa facere clamo
atque testor. Audite, audite consulem, iudices, nihil
dicam adrogantius, tantum dicam totos dies atque
noctes de re publica cogitantem! Non usque eo L.
Catilina rem publicam despexit atque contempsit ut ea 10
copia quam secum eduxit se hanc civitatem oppres-
surum arbitraretur. Latius patet illius sceleris contagio
quam quisquam putat, ad pluris pertinet. Intus, intus,
inquam, est equus Troianus; a quo numquam me
consule dormientes opprimemini. 79. Quaeris a me ec- 15
quid ego Catilinam metuam. Nihil, et curavi ne quis
metueret, sed copias illius quas hic video dico esse
metuendas; nec tam timendus est nunc exercitus L.
Catilinae quam isti qui illum exercitum deseruisse
dicuntur. Non enim deseruerunt sed ab illo in speculis 20
atque insidiis relicti in capite atque in cervicibus nostris
restiterunt. Hi et integrum consulem et bonum impera-
torem et natura et fortuna cum rei publicae salute
coniunctum deici de urbis praesidio et de custodia
civitatis vestris sententiis deturbari volunt. Quorum 25
ego ferrum et audaciam reieci in campo, debilitavi in
foro, compressi etiam domi meae saepe, iudices, his
vos si alterum consulem tradideritis, plus multo erunt
vestris sententiis quam suis gladiis consecuti. Magni
interest, iudices, id quod ego multis repugnantibus egi 30
atque perfeci, esse Kalendis Ianuariis in re publica duo
consules. 80. Nolite arbitrari, mediocribus consiliis
aut usitatis viis eos uti. Non lex improba, non perniciosa
largitio, non auditum aliquando aliquod malum rei
publicae quaeritur. Inita sunt in hac civitate consilia, 35

iudices, urbis delendae, civium trucidandorum, nominis
Romani exstinguendi. Atque haec cives, cives, inquam,
si eos hoc nomine appellari fas est, de patria sua et
cogitant et cogitaverunt. Horum ego cotidie consiliis
40 occurro, audaciam debilito, sceleri resisto. Sed moneo,
iudices. In exitu iam est meus consulatus; nolite mihi
subtrahere vicarium meae diligentiae, nolite adimere
eum cui rem publicam cupio tradere incolumem ab his
tantis periculis defendendam.

45 XXXVIII. 81. Atque ad haec mala, iudices, quid
accedat aliud non videtis? Te, te appello, Cato; nonne
prospicis tempestatem anni tui? Iam enim in hesterna
contione intonuit vox perniciosa designati tribuni, conlegae tui; contra quem multum tua mens, multum
50 omnes boni providerunt qui te ad tribunatus petitionem
vocaverunt. Omnia quae per hoc triennium agitata
sunt, iam ab eo tempore quo a L. Catilina et Cn. Pisone
initum consilium senatus interficiendi scitis esse, in hos
dies, in hos mensis, in hoc tempus erumpunt. 82. Qui
55 locus est, iudices, quod tempus, qui dies, quae nox cum
ego non ex istorum insidiis ac mucronibus non solum
meo sed multo etiam magis divino consilio eripiar atque
evolem? Neque isti me meo nomine interfici sed vigil-
antem consulem de rei publicae praesidio demoveri
60 volunt. Nec minus vellent, Cato, te quoque aliqua
ratione, si possent, tollere; id quod, mihi crede, et agunt
et moliuntur. Vident quantum in te sit animi, quantum
ingeni, quantum auctoritatis, quantum rei publicae
praesidi; sed, cum consulari auctoritate et auxilio
65 spoliatam vim tribuniciam viderint, tum se facilius
inermem et debilitatum te oppressuros arbitrantur.
Nam ne sufficiatur consul non timent. Vident in tuorum

potestate conlegarum fore; sperant sibi D. Silanum,
clarum virum, sine conlega, te sine consule, rem publicam
sine praesidio obici posse.   70

83–86. The safety of the state lies in the votes of the jury.

83. His tantis in rebus tantisque in periculis est tuum,
M. Cato, qui mihi non tibi, sed patriae natus esse videris,
videre quid agatur, retinere adiutorem, defensorem,
socium in re publica, consulem non cupidum, consulem,
quod maxime tempus hoc postulat, fortuna constitutum 5
ad amplexandum otium, scientia ad bellum gerendum,
animo et usu ad quod velis negotium sustinendum.
XXXIX. Quamquam huiusce rei potestas omnis in
vobis sita est, iudices; totam rem publicam vos in hac
causa tenetis, vos gubernatis. Si L. Catilina cum suo 10
consilio nefariorum hominum quos secum eduxit hac de
re posset iudicare, condemnaret L. Murenam, si inter-
ficere posset, occideret. Petunt enim rationes illius ut
orbetur auxilio res publica, ut minuatur contra suum
furorem imperatorum copia, ut maior facultas tribunis 15
plebis detur depulso adversario seditionis ac discordiae
concitandae. Idemne igitur delecti ex amplissimis
ordinibus honestissimi atque sapientissimi viri iudica-
bunt quod ille importunissimus gladiator, hostis rei
publicae iudicaret? 84. Mihi credite, iudices, in hac 20
causa non solum de L. Murenae verum etiam de vestra
salute sententiam feretis. In discrimen extremum
venimus; nihil est iam unde nos reficiamus aut ubi lapsi
resistamus. Non solum minuenda non sunt auxilia quae
habemus sed etiam nova, si fieri possit, comparanda. 25
Hostis est enim non apud Anienem, quod bello Punico
gravissimum visum est, sed in urbe, in foro – di im-

mortales! sine gemitu hoc dici non potest – non nemo
etiam in illo sacrario rei publicae, in ipsa, inquam, curia
30 non nemo hostis est. Di faxint ut meus conlega, vir
fortissimus, hoc Catilinae nefarium latrocinium armatus opprimat! ego togatus vobis bonisque omnibus adi-
utoribus hoc quod conceptum res publica periculum
parturit consilio discutiam et comprimam. 85. Sed
35 quid tandem fiet, si haec elapsa de manibus nostris in
eum annum qui consequitur redundarint? Unus erit
consul, et is non in administrando bello sed in sufficiendo
conlega occupatus. Hunc iam qui impedituri sint * * *
illa pestis immanis importuna Catilinae prorumpet,
40 qua po * * * minatur; in agros suburbanos repente ad-
volabit; versabitur in urbe furor, in curia timor, in foro
coniuratio, in campo exercitus, in agris vastitas; omni
autem in sede ac loco ferrum flammamque metuemus.
Quae iam diu comparantur, eadem ista omnia, si or-
45 nata suis praesidiis erit res publica, facile et magistratu-
um consiliis et privatorum diligentia comprimentur.

   XL. 86. Quae cum ita sint, iudices, primum rei
publicae causa, qua nulla res cuiquam potior debet esse,
vos pro mea summa et vobis cognita in re publica
50 diligentia moneo, pro auctoritate consulari hortor, pro
magnitudine periculi obtestor, ut otio, ut paci, ut saluti,
ut vitae vestrae et ceterorum civium consulatis; deinde
ego idem et defensoris et amici officio adductus oro atque
obsecro, iudices, ut ne hominis miseri et cum corporis
55 morbo tum animi dolore confecti, L. Murenae, recentem
gratulationem nova lamentatione obruatis. Modo
maximo beneficio populi Romani ornatus fortunatus
videbatur, quod primus in familiam veterem, primus
in municipium antiquissimum consulatum attulisset;

nunc idem in squalore et sordibus, confectus morbo, 60
lacrimis ac maerore perditus vester est supplex, iudices,
vestram fidem obtestatur, vestram misericordiam im-
plorat, vestram potestatem ac vestras opes intuetur.

*87–89. Cicero asks the jury to have pity on Murena and not to take
the consulship from him. If they do, he will have nowhere to
go.*

87. Nolite, per deos immortalis! iudices, hac eum
cum re qua se honestiorem fore putavit etiam ceteris
ante partis honestatibus atque omni dignitate fortu-
naque privare. Atque ita vos L. Murena, iudices, orat
atque obsecrat, si iniuste neminem laesit, si nullius auris 5
voluntatemve violavit, si nemini, ut levissime dicam,
odio nec domi nec militiae fuit, sit apud vos modestiae
locus, sit demissis hominibus perfugium, sit auxilium
pudori. Misericordiam spoliatio consulatus magnam
habere debet, iudices; una enim eripiuntur cum con- 10
sulatu omnia; invidiam vero his temporibus habere
consulatus ipse nullam potest; obicitur enim contioni-
bus seditiosorum, insidiis coniuratorum, telis Catilinae,
ad omne denique periculum atque ad omnem iniuriam
solus opponitur. 88. Qua re quid invidendum Murenae 15
aut cuiquam nostrum sit in hoc praeclaro consulatu non
video, iudices; quae vero miseranda sunt, ea et mihi
ante oculos versantur et vos videre et perspicere potestis.
XLI. Si, quod Iuppiter omen avertat! hunc vestris
sententiis adflixeritis, quo se miser vertet? domumne? 20
ut eam imaginem clarissimi viri, parentis sui, quam
paucis ante diebus laureatam in sua gratulatione con-
spexit, eandem deformatam ignominia lugentemque

videat? An ad matrem quae misera modo consulem
25 osculata filium suum nunc cruciatur et sollicita est ne
eundem paulo post spoliatum omni dignitate con-
spiciat? 89. Sed quid eius matrem aut domum appello
quem nova poena legis et domo et parente et omnium
suorum consuetudine conspectuque privat? Ibit igitur
30 in exsilium miser? Quo? ad Orientisne partis in quibus
annos multos legatus fuit, exercitus duxit, res maximas
gessit? At habet magnum dolorem, unde cum honore
decesseris, eodem cum ignominia reverti. An se in con-
trariam partem terrarum abdet, ut Gallia Transalpina,
35 quem nuper summo cum imperio libentissime viderit,
eundem lugentem, maerentem, exsulem videat? In
ea porro provincia quo animo C. Murenam fratrem
suum aspiciet? Qui huius dolor, qui illius maeror erit,
quae utriusque lamentatio, quanta autem perturbatio
40 fortunae atque sermonis, cum, quibus in locis paucis
ante diebus factum esse consulem Murenam nuntii
litteraeque celebrassent et unde hospites atque amici
gratulatum Romam concurrerent, repente exstiterit
ipse nuntius suae calamitatis!

90. *Cicero appeals to the jury to acquit Murena for the sake of his
family and home and commends him to them.*

90. Quae si acerba, si misera, si luctuosa sunt, si
alienissima a mansuetudine et misericordia vestra,
iudices, conservate populi Romani beneficium, reddite
rei publicae consulem, date hoc ipsius pudori, date patri
5 mortuo, date generi et familiae, date etiam Lanuvio,
municipio honestissimo, quod in hac tota causa frequens
maestumque vidistis. Nolite a sacris patriis Iunonis

Sospitae, cui omnis consules facere necesse est, domesticum et suum consulem potissimum avellere. Quem ego
vobis, si quid habet aut momenti commendatio aut 10
auctoritatis confirmatio mea, consul consulem, iudices,
ita commendo ut cupidissimum oti, studiosissimum
bonorum, acerrimum contra seditionem, fortissimum
in bello, inimicissimum huic coniurationi quae nunc
rem publicam labefactat futurum esse promittam et 15
spondeam.

NOTES

(The pages upon which comment is made are shown
in shoulder headings)

Sections 1–2

I. 1. line 1. **Quae precatus ... sum:** This or a similar form
of words is used more than once by Cicero for the beginning of a
speech and is quoted with approval by Quintilian, the famous
teacher of rhetoric, who lived in the first century of our era. He
held that the cretic (– ∪ –) was the best rhythm with which to
begin. **sum** is to be taken with *precatus*; the auxiliary verb is
often found separated from the participle in tenses formed with
parts of the verb *esse*. **a dis immortalibus:** With the deponent
verb *precari* the thing which is prayed for is regularly found in
the accusative case, while the person to whom the prayer is
addressed is found either in the accusative (with or without *ad*)
or, as here, in the ablative with *a*. **Quae** looks forward to *ut*
and is picked up by *eadem*; English would not start with a
relative, but the sentence must be rephrased in some such way
as ' Even as I prayed ... that ... , so now again I pray ...'.

l. 1. **iudices:** ' gentlemen of the jury ' is our traditional
equivalent, not ' judges '. For information concerning the
legal background of this case and the composition of the jury,
see Introduction, p. xxiif. This speech is *ad iudices* and deals
with a criminal case or *causa publica*. A political speech to the
people was an *oratio ad Quirites* and to the Senate *ad Senatum*.

l. 2. **more institutoque maiorum:** In this passage Cicero uses
the long established formulae intentionally since ' the practice
of our ancestors ' was a very strong influence in Roman life
and would tend to give a jury confidence in the speaker.

l. 2. **illo die quo:** Ablatives of time when; ' on that day on
which '.

l. 2. **auspicato:** The magistrate presiding over a meeting
took the auspices on the morning of the meeting on the Campus

50

Martius and according as they proved favourable or unfavourable the *comitia* was held or postponed.

The perfect participles of a number of verbs were regularly
used impersonally in the Ablative Absolute from earliest times
and, from the time of Cicero, this construction spread more
widely. The ablative noun is implied in the participle and is
cognate; ' the auspices having been taken '. The construction is
parallel to the impersonal passive of finite tenses (e.g. *pugnatum
est*: ' a battle has been fought ') and most of such ablative
singular participles became virtually adverbs – e.g. *consulto*:
' deliberately ', ' on purpose '. See E. C. Woodcock, *A New
Latin Syntax*, 93, *Note* (2) p. 74.

l. 3. **comitiis centuriatis**: It was, according to tradition,
founded by the king, Servius Tullius, but is unlikely to have
existed before the second half of the fifth century. It enacted
laws, elected magistrates *cum imperio* (i.e. praetors and consuls
of the annual magistrates) and censors, declared war and peace,
and inflicted the death penalty. It met outside the *pomerium*
which was a line demarcating the limits of the city as constituted by the augurs, since a meeting of the citizens under arms
was not permitted within those limits and the centuries from
which the assembly got its name were in origin military units.
By this time the voting centuries were no longer identical with
military units but the old practice continued and it normally
met in the Campus Martius, which lay outside the city boundary.

l. 3. **renuntiavi**: ' declared duly elected '. The usual word for
the declaration of the result of an election by the presiding
magistrate.

l. 4. **ut ... eveniret**: Indirect command after *precatus ...
sum*.

l. 4. **ea res**: The election of Murena as consul.

l. 4. **mihi fidei magistratuique meo**: ' for myself, my honour,
and my office '. Part of a traditional formula. **magistratuique
meo**: The speech was delivered near the end of Cicero's consulship. See Introduction, p. ix.

l. 4. **populo plebique Romanae**: This phrase looks back to a
time when patricians alone formed the *populus* or citizen body

enjoying full political rights at Rome, while the plebeians were excluded from the religious colleges, the magistracies, the Senate, and were not permitted to marry patricians.

l. 5. **bene atque feliciter:** A traditional formula; ' with all good fortune '.

l. 6. **ob ... obtinendum:** Probably best translated by a clause: ' since that same man's acquittal must be assured and his consulship preserved '. **una cum:** ' together with '. The thought in this rather compressed phrase is that Murena must be acquitted and his civil rights thus preserved, in order that he may enter the office of consul to which he has already been elected.

l. 7. **et ut:** Still after *precor*.

l. 7. **mentes atque sententiae:** mentes is what the jury thinks and **sententiae** the expression of their views in their voting.

l. 8. **voluntatibus suffragiisque consentiant:** Because the Roman people would not wish the man whom they had elected consul to be barred from office by an unfavourable verdict.

l. 9. **eaque res:** *consensus* ' agreement ' implied from *consentiant*.

l. 10. **otium concordiamque:** These words would have had more meaning for Cicero at this time than is at first sight apparent. **otium** means ' peace within the community '; **concordiam,** a halt to the struggles between the orders. The phrase *concordia ordinum* might be said to sum up Cicero's political aspirations after the collapse of the Catilinarian Conspiracy. See Introduction, p. xii.

l. 11. **sollemnis:** Properly in religious language ' annual ', hence ' appointed ' and when the religious idea is strong ' solemn ', ' religious '.

l. 11. **comitiorum:** ' at elections '. Possessive genitive.

l. 12. **vim:** ' weight ', ' power '.

l. 12. **religionem:** ' sanctity '.

l. 14. **eis quoque hominibus:** Although the prayer was, strictly speaking, only for himself, if it was as effective as the occasion warranted, then it would include those elected as well.

l. 15. **me rogante:** ' when I held the elections '. The complete phrase is *consul populum consulem rogat*. The ablative of the present participle ends in ' *e* ' when the use of the participle is substantival or (as here) verbal. In the normal adjectival usage it ends in ' *i* '.

l. 15. **fauste feliciter prospereque:** Another traditional formula.

2. line 16. **Quae cum ita sint:** In translating, watch the difference between Latin and English word order and remember that English does not use the relative pronoun at the beginning of a sentence to link it with what has gone before.

l. 17. **potestas:** Cicero here asserts that the power of the jurors is close to that of the gods. In another speech he says that their power comes next to the *numen* of the gods.

l. 18. **certe communicata vobiscum:** ' at least shared with you '.

l. 18. **idem:** Cicero.

l. 19. **fidei:** Here ' protection '.

l. 21. **beneficium populi Romani:** ' the office conferred upon him by the Roman people ' i.e. his consulship.

l. 21. **cum . . . salute:** ' to the preservation of yourselves and of the whole citizen body '.

Section 2

l. 1. **Et quoniam:** This period can quite well be translated as a single sentence. English might, however, find a break after *dicam* preferable. The pattern is: **quoniam . . . reprensa est, ante quam . . . instituo, . . . dicam, non quo . . . sit . . . , sed ut . . . possim.**

l. 1. **officio:** My service to Murena.

l. 2. **etiam ipsa susceptio:** ' even the very fact that I have undertaken '.

l. 3. **reprensa:** Agrees with *susceptio* only, being the nearer of more than one subject.

l. 3. **instituo:** It is regular usage in classical Latin that when the main verb – here *dicam* – refers to the future and is positive, either the present indicative or the present subjunctive is used after *ante quam* and *prius quam* referring to the future. When it is negative, the future perfect indicative is used. The few examples of the use of the future simple occur only in early or later Latin. See Woodcock, 227, p. 184.

l. 4. **non quo ... sit:** ' not because at this of all times the defence of my role is more important to me than his acquittal '. This subjunctive shows that the speaker has rejected the reason he has given. In classical Latin such repudiated reasons are usually introduced by *non quod* or *non quo*. The latter is more common in Cicero. See Woodcock, 243, p. 199.

l. 6. **ut:** ' because '.

l. 6. **facto:** ' course of action '.

l. 7. **honore fama fortunisque: honore** is ' office ' not ' honour '. By the *lex Calpurnia de ambitu* of 67 anyone found guilty of bribery was deprived of the consulship to which he had been elected and was ineligible for future office. **fama:** ' his good name '. **fortunisque omnibus:** This law also imposed a heavy fine for those found guilty of the offence and barred them from the Senate, thereby ruining their future political career. See also Introduction, p. xxiv.

Sections 3–5

II. 3. line 1. **Et primum:** The natural English word-order will be quite different to the Latin.

l. 1. **M. Catoni:** For Cato and Stoic ethics, see Introduction, p. xxxii, and Appendix, p. 140.

l. 1. **ad certam ... derigenti:** ' who organises his life according to the fixed pattern of a system '. **normam:** ' rule ', ' pattern '. **rationis:** A philosophical system.

l. 2. **diligentissime ... omnium:** ' weighing with the most scrupulous care the relative importance of each duty '. **momenta:** (=*movimenta*) Considerations which turn the scales for a Stoic who is considering which is the morally right course of action when he is faced by a number of alternatives. The Stoics had a strong concept of moral duties – *officia*.

l. 4. **rectum**: Another technical term from Stoic ethics. ' a right action '.

l. 4. **legis ambitus latorem**: ' the author of a law against bribery '. The *lex Tullia de ambitu* of this year which supplemented the *lex Calpurnia* mentioned above increasing the number of offences possible and inflicting more severe penalties. See Introduction, p. xxiv.

l. 5. **gesto consulatu**: *Consulatum gerere* means ' to conduct the office of consul '.

l. 6. **attingere**: ' to touch ' in the sense of ' to have anything at all to do with '.

l. 6. **reprehensio**: ' criticism '. Cato's complaint is that it is improper for Cicero to have introduced a law against bribery, shown himself ready to act vigorously against transgressors of the law – *tam severe gesto consulatu* – and then defend a man accused of that very offence.

l. 7. **quibus maxime debeo**: The jury could reasonably expect Cicero to be eager to explain to them his apparent inconsistency in order to persuade them that they could accept his case in full confidence of his reliability.

l. 8. **gravissimo atque integerrimo**: ' venerable and upright '. Two qualities which claim for Cato the right to expect an answer to his charge.

l. 9. **rationem ... probem**: ' justify my course of action '.

l. 9. **A quo tandem**: Cicero's reply which is, of course, no answer at all to Cato. **tandem**: ' I ask you ' as frequently in commands and questions.

l. 10. **aequius**: ' more appropriate '.

l. 12. **coniunctior**: ' more closely tied '.

l. 13. **magnis ... sustentata**: A reference to his suppression of Catiline.

l. 14. **Quod si**: ' But if in a case for the recovery of such goods as have been formally sold, a man who has assumed the contractual obligation ought to incur the risk of a court decision, then surely with still more justice in the trial of a consul-elect that consul who has declared him elected rather than any other should be the guarantor of the honour conferred by the Roman people and defend it from all danger.' In this sentence, complicated by the legal terminology, Murena's consulship is a *res mancipi* of which Cicero is the seller and Murena the purchaser. A *res mancipi* is something that changes hands by the formal process of *mancipatio* (derived from *manus* and *capio*) = a taking in the hand. In this process the purchaser took hold of what was to become his property in the presence of six adult witnesses and at such a sale always received a guarantee of title (hence the *nexus* or contract) by which the seller, should his right to the object be challenged, either had to prove his right or reimburse the purchaser for any loss he might suffer. The *periculum iudicii* is the risk of a court assigning the property to a third party; an *auctor* is a person who guarantees that he has the right to sell an object to another.

l. 18. **benefici:** The consulship, as in 2, l. 21.

l. 18. **periculi:** ' from danger '.

4. line 19. **non nullis in civitatibus:** e.g. in Athens.

l. 20. **summo honore:** ' the highest office '.

l. 23. **auctoritatis ... facultatis:** Partitive genitives to be taken with *minus*. ' authority ', ' prestige ' ... ' eloquence '.

l. 23. **Quod si:** ' But if those who are just sailing into harbour from the open sea are usually extremely eager to give those about to weigh anchor an account of storms, pirates and places of danger, ...' **solventibus:** sc. *navem*. **praecipere aliquid alicui:** ' to give someone information or warning about something '. **praedonum:** In spite of Pompey's success against the pirates in 67, piracy soon returned to the Mediterranean and was only finally eliminated in classical times by Augustus. **locorum:** It is not immediately clear what exactly this word means, but the context requires that it indicate a third source of danger for those setting sail.

This elaborate nautical metaphor gives appropriately increased weight to the theme which is central to Cicero's argument in the speech. He, the consul, must ensure that there are two good consuls ready to face Catiline in 62. Note how, elsewhere in the speech, rhetorical devices and language are introduced to add weight to argument. At the end, for example, the danger of Catiline is stressed in this way.

l. 26. **quod . . . faveamus:** ' because we naturally desire to help those . . .'.

l. 28. **ingrediantur:** A consecutive subjunctive referring to a class of people.

l. 28. **quo . . . animo:** ' with what feelings '. **tandem:** See 3, l. 10.

l. 29. **prope . . . videntem:** ' who after a severe buffeting am just coming into sight of land '. Cicero compares his consulship with a stormy voyage. For the sequence of events at the end of his consulship see Introduction, p. xix f.

l. 30. **cui:** Dative of the agent with *subeundas*.

l. 30. **tempestates:** It is crucial to Cicero's case that there are storms to come which require that there be two consuls in the New Year to deal with them. See below.

l. 31. **boni consulis:** ' the duty of a conscientious consul '. A genitive of description derived from the idea of possession inherent in the case. It is explained as an idiomatic extension of the possessive genitive predicated with *esse* as found in such sentences as: *liber est pueri* = ' the book is the boy's'.

l. 33. **alio loco:** In 79, p. 43.

l. 33. **salutis:** Partitive genitive with *quantum*. ' how much it matters to the safety of the state that . . .' This because Catiline and his followers are still at large.

5. line 35. **Quod . . . est:** ' And if this is the case '.

l. 35. **non tam:** In this sentence **officium,** his duty towards a personal friend, is contrasted by Cicero with **res publica,** his responsibility towards the state; **me** is Cicero as a private individual, while **consulem** refers to him in his official capacity as a magistrate.

III. line 38. **Nam quod:** ' But as to the fact that ' answering an opponent's objection. See 3, l. 4 f. The argument is ' I agree that I was the author of a law against bribery, but I did not therefore stop my practice of defending citizens from danger.

If bribery took place, it would be wrong for me to defend it
even had I not brought in a law against it. I say, however,
that Murena is innocent, so how does my law make it wrong
for me to appear on his behalf?' Both Cato and Cicero in this
argument and counter-argument have pre-judged the very
point at stake.

l. 38. **certe ita tuli ut . . . non:** 'I certainly passed it without
. . .' This restrictive use of consecutive clauses with *ita* leading
up to them is common in Cicero, but is not a natural English
mode of expression. The imperfect subjunctive **abrogarem**
indicates his intent at the time when he introduced the law.

l. 39. **eam:** sc. *legem* though not in the full legal sense as at
the beginning of the sentence, but rather 'a practice that has
hardened into a rule '.

l. 39. **civium:** Looking back to the previous sentence and the
consul's duty to defend the common safety.

l. 40. **Etenim:** This word shows that Cicero is giving his
reason for his previous sentence.

l. 41. **largitionem:** 'bribery '.

l. 42. **defenderem:** 'maintain ', 'argue '.

l. 44. **quid est quod:** 'how does the fact that '.

Section 6

6. line 1. **Negat:** Repeated from 3, l. 4 *sc.* Cato.

l. 1. **eiusdem severitatis:** *Catilinam expulisse* and *pro L.
Murena dicere* are the two substantival phrases which are
being compared and to which this Genitive of Description
refers.

l. 2. **molientem:** In one of its regular meanings 'trying to
bring about ', 'plotting '.

l. 2. **verbis:** In his warnings to his fellow-citizens of Catiline's
designs and in particular by his Catilinarian Orations.

l. 2. **paene imperio:** Catiline left the city as a result of the
revelations in the First Catilinarian Oration immediately after
its delivery. Cicero had not directly used his *imperium*, the

authority bestowed upon him by his consulship, to drive
Catiline from the city but had called upon him in his speech to
leave. See Introduction, p. xx.

l. 3. **pro L. Murena dicere:** Cato implies that Murena's
guilt is obvious by his assertion that a speech in defence of
Murena argues less severity (on Cicero's part) towards him than
he showed towards Catiline.

l. 4. **partis ... docuit ... egi ... personam ... impositam
sustinui:** All these words sustain a metaphor from the stage,
not unique in Cicero's speeches. **partis:** Plural in this sense,
as in all classical authors; later writers use the singular.
personam: ' role '.

l. 7. **huius imperi:** His powers as consul. The suggestion
that these words may also refer to the *senatus consultum de re
publica defendenda* is unnecessary since the decree did not add
any powers to the consular *imperium*, but merely instructed the
consuls to use it with particular vigilance.

l. 8. **dignitas:** The authority and prestige given by tradition
to a Roman consul facing a national crisis.

l. 9. **desiderabat:** ' required '. This verb is in the indicative
although in a temporal *cum* clause in past time since the meaning is solely temporal as suggested by the introductory *tum*.

l. 10. **cogebar:** i.e. by my position in the state. **volebam:**
i.e. following my natural inclinations. Translate: ' I overcame
my natural inclinations and displayed the vigour required by
the situation '.

l. 11. **cum:** ' since '. Note the mood of the verb.

l. 11. **causae:** ' reasons '.

l. 12. **tandem:** Again ' I ask you ' as in 3, l. 10.

l. 13. **naturae ... servire:** ' to gratify my nature and usual
practice '. **consuetudini:** Cicero spoke more frequently for the
defence than the prosecution. One of the recognised roads to
political power was a series of successful speeches for the
defence. In this way the aspiring statesman collected a circle
of influential men and their clients who repaid their debt of
gratitude with political support. Cicero's *misericordia* and

humanitas would usually contain a generous portion of self-interest. One of the problems involved in this practice was to avoid making political enemies of the prosecution. Cicero's skill in this respect repays careful study. See also note on *Omnes . . . concurrimus* 45. l. 44, p. 109. and Introduction, p. x f.

l. 14. **officio defensionis meae:** ' my obligation to act for the defence '.

l. 14. **ratione accusationis tuae:** ' the grounds for your accusation '.

l. 15. **alia in parte:** See 67 ff. pp. 36–37 and 78 ff., pp. 42–45.

l. 16. **nobis:** ' by me '.

Sections 7–10

7. line 1. **me:** To be taken with *commovebat.*

l. 1. **sapientissimi atque ornatissimi:** Literally ' very learned and very distinguished '; conventional epithets (*sapiens* in particular of a jurist). Cf. our ' my learned friend '. Sulpicius led for the prosecution. See Introduction, p. xxxi.

l. 2. **conquestio:** ' complaint '. It is not used frequently in this sense but is often found as a technical term meaning 'an appeal to the emotions '.

l. 3. **qui:** Sulpicius.

l. 3. **gravissime ... ferre:** ' that he was grievously and bitterly hurt that '.

l. 4. **familiaritatis necessitudinisque:** These genitives are said to be partitive in origin and to suggest an incomplete mental hold upon something.

l. 5. **Huic ... satis facere:** ' to justify myself in his eyes '. A legal phrase, as is **adhibere arbitros** ' to employ you as umpires '. A *iudex* came to his decision according to laws, an *arbiter* according to equity.

l. 7. **cum ... tum:** Translate the *cum* by ' while ' and omit the *tum.*

l. 7. **in amicitia:** ' in a matter involving friends '.

l. 8. **accuseris:** Cicero prefers the ending *-re* in the second person singular passive, except in the present indicative.

This is one of the few exceptions. This subjunctive introduces a general proposition for which English normally uses ' you ' or ' one ' as the subject of the verb.

l. 8. **Ego . . . confiteor:** The sentence will run more naturally in English if this verb is taken first and the order of translation be: **confiteor me . . . debuisse et arbitror praestitisse.**

l. 9. **petitione:** ' candidature '. Cf. *consulatum petenti* below. Sulpicius was a consular candidate for 62 and a rival of Murena. Note Cicero's close political ties with opposing counsel – these explain much of the tone of this speech. See note on *consuetudini*, 6, l, 13, p. 59.

l. 9. **studia atque officia:** *Studium* is zeal for anyone, hence ' affection ', ' devotion ', while *officia* are acts owed by anyone to another to whom he is under a debt of obligation. The word was frequently used in the case of clients' activities on behalf of a patron.

l. 10. **pro nostra necessitudine:** ' as our close relationship requires '. **pro:** ' in accordance with '. *necessitudo* is any close tie.

l. 11. **praestitisse:** ' fulfil ', ' discharge '. Sc. *studia atque officia.*

l. 11. **a me:** ' on my part '.

l. 12. **esset:** By this imperfect potential subjunctive Cicero expresses his view of what could have happened in the past but can no longer occur. ' Nothing . . . which could have been required of. . . .'

l. 12. **gratioso:** Used substantively. A man possessing *gratia* ' influence '. The singular of an adjective is used as a noun either when a collective noun or, as here, when closely linked with another noun.

l. 13. **ratio:** ' state of affairs ', ' situation '.

l. 14. **Sic . . . persuadeo:** ' It is my view and my belief that '.

l. 15. **me . . . debuisse:** Take in the order: **me debuisse tibi tantum contra honorem Murenae quantum . . . honorem:** Advancement to public office. **postulare:** ' to require as of right '.

l. 16. **salutem:** As in 1, l. 7. ' acquittal '. Cicero maintains that his obligations to Sulpicius in view of their *necessitudo* made it his duty to support Sulpicius' candidature for the consulship to the extent that Sulpicius felt able to call upon him. He is under no such obligation to assist his prosecution of Murena.

8. line 17. **tum cum peteres ... studui:** When in narrative the action or circumstances contained in the *cum*-clause give the background to the action of the main verb, the verb of the *cum*-clause is in the subjunctive mood. This occurs even though the characterising or descriptive idea which had originally been responsible for the subjunctive is so weak that the clause must be classed as purely temporal and would therefore be expected to have its verb in the indicative. See Woodcock, 235, p. 191.

l. 17. **peteres ... petas:** There is play here on the meanings of *petere*. *Consulatum petere* = ' to be a candidate for the consulship' and *Murenam petere* = ' to attack Murena '.

l. 18. **cum ... petas:** ' since you are attacking Murena himself '. The subjunctive is causal as the clause gives the reason why Cicero does not feel obliged to support Servius.

l. 18. **eodem pacto:** ' in the same way '. Originally the ablative of a neuter noun *pactum* derived from the verb *paciscere* = ' to bargain, covenant' found in Classical Latin only in the perfect participle passive.

l. 19. **hoc:** ' this view '.

l. 19. **concedi:** ' be entertained '.

l. 21. **alienissimos** ' complete strangers '.

IV. line 22. **in capitis dimicatione ... in honoris contentione:** ' in a contest involving his civil rights ... in a struggle for office '. The objective genitive is not confined to use with nouns derived from transitive verbs, but from the earliest times examples are found qualifying nouns connected with intransitive verbs which may require a dative, ablative, or prepositional phrase to complete the sense (e.g. *contendere de honore*).

l. 23. **idcirco:** This word looks forward to the causal clause introduced by **quod. obruetur:** ' will be overriden '. Because

Cicero's friendship with Murena did not stop him from support-
ing Sulpicius when he was a candidate for office, it does not
mean that Murena will be sacrificed in the present case.

l. 24. **Quae:** ' My friendship with Murena '. **causa:** *sc.* ' of
my defending Murena '.

l. 25. **tamen:** Regularly first word in a clause when used with
a corresponding concessive or conditional particle or conjunction.

l. 25. **dignitas:** The respect felt to be due to any man who
holds a position of responsibility in the state.

l. 25. **honoris . . . amplitudo:** To be taken together. **amplitudo:** ' distinction '. A more general word than *dignitas* or
auctoritas which both had distinct meanings in the Roman
political scene.

l. 26. **mihi . . . infamiam inussisset:** ' would have branded
me with the disgrace of '.

l. 27. **hominis . . . amplissimi:** ' a man distinguished by his
own achievements and the honours conferred upon him by the
Roman people '. **suis:** Refers to his *dignitas.* **populi Romani:**
i.e. *honoris eius.* **ornamentis:** An instrumental ablative such
as is regularly found with verbs and adjectives denoting fulness.

l. 28. **causam tanti periculi:** ' a case involving so great a
risk '. A Genitive of Description. Cf. note on *boni consulis*,
4, l. 31. p. 57.

l. 30. **neque est integrum:** ' nor am I at liberty ' – for the
reasons given in the following sentence.

l. 32. **pro:** ' by virtue of '.

l. 33. **sic existimo:** This sentence is corrupt in the MSS, but
the meaning of the text as restored by Clark is that Cicero
thinks that, since his efforts have been so greatly rewarded, to
discontinue them now that he has obtained the consulship
would be the mark of a cunning and ungrateful man. Cunning,
because the purpose behind them would be revealed as springing
from self-interest, and ungrateful because we should be grateful
for our rewards.

l. 33. **exceperis . . . sis:** A ' generalised ' second person.

l. 34. **hominis ... ingrati:** 'the mark of a cunning and ungrateful man '.

9. line 35. **te auctore:** ' on your authority '. Cicero says that he will abandon his efforts gladly, if Sulpicius accepts the responsibility for his being able to do so without reproach.

l. 36. **inhumanitatis:** ' lack of feeling '.

l. 37. **ego vero:** ' I for my part '. **vero:** This stresses *ego* contrasted with *te* above.

l. 39. **improbitatem:** ' lack of principle '.

l. 41. **officiosus:** ' obliging '. Closely connected with *officium*, it often suggests the readiness to serve or do one's duty to one's superiors.

l. 42. **coniecturam:** ' inference '.

l. 42. **studio:** ' profession '.

l. 45. **respondere:** ' to give an opinion '. The usual legal term for the reply of a lawyer consulted professionally.

l. 45. **te advocato:** ' when your opinion has been taken '. An *advocatus* was originally anybody who came into court to support a litigant by his presence. Only later did the word come to mean ' advocate ' in our sense.

l. 46. **causa cadere:** ' to lose one's case '.

l. 47. **tui fontes:** ' your sources ', ' abundant supplies '. *sc.* of legal knowledge. This word is frequently used figuratively.

l. 47. **inimicis tuis:** The orator's love of a neat antithesis – **inimicis : amicis** – causes him to write **inimicis** for *adversariis amicorum tuorum*.

10. line 49. **tua familiaritas:** ' my close friendship with you '.

l. 49. **removisset:** i.e. had made me unwilling to undertake the defence of Murena.

l. 50. **Q. Hortensio, M. Crasso:** See Introduction, p. xxix f.

l. 50. **clarissimis:** ' distinguished '. A regular honorific title of leading public figures such as magistrates or senators.

l. 51. **gratiam:** ' good-will '.

l. 51. **magni aestimari:** ' is highly prized '. **magni:** An adverbial genitive used in expressions of price and value. This use is most probably to be derived from the Genitive of Description.

l. 54. **patronum:** In the early days of the city members of the leading families in Rome attached to themselves poorer citizens whom they helped with legal or financial aid in return for political support. This help came to be considered so important that the praetor used to promise in his edict that he would assign an advocate to anyone who was without legal assistance.

l. 56. **quod . . . amicitiae:** ' any concession that should be made to friendship '.

l. 58. **non secus ac si . . . esset:** ' as if it were '.

l. 59. **isto in loco:** The seats provided in court for the counsel for the prosecution.

l. 59. **officio, fidei, religioni:** ' duty, honour, conscience '. An example of the figure of speech known as *gradatio* or climax.

l. 61. **contra . . . dicere:** Cicero makes a telling end to the *exordium* or introduction by contrasting his opposition to one friend's efforts with his support for the other in his dangerous situation. This contrast leads easily to the use of abstract for concrete to heighten the effect: **pro amici periculo** = ' for a friend in danger '.

Sections 11–12

V. 11. line 1. **tris . . . partis:** In the speech for the prosecution the charges would have been arranged under their various headings (*partitio*) – in this case three in number. The rebuttal (*confutatio*) of these charges was similarly divided. The first part (11–14) deals with the charges brought against Murena's life and personal character (**in reprehensione vitae**). Quintilian praised this *partitio* for its clarity and simplicity.

l. 3. **in contentione dignitatis:** ' in a comparison of the respective merits of the consular candidates '.

l. 3. **in criminibus ambitus:** ' in charges of corruption '. *Ambitus* was originally ' a going round ' or canvassing for public office. This in itself was not illegal but the electoral corruption which came to accompany the practice and grew to scandalous proportions in the second century was the target for a series of laws *de ambitu* aimed at its elimination. The *quaestio de ambitu* was one of the seven standing courts established by Sulla in his reforms of 81 but the succession of laws thereafter shows how difficult it was to stamp out this malpractice in spite of the heavy penalties. For a full account see Introduction, p. xxiii.

It is easy for us to enjoy a feeling of moral superiority over the Romans in this matter, but we should remember that Roman politicians did not enjoy the modern opportunities of buying votes with the tax-payers' money and it was a short step from the client system to open bribery.

l. 5. **gravissima ... levis:** Probably no more than another neat and conventional antithesis. It would be reasonable, however, for a jury to expect that Murena's corruption was not a single lapse and that they would hear a lengthy tale of dishonesty.

l. 6. **illos:** The prosecution.

l. 6. **lex ... accusatoria:** The modern advice is: ' No case; abuse opponent's counsel.' Roman lawyers followed this maxim whether there was a case or not and the prosecution's custom of trying to prejudice a jury against the defendant by impugning his character was so common that it could reasonably be called a *lex*, ' rule ' or ' law '.

l. 7. **vera ... facultas:** ' any true ground '.

l. 8. **Obiecta est ... Asia:** ' Asia is cast in his teeth '. Asia was notorious for the ease with which it corrupted Roman officials. Even if we allow for the rhetorical tendency of Roman writers to contrast the debilitating effects of oriental wealth and luxury with the native Italian rectitude, we may still recognise that the opportunities for corruption in the East were greater than elsewhere. And even if our picture of Roman conduct in the provinces is coloured by the fact that much of our evidence is drawn from speeches prosecuting the least satisfactory Roman governors and generals, we should remember that for each of these guilty men there would have been many honest and hard-working officials. Yet Cicero himself refers to it in a letter to his brother as *corruptrix provincia* and he had personal experience.

l. 8. **quae:** Note the adversative force here; 'this province, however'.

l. 9. **expetita est:** Stronger than *petita*; 'deliberately sought'.

l. 9. **in militari labore peragrata:** 'traversed during the course of hard service in the field'. Cicero declares that Murena did not go to Asia in the pursuit of pleasure and luxury but to fight. And he would have been open to censure, had he not done so, on the grounds either that he was afraid of the enemy or his father, or that he had been rejected by his father. He then suggests that if a triumph attracted Murena he could still have shared his father's without bringing any military distinction of his own to it.

l. 10. **Qui si ... non meruisset:** Remember to change the linking relative and word order to obtain idiomatic English. 'And if he had not served (*merere* sc. *stipendia* = to perform military service) under the general, his father'. **non:** Negatives the single word *meruisset*.

l. 10. **patre suo:** L. Licinius Murena took part in the battle of Chaeronea in 86 in which Sulla defeated Mithridates' general, Archelaus. He was left as propraetor of Asia in command of the two legions which had deserted Fimbria and joined Sulla. An ambitious man, he broke the terms of the Treaty of Dardanus agreed between Sulla and Mithridates in 84 and attacked the king, ravaging his territory. In spite of verbal instructions from the Senate to cease hostilities, Murena continued his attacks until he was defeated with heavy loss and compelled to retreat into the mountains of Phrygia. In 81 Sulla sent A. Gabinius with orders to Murena to stop fighting. Murena returned to Rome later that year and celebrated what must be one of the least-deserved triumphs in the history of Rome.

l. 12. **imperium:** What we know of his father's character and behaviour suggests that he may well have been a man under whom a son would have hesitated to serve.

l. 12. **a parente repudiatus:** Rejected by his father as not fit to serve under him. The general's staff was a proper place for his friends and family in Roman eyes. Cf. *pietatis.* 12. l. 29. The client system ensured that *a fortiori* it was felt only proper to employ members of one's family. Many famous generals – Pompey, for example – served their military apprenticeship under their fathers.

l. 13. **An:** This conjunction is used to introduce a question which appears to be simple but is in fact the second part of an alternative question of which the first is not expressed. ' Or perhaps . . .' The omission of the first alternative implies that it can be quickly dismissed.

l. 13. **cum:** ' although '.

l. 13. **in equis . . . filii:** A general's youngest children rode in the triumphal chariot with him. Those old enough, but not yet of an age to to wear the *toga virilis,* rode on the horses drawing the chariot. Adult sons rode on their own horses behind their father. **praetextati:** Wearing the *praetexta,* the *toga* bordered with purple worn by the higher magistrates and by free-born children below the age of seventeen. **triumphantium:** To be taken with both *equis* and *filii.* **potissimum:** ' in preference to all others '.

l. 14. **huic . . . fuit:** ' should he have avoided adorning his father's triumph with decorations for bravery so that . . .' **huic:** Dative of the agent with the gerundive *fugiendum.* As a son of the general he would be part of the triumphal procession anyway. Does the prosecution not expect him to have taken such an active part in his father's campaign that he is almost a fellow-*triumphator* with his father?

12. line 17. **vero:** ' indeed ', ' certainly '.

l. 18. **adiumento . . . solacio . . . gratulationi:** Predicative datives with *parenti,* the usual accompanying dative of the person interested. **gratulationi:** ' a cause for congratulation to '.

l 19. **habet:** ' contains ', ' involves '.

l. 22. **Asiae nomen:** Genitive of Definition. ' the word " Asia " '.

l. 23. **laus . . . memoria . . . honos et gloria:** An example of the figure of speech known as *expolitio* in which the same idea is expressed in a variety of different ways.

l. 25. **susceptum . . . dedecus:** A complex form of expression. The *flagitium in Asia susceptum* is responsible for the *dedecus ex Asia deportatum*. The misdeeds in the province are responsible for the bad reputation with which he returns from it. **deportatum:** A technical term for bringing anything back from a province. It may be something concrete, e.g. *praeda* or abstract, e.g. *gloria, benevolentia, dedecus.* Doubtless the *praeda* and *dedecus* were not clearly separated in men's minds.

l. 26. **Meruisse . . . meruisse . . . fuisse:** The subjects of the sentence.

l. 26. **in eo bello:** The Third Mithridatic War. See Introduction, p. xvi f.

l. 28. **virtutis . . . pietatis . . . felicitatis:** More Genitives of Description. **pietatis:** cf. note on *a parente repudiatus* 11. l. 12. p. 68. **finem . . . felicitatis:** ' that his father's victory and triumph brought his service to an end was a proof of his good fortune '. In the ancient world luck was held to play a much larger and more honourable part in a general's success than is allowed to it today. There would be no hint of incongruity to Roman ears in linking *felicitas* with *virtus* and *pietas* as three qualities to applaud in the defendant. Cf. note on. ' *Me saucium* ' 38, l. 8, p. 102.

l. 30. **quidem:** Adversative, introducing the opposing view.

l. 31. **loci:** Partitive Genitive with *nihil*.

l. 32. **occupavit:** The ideas of ' occupying ' and ' forestalling ' are both present. Praise by taking up all the available room beforehand has left no place for slander.

Sections 13–14

VI. 13. line 1. **Saltatorem:** ' dancer ', ' mountebank'. Dancing by oneself was regarded by the Greeks and Romans as indecent.

l. 2. **vehementis accusatoris:** The suggestion is that the prosecutor is tempted to overstate his case because of its fundamental weakness.

l. 3. **maledici conviciatoris:** Abuse because the prosecutor has no case.

l. 3. **ista:** i.e. enough to make this sort of behaviour unworthy of you.

l. 5. **trivio:** ' the gutter '. Lit. ' cross-road ' and hence in general ' highway '.

l. 5. **scurrarum:** A *scurra* was a parasite, a man who dines out on his wit and conversation.

l. 6. **sed circumspicere:** sc. *debes.* i.e. The implications of this insult must be considered.

l. 8. **Nemo . . . fere:** ' Scarcely anyone '.

l. 9. **nisi forte:** ' unless perhaps '. Ironical.

l. 10. **honesto:** ' respectable '.

l. 10. **Tempestivi:** One which had begun before the usual time.

l. 11. **amoeni loci:** ' in delightful surroundings '. This adjective is used of objects pleasant to the eyes, particularly of natural beauty.

l. 11. **multarum deliciarum:** (Sensual) ' pleasure ', ' sport '; also of girls ' darling ', ' beloved '.

l. 11. **comes . . . saltatio:** ' dancing is the final accompaniment '.

l. 12. **Tu . . . potest:** Dancing is the culmination of a debauch. Yet while the prosecution accuses Murena of dancing, it makes no mention of any of the deplorable behaviour which was an essential prelude. **mihi:** Ethic Dative. Essentially a colloquial usage, the dative of a pronoun indicates a person who regards the action of the verb with interest. ' So far as I can see '.

l. 12. **adripis:** ' you light upon '.

l. 13. **relinquis:** ' you leave out '.

l. 17. **voluptatis nomen habent:** ' are called pleasure '. A Genitive of Definition instead of a noun in apposition.

l. 18. **umbram:** ' shadow ' in the sense of inseparable companion,

14. line 21. **Sic ... ut:** English idiom would not use a consecutive clause here. ' My defence ... is that ...'

l. 23. **petulans dictum:** ' improper joke '.

l. 23. **Bene habet:** Colloquial ' Good '.

l. 24. **nostris laudibus ... confessione:** Instrumental ablatives. **confessione:** Somewhat of an exaggeration. The confession is based upon the prosecution's inability to produce more damning accusations.

l. 26. **virum ... hominem:** ' public figure ... private individual '.

l. 27. **ad contentionem dignitatis:** ' a comparison of merits ' as in 11, l. 3.

Sections 15–18

VII. 15. line 1. **Summam ... dignitatem:** The respect due to an old and distinguished family. Cicero begins his contrast between the rival claims of Murena and Sulpicius, which if not handled tactfully could get him into personal difficulties with the prosecution, with a passage to ensure that Sulpicius will not hold this part of the speech against him too strongly. The whole of this passage is an excellent example of Cicero's forensic skill and statesmanship.

l. 7. **Quo loco:** ' And if on this point you assume that only a patrician is well-born '. The *gens Licinia* of which Murena was a member was plebeian.

l. 9. **plebes in Aventinum sevocanda:** Five secessions of the plebeians, usually to the Aventine, are recorded in the early history of Rome. The first is traditionally dated to 494 and the last, the occurrence of which is not seriously disputed, took place in 287. In a *secessio* the plebeians withdrew completely from the life of the city.

l. 11. **proavus:** L. Licinius Murena, likely to have been praetor not later than 147, because he was in all probability an ex-praetor when appointed to the commission set up to assist L. Mummius in reorganising Greece 146–145.

l. 11. **avus:** L. Licinius Murena was praetor not later than 101.

l. 12. **pater:** Murena's father is dealt with in full in the note on *patre suo* 11, l. 10, p. 67.

l. 12. **amplissime atque honestissime:** Conventional epithets. Even Cicero found it difficult to spread himself on this episode in Murena's family history.

l. 13. **faciliorem gradum:** ' an easier path '. This is probably true. The Roman electorate displayed a steady conservatism in their choice of magistrates and for a candidate to have behind him an illustrious succession of office-holding ancestors was an undoubted asset. The praetorship brought with it an *imperium* and, in earlier times at least, a lesser degree of *nobilitas*. The son was only going one step further than his father.

l. 14. **patri debitus:** A man whose father and grandfather had been praetors and who had himself been praetor, pro-praetor and celebrated a triumph could with reason have looked forward to a consulship. Had he lived, he might well have been elected in due course.

16. line 15. **nobilitas:** Some confusion has existed in the past concerning the meaning of *nobilitas, ignobilitas* and *novitas* as used in this and subsequent sections. This confusion has been occasioned by the fact that until the end of the previous century these terms had been used with a wider meaning than is the case here. A *nobilis* had been a man who had either himself held any curule office or who had a holder of such office among his ancestors. At the end of the Republic, however, the word was only used with reference to the consulship. The author of the electioneering handbook, *Commentariolum Petitionis*, makes this clear when he talks of *novos homines praetorios*. These words must be understood in their strict sense throughout this passage. See D. Earl, *The Moral and Political Tradition of Rome* (Thames and Hudson, 1967), p. 12.

Of course plebeians could be every bit as noble as patricians. The *gens Sulpicia*, however, was one of the oldest patrician *gentes* and could produce a consul as far back as 500 – hence *summa*.

l. 16. **litteratis:** ' men of letters '. A *litteratus* is a man of genuine learning as opposed to a *litterator*, one who dabbles in literature.

l. 17. **historicis:** ' antiquarians ' not ' historians '.

l. 18. **obscurior:** ' less well-known '.

l. 18. **Pater . . . loco:** The fact that he was *equestri loco* means that he had not reached the quaestorship which, under Sulla's legislation enacted during his dictatorship in 81, was made the requirement for admission to the Senate.

l. 18. **nulla . . . celebratus:** Cicero is probably using this phrase to give what credit he can to recent members of Sulpicius' family. It would appear in the context to mean that, unlike the father, the grandfather was at least a senator, although he did not reach curule office.

l. 19. **sermone:** ' conversation '.

l. 20. **ex annalium . . . eruenda:** Abstract for concrete. ' must be dug up from ancient records '. **annalium:** As the word implies, *annales* are a record in which the events of each year are preserved separately. The accounts of early Rome are scanty but from about 300 onwards there are regular records of magistrates and events of religious importance. These records would thus contain the evidence of Sulpicius' *nobilitas*.

l. 21. **in nostrum numerum:** As a *novus homo*. Cicero's *novitas* was rather different from the Roman variety. At Arpinum his was one of the leading families. He was in his own words *domi nobilis*, but at Rome he had been only equestrian and even to enter the Senate was a big step forward for him.

l. 24. **summa . . . amplitudine:** The consulship. Although unsuccessful on this occasion, he became consul in 51.

l. 25. **Q. Pompeio:** A friend of the famous Scipio Aemilianus, he was consul in 141 and served in Hispania Citerior. He was proconsul for the next two years and then censor in 131. He was the first member of the *gens Pompeia* to become consul and the first plebeian censor.

l. 25. **fortissimo viro**: His military career in Spain was somewhat chequered. Having failed to take or blockade Numantia he received thirty talents for accepting terms, but on the arrival of his successor he disowned the agreement with the Senate's connivance and went unpunished. He was shortly afterwards accused of extortion and acquitted.

l. 26. **virtutis**: Partitive genitive with *minus*.

l. 27. **M. Aemilio**: M. Aemilius Scaurus was consul in 115, censor in 109, consul *suffectus* in 108, and for a number of years *princeps senatus*. Cicero regarded him as the leading Optimate of his time and he played a prominent part in politics on the optimate side at the end of the second and beginning of the first centuries. His family, however, had not held high office for three generations (Cf. **memoriam prope intermortuam generis** l. 30 below) and he was therefore in men's minds a *novus homo*.

l. 27. **Etenim**: A slightly awkward order. Take thus: **eiusdem . . . est . . . tradere . . . posteris . . . amplitudinem . . . quam . . . acceperit (quod . . . fecit) et . . . renovare . . . memoriam (ut Scaurus)**. The infinitives are the subject of *est*, and with *acceperit* an indefinite subject must be supplied.

l. 27. **animi atque ingeni**: ' qualities of character and natural ability '. Cicero argues that it is no less distinguished for a man to ennoble his family than for a *nobilis* to revive his family's past splendours.

VIII. 17. line 31. **Quamquam**: Take in the order **Quamquam ego putabam . . . perfectum esse** (impersonal) **. . . ne . . . obiceretur . . . qui** (antecedent *ego*) **. . . agebam**. ' And yet . . .'. The MSS have at the end of this sentence a variety of readings which provide difficult, if not impossible, Latin and cannot be construed satisfactorily. Badham's *id agebam* provides the right sense. Cicero is claiming that his efforts are responsible for ending the reproach of *ignobilitas* and it is therefore desirable for him to be the subject of a verb which must describe how this was done.

l. 32. **ignobilitas:** ' lack of nobility '.

l. 33. **Curiis:** ' men like the famous Manius Curius Dentatus' and similarly with the other plurals. Curius defeated the Samnites and in 275 won the Battle of Beneventum against Pyrrhus, king of Epirus, who had invaded Italy. He was consul in 290, 275 and 274; censor in 272.

l. 34. **Catonibus:** M. Porcius Cato, the Censor, consul in 195 and advocate of the destruction of Carthage.

l. 34. **Pompeiis:** See note on *Q. Pompeio* 16, l. 25. p, 73.

l. 35. **Mariis:** C. Marius, consul in 107, 104, 103, 102, 101, 100 and 86; reorganiser of the Roman army and conqueror of Jugurtha and the Germanic tribes, the Teutones and Cimbri.

l. 35. **Didiis:** T. Didius, consul in 98, who fought in Macedonia and Spain.

l. 36. **Caeliis:** C. Caelius Caldus, a partisan of Marius and consul in 94.

l. 37. **tanto intervallo:** Cicero was proud of the fact that he was the first *novus homo* to become consul for many years. He returns to this theme in his speech *de lege agraria* where he talks of a 'perlongo intervallo'. The last consul certainly a *novus homo* was M. Herennius in 93; possibly C. Norbanus in 83 ennobled his family. Both, however, had had senatorial families. The period after Sulla's reforms was not one likely to favour new men.

l. 37. **claustra ... nobilitatis:** ' the barrier protecting nobility '.

l. 38. **apud maiores nostros:** The traditional date for the first plebeian consul is 366 when L. Sextius Lateranus entered office, having as tribune in the previous year with his colleague C. Licinius Stolo carried the Licinio-Sextian rogations. These rogations which they had proposed in 376 provided that at least one consul should be a Plebeian.

l. 40. **familia vetere at inlustri:** A reasonable claim. Cf. 15, ll. 11-13

l. 41. **equitis Romani filio:** cf. note on *in nostrum numerum* 15, l. 21, p. 73.

l. 42. **de generis novitate:** These words have been mistakenly interpreted as meaning that the reproach against Murena's family was that it was not as old as that of Sulpicius. This interpretation has been caused by the belief that because his family had for three generations held curule office it could not be reproached with *novitas* in the sense that he was a *novus homo*. The note on *nobilitas* 16, l. 15 p. 72 shows that *novitas*, if used with the meaning ' the position of a *novus homo* ', must at this period indicate *novitas* with reference to the consulship. The meaning of this sentence is that whereas Cicero had thought that he had caused *virtus*, the quality peculiar to the *novus homo*, to be as valuable an asset to consular candidates as *nobilitas*, the quality peculiar to the noble, he now finds *novitas* or the lack of *nobilitas* being held up by the prosecution as a disadvantage. Translate: ' about his family's lack of nobility '. See Earl, *The Moral and Political Tradition of Rome* p. 46 ff.

l. 43. **duobus patriciis:** L. Sergius Catilina (the conspirator) and P. Sulpicius Galba.

l. 46. **id:** Defeating patrician opponents; **crimen** is the complement.

l. 47. **profecto:** ' then surely '.

Section 18

18. line 1. ' **Quaesturam ... prior.**': There were originally two quaestors, at first nominated by the consuls, but since 449 elected by the *comitia populi tributa*. This assembly was summoned by consuls or praetors and elected quaestors and curule aediles, passed laws, and held trials. When the office was opened to plebeians in 421 the number of quaestors was increased to four and later, in 267 or 241, it was raised to eight. Sulla further increased the number to twenty.

The candidate who first got the vote of a majority of the thirty-five tribes was declared elected first and Sulpicius is represented as saying that his election was announced before Murena's and he therefore has greater *dignitas*. Cicero's answer is that priority of announcement does not necessarily mean superior merit. Two or more candidates may be equally deserving of office – *pares dignitate* – but the name of one of them must in the electoral procedure be announced first. The following sentence is an indication of the weakness of any answer Cicero may give. See also 35, l. 1. p. 20

It is a different story at the beginning of his speech *de imperio Cn. Pompei* where in the election of the praetors Cicero's name was announced first. Cicero's reply to Sulpicius' point looks suspiciously thin, particularly when we recall the importance attached to order of precedence by the Romans.

l. 2. **Non est respondendum:** It is not worth my while to reply to all the prosecution's allegations.

l. 3. **fugit:** ' escaped your notice '.

l. 8. **pari momento sortis fuit: momento** is that which turns the scale. An Ablative of Description which derives from the use denoting attendant circumstances. What follows shows that this phrase means that they were equally unimportant.

l. 8. **lege Titia:** Possibly a law of Sex. Titius, a tribune in 99.

l. 8. **provinciam:** A *provincia* was originally the sphere of action of any magistrate and only later came to be particularly associated with Rome's possessions overseas. The quaestors' provinces were decided by the Senate before the new quaestors entered office. They were then distributed among the quaestors either by decision of the superior magistrates and confirmed by the Senate, or by lot (**sortiuntur** below).

The quaestors can be divided into three groups:

(i) *Quaestores urbani*, two in number, were required to remain in Rome throughout their term of office and their main function was to assist the consuls. They were chiefly concerned with criminal prosecutions and control of the treasury.

(ii) Quaestors who were attached to provincial governors and commanders in the field with duties largely, if not entirely, connected with finance.

(iii) *Quaestores classici*, four in number and established after the subjugation of Italy, dealt primarily with naval matters

and coastal defence. Their headquarters were at Ostia, at
Cales in Campania, in Cisalpine Gaul probably at Ariminum,
and at a fourth place not mentioned in any extant document
but believed to have been Lilybaeum in Sicily.

It is easy to appreciate that a busy port like Ostia with its
attendant problems of the corn-supply would be a headache
for the quaestor in charge.

l. 10. **adclamari:** Always of a hostile noise in Cicero.

l. 11. **gratiosam:** Bringing *gratia* or influence to its quaestor.

l. 12. **nomen:** ' reputation '.

l. 13. **campum:** ' field ' in the sense of ' scope '.

l. 13. **cognosci:** ' to become recognised '.

Sections 19–22

19. line 1. **Reliqui temporis spatium:** The period after the
quaestorship.

l. 2. **tractatum:** ' employed '.

IX. line 3. **militiam:** An ironical comparison of 'military
service ' in the law-courts with Murena's campaigns.

l. 4. **respondendi, scribendi, cavendi:** All technical legal
terms: giving legal opinions, engrossing legal documents,
warning clients of legal pitfalls.

l. 5. **ius civile:** Note the asyndeton to convey the idea of a
busy life and constant occupation with his legal work.

l. 5. **didicit:** ' he has been deeply involved in ' rather than
' learned '.

l. 7. **difficultatem exsorbuit:** ' has swallowed their captiousness '.

l. 9. **laus:** ' merit '.

l. 9. **grata hominibus:** ' appreciated by his fellows '. The
suggestion implied by the juxtaposition of **hominibus** to **unum
hominem** is that there were many. **unum** is inserted to
strengthen this suggestion and to make the contrast with
multis.

l. 9. **elaborare:** 'take great pains'. The word implies both perseverance and eventual success.

20. line 12. **legatus, L. Lucullo:** *Legati* were officers serving on the staff of a provincial governor or commander without set duties. They were normally senators, often more experienced men than Murena could have been at this stage of his career, but he served with distinction in this capacity from 73 to 69. See Introduction, p. xxviii.

L. Licinius Lucullus (*c.* 117-56) had been appointed to an extraordinary proconsular command in 74 to fight Mithridates. In the three following years he defeated him and saved the province of Asia from a financial crisis by his firm and just settlement which earned him the hatred of the equestrian order. This hatred was caused by the resulting loss of profit and it was in no small measure responsible for the ending of his command.

Note the use of the dative rather than the genitive which can be reproduced in English: 'He was staff-officer to Lucullus'.

l. 15. **istam:** 'which you cast in his teeth'. Cf. note on *Obiecta est . . . Asia* 11, l. 8, p. 66.

l. 15. **refertam et . . . delicatam:** 'crammed (*sc.* with wealth) and full of luxury'. The nouns **avaritiae . . . luxuriae** correspond with the two adjectives.

l. 18. **ut . . . imperator:** A neat rhetorical antithesis rather than a considered opinion of the military capacity of the two men. Yet, if Cicero is assuming any reasonable knowledge of the facts on the part of his audience, this cannot be too far from the truth or it would harm his own case.

l. 20. **praesente:** To lend his moral support as an *advocatus*. His presence should guarantee the veracity of Cicero's praise of Murena, but if anyone thinks that Lucullus has agreed to a distortion of the truth because of Murena's danger, he can read the facts in Lucullus' official despatches.

l. 23. **tantum laudis:** Note the different patterns of the Latin and the English idiom. Not in English 'as much . . . as neither . . . nor' but 'bestowed more commendation than a general who sought it for himself or grudged it to others was under obligation to bestow when apportioning praise '.

21. line 26. **honestas:** ' distinction ' not ' honesty '.

l. 27. **quam:** ' which I would judge equal and to which I would attribute the same merit '.

l. 27. **si ... liceat:** Cicero shows Servius every courtesy.

l. 28. **agitat:** ' derides ', ' attacks ', ' ridicules '. **insectatur:** A stronger word than *agitat*. ' inveighs against ', ' pursues relentlessly '.

l. 30. **operarum:** ' this daily round of jobs '. A contemptuous reference to the lawyer's (sc. *forensium*) life. The superstition that Latin authors, including Cicero, found ' -*orum* -*orum* ' or ' -*arum* -*arum* ' an ' ugly repetition ' dies hard. Cf. *interimendorum sacrorum*, l, 33. p. 15. For the facts, see L. E. Eyres, ' -orum -ndorum ' in *Didaskalos* No. 2, (1964), pp. 90–95.

l. 31. ' **Apud exercitum ...** ': The following verbs are in the subjunctive because the questions are deliberative and are used as a form of repudiation to express indignation or surprise. Sulpicius must have voiced the condescending indignation of the man who has all the time been at the centre of government for the military man returning to politics from an overseas posting in which he has lost contact with the political scene.

l. 34. **Primum:** Watch the word order in translation.

l. 34. **ista nostra adsiduitas:** ' that continuous presence of ours (*sc.* lawyers) '.

l. 37. **in oculis:** ' before men's eyes '. Cicero says that it is advantageous to a politician's popularity for him to be observed by others, but people can see too much of him. It is therefore no bad thing for him to be off the political stage for a time, since people might then miss him and want him back again. **mei satietatem:** ' boredom with me '. An objective genitive; similarly **nostrum** below.

l. 37. **gratiam:** ' esteem ', ' regard ' (of others for Cicero).

22. line 40. **ad ... contentionem:** ' to the comparison of professions and skills '. In fact both the army and the law-courts could play their part in the careers of politically

ambitious Romans. A lawyer, by a judicious choice of his cases, particularly as counsel for the defence, could build up a following of political supporters. Cf. note on *consuetudini* 6, l. 13. p. 59.

Military service had the disadvantage of removing a man from the political life of the capital and the fifties show the ways in which men sought to overcome this difficulty by political alliances and the use of tribunes in Rome or legates in their provinces. Yet a candidate for office returning from a successful command brought with him not only the popularity of a victorious general but often the resources to finance his election campaign and in the background the hint – and as time went on, more than the hint – of troops whose first loyalty was to their commander.

l. 41. **qui:** ' how '.

l. 43. **multo ... dignitatis:** ' is much more valuable '.

l. 43. **gloria:** Ironically in its application to the law.

l. 44. **de nocte:** Very early rather than very late. The Romans regularly started their day much earlier than we do. ' even before dawn '.

l. 47. **actionem instituis ... instruit:** The word-play can be reproduced in English by ' draw up '. **actionem:** The general term for all the legal procedure involved in a case.

l. 48. **capiantur:** Common to both legal and military terminology ' are convicted ' or ' are captured ', though rarely found in the first sense.

l. 49. **tenet:** sc. *mente*; ' understands '.

l. 49. **ut:** ' how '.

l. 49. **aquae ... arceantur:** An *actio aquae pluviae arcendae* could be brought if anyone caused rainwater from his property to flow onto his neighbour's land and cause damage. The right to allow water to drip from the eaves of your house onto another's land was known as *ius stillicidi*. The climate and terrain of both Greece and Italy led to repeated trouble between neighbours caused by poor drainage of surface water and to frequent law-suits.

l. 51. **regendis:** 'defining'. Used in boundary disputes with the idea of 'limiting' involved, as opposed to **propagandis** 'extending' frontiers.

X. line 53. **Haec:** Cicero waxes eloquent in praise of *res militaris*, making an effective climax to this section.

l. 56. **praeclara:** Ironical 'this fine profession of ours'.

l. 57. **latet:** 'lies safe'.

l. 58. **increpuit:** 'has been noised abroad'.

l. 58. **suspicio tumultus:** 'a hint of war'. **tumultus:** war in Italy or Cisalpine Gaul. This would bring about a *iustitium* or cessation of all public business.

Sections 23–25

23. line 2. **filiolam:** An affectionate diminutive. 'dear little daughter'.

l. 2. **osculari:** 'fondle', 'caress'.

l. 3. **istud nescio quid:** Contemptuous.

l. 5. **virtutibus:** Ablative of Cause derived from the instrumental use of this case. The other ablatives are to be taken with **dignissimum.**

l. 8. **nullam ... viam:** Cicero must have had his tongue in his cheek. He goes on in the next section to differentiate between the pedantry of academic lawyers and the power of persuasive rhetoric whether in court or at the hustings. While it might in some cases be legitimate to say that a certain lawyer is either one or the other, it is not generally speaking a valid distinction and certainly not fair in the case of Sulpicius.

l. 9. **munitam:** The usual word for building a road.

l. 10. **Omnes ... artes:** If a profession is to win for its practitioners the support of the people, it must confer on them *dignitas* or personal distinction and a *utilitas* or advantage which will bring them the people's *gratia.*

l. 10. **quae ... concilient:** A consecutive clause. 'which are such as to win'.

l. 11. **pergratam:** Active in meaning; 'which confers exceptional *gratia* '.

XI. 24. line 12. **Summa dignitas:** Successful military commanders have *dignitas* because they are generally thought to be responsible for the safety of city and empire; **summa etiam utilitas:** This because we are protected by the advice they give and the danger they run.

l. 14. **statu:** 'condition', 'constitution'. Remember that at this time one of the consuls is away from Rome dealing with Catiline's forces in the field. See Introduction, p. xxi.

l. 17. **Gravis:** 'important'.

l. 19. **posse:** In apposition to **facultas.** The *dignitas* or *auctoritas* of a man of standing was expected to be able to sway the voting at an election or trial. As a result, senior magistrates and ex-magistrates were notoriously touchy on order of precedence in speaking in a meeting. The most senior spoke first and what he said was expected to carry most weight. But anyone who had the *facultas* of influencing a meeting more than was expected of him from his rank added to his *dignitas* and increased his chances of election. Cf. l. 24. below: '**etiam non nobiles consulatum consecuti sunt**', like Cicero himself.

l. 18. **valuit:** 'has been instrumental in'.

l. 22. **comprimat ... flectat ... resistat:** Consecutive subjunctives.

l. 22. **tribunicios furores:** From the time of the Gracchi onwards, apart from a few years after the introduction of Sulla's constitution, the history of the tribunate was a turbulent one. Physical violence, bitter quarrels, and attacks upon established authority were all part of the scene and Cicero may have particularly in mind his own speech against P. Servilius Rullus earlier in the year.

l. 23. **largitioni:** Bribery by means of land allotments or cheap corn.

l. 25. **plurimas gratias:** 'popularity with the largest number'.

l. 27. **isto vestro artificio:** Contemptuous.

25. line 28. **dignitas ... esse:** Cicero, as a lawyer, changes

the opinions he expresses in his speeches to suit each case. Elsewhere he speaks much more highly of the profession of the law.

l. 28. **tenui:** With two meanings. ' trifling ' and ' quibbling,' ' hair-splitting '.

l. 29. **singulis litteris:** Spelling.

l. 30. **interpunctionibus:** ' divisions between words '. An *interpunctio* is a mark between words, the method of dividing words in ancient writing when no space was left between them. It is also a mark in a written model prepared by a lawyer for his client to learn by heart which indicates the correct intervals between the clauses to show their interdependence. We hear of an argument about the will of a man who had left instructions that his body was to be buried INCULTOLOCO. Did he mean *in culto loco* or *inculto loco*?

l. 32. **vestris mysteriis:** Only lawyers could know and interpret the law during the early years of Rome before it had been published.

l. 33. **Posset agi lege:** An impersonal passive; the first of two alternative indirect questions without any introductory word. Legal business could only be transacted on certain days of the year – *fasti* – and not on others – *nefasti*.

l. 34. **fastos:** The *Fasti calendares* which marked F and N against *dies fasti* and *nefasti*.

l. 35. **potentia:** Power improperly held.

l. 35. **qui consulebantur:** The *pontifices*, originally all patricians, in charge of the calendar.

l. 36. **Chaldaeis:** Famous as astrologers. The *pontifices* were asked if a day was *fastus* in the same way as an astrologer if it was propitious.

l. 37. **Cn. Flavius:** The son of a *libertus* of Appius Claudius Caecus, he was Appius' secretary and had access to a manuscript of his *Legis Actiones*. This he published and thus for the first time gave the people knowledge of Civil Law and its procedure. For this service he was made tribune, praetor, curule aedile and in his aedileship (304) displayed in the Forum the list of days on which *legis actio* was permitted. Such at least is the story, but it is unwise to accept too readily the details of accounts of events of this early period.

l. 37. **qui . . . confixerit:** The crow was said to attack other animals in the eyes and this became a proverbial saying for catching someone out in the way in which he usually catches others.

l. 38. **ediscendis:** Ablative ' by learning off '; *sc.* whether they were *fasti* or *nefasti*.

l. 40. **compilarit:** ' got together '.

l. 41. **ratione:** ' list '.

l. 42. **verba quaedam:** ' legal formulae '.

l. 43. **interessent:** ' might be involved in '.

Sections 26–27

XII. 26. line 1. **bellissime:** Colloquial. ' perfectly well '.

l. 3. **FUNDUS:** The drama enacted in court can be reconstructed from this passage as follows:—

Plaintiff: Fundus ... Voco
Defendant: Unde ... Revoco
Praetor: Suis ... Viam

The parties now come forward with their witnesses to the symbol of the disputed object.

Praetor: Redite Viam

The parties return with the symbol.

Plaintiff: Eum ... Aio

The defendant repeats these words.

(The praetor then tells the two parties to depart and they lay down the symbol.)

Plaintiff: Anne ... Vindicaveris?

(There then follows a further exchange between the plaintiff and the defendant.)

l. 3. **inquit:** *sc.* the lawyer.

l. 4. **cedo:** An old form of the second person singular of the imperative. Literally it means ' give '. Here it is used, as frequently, to draw attention to something.

l. 5. **EX IURE QUIRITIUM**: ' According to the legal rights of Roman citizens '.

l. 6. **INDE IBI**: ' Therefore I call you from the praetor's court to join hands with me on the property '. Originally the formal joining of hands and laying claim to the property in dispute took place on the site in the presence of the praetor (*in iure*). As the area in Italy over which Roman law held good expanded and the praetors found this an impossible burden, the custom was changed by consent. The parties concerned now went to the site and joined hands *ex iure*, without the praetor being present, and then brought back to the court a lump of earth as a symbol of the disputed land. Note that **INDE** is causal in sense.

l. 7. **loquaciter**: To be taken with *litigioso*.

l. 8. **ille**: The defendant.

l. 9. **tibicinis Latini**: These musicians were traditionally Latins, not Roman citizens. As, when accompanying actors on the stage, they crossed over from one to another, so the lawyer crosses over from plaintiff to defendant.

l. 11. **REVOCO**: ' I call you in turn ' not ' recall '.

l. 11. **pulchrum**: Colloquial. ' fine '.

l. 13. **carmen**: A set form of words, not necessarily in verse. ' chant '.

l. 13. **cum ... illo**: ' of which this is the most ridiculous part '.

l. 14. **SUPERSTITIBUS**: ' witnesses '.

l. 15. **ISTAM VIAM**: To the property.

l. 16. **sapiens ille**: Contemptuous again.

l. 18. **barbatos**: Shaving was introduced about the end of the fourth century.

l. 21. **IN IURE**: ' in court '. This phrase appears to be part of a formula found in lawsuits dealing with disputed titles.

l. 22. **ANNE TU**: ' would you state the grounds upon which your claim is based '.

l. 23. **tenebant**: ' knew ', ' understood '.

l. 25. **excussa:** ' examined '.

l. 25. **prudentiae:** ' common sense '.

l. 26. **fraudis:** Either ' pitfalls ' or ' harm ', ' danger '.

27. line 28. **iure consultorum:** The normal form is *iuris consultus.*

l. 28. **ingeniis:** ' subtleties '.

l. 29. **Mulieres omnis:** A woman was held to be incapable, by reason of the feebleness of her intellect, of looking after herself and was therefore always the ward of a guardian. She could, however, choose her own guardian on whom she would have imposed her own terms of guardianship beforehand.

l. 31. **continerentur:** A final clause. ' to be controlled '.

l. 32. **Sacra:** Property at Rome often carried with it the expensive obligation of performing certain religious rites in honour of the deity connected with the family or *gens* owning the property and they were known as *sacra privata.*

l. 32. **horum:** Lawyers.

l. 33. **senes ... reperti sunt:** A woman burdened with *sacra* could avoid their performance by undergoing *coemptio*, a secular form of marriage as opposed to *confarreatio* or *usus*, with an old man who did not have either children or money. The husband who after marriage owned her property including the obligation to perform the *sacra*, immediately freed her from it and returned her property piecemeal as gifts or *dona.* The obligation however remained with him but, as he left neither property nor children, it became extinct (*interire*) at his death which, it was hoped, would soon occur.

l. 35. **aequitatem ... tenuerunt:** ' they have abandoned the spirit of equity and retained only the letter '. Cf. *aequitatis* 41, l. 11. p. 24.

l. 36. **alicuius:** A lawyer.

l. 36. **exempli causa:** ' in a model case ', ' in the formula ' not ' for instance '.

l. 36. **id nomen:** Gaia.

l. 38. ' **Gaias** ': In the formula of *coemptio* the woman's name was Gaia.

l. 40. ' diem tertium . . .' . . . oporteret: Cicero is only holding up to ridicule what would seem to the layman of his day a petty legal quibble. The difference between a *iudex* and an *arbiter* is essentially that an appeal to the former is for a fixed sum, but that to the latter is for an amount to be determined according to the circumstances. This distinction widens into that between law and equity and leads to the modern contrast between judgement and arbitration. This passage shows the difficulty found by Roman jurists in deciding when the word *iudex* and when the word *arbiter* was to be used.

Section 28

XIII. 28. line 1. dignitas . . . consularis: ' a claim to the consulship '.

l. 1. ista scientia: The legal profession.

l. 3. constaret: A causal subjunctive.

l. 3. gratiae: ' popular support '. The following sentence explains why. The profession bestows its benefits on all alike and cannot therefore win popularity by giving one man an advantage over his political opponents.

l. 4. promptum: ' available '.

l. 5. gratum: ' conferring *gratia* '.

l. 6. benefici conlocandi: The friendships of Roman political life involved exchanges of assistance as carefully calculated as transactions in the world of commerce from which the word *conlocandi* is drawn. These calculations involved the use of a complex vocabulary which indicated the relationship between the parties involved. A *beneficium* is a kindness which created an obligation, while an *officium* was a service in repayment of such obligation. *Conlocare* means ' to invest money '.

l. 7. ' LICET CONSULERE? ': In the days before their secrets were revealed lawyers were approached by clients with these words to which the lawyers replied: ' *Consule* '. The argument is that now that the law is open to all not only do lawyers have no chance of conferring a favour but they are not even asked for it.

l. 8. **in ea prudentia:** ' in the possession of knowledge '. *Sc.* of the forms of action.

l. 10. **rebus prolatis:** The regular form of words for the suspension of public business during holidays, war, or public disorder.

l. 10. **Peritus:** You cannot call a man expert in a subject about which, as a result of general knowledge of it, there is no disagreement.

l. 13. **perpaucis ... litteris:** ' a very few documents '. The *ius privatum* consisted only of the XII Tables, a few laws and forms of procedure, and the praetors' *edicta*.

l. 14. **si ... moveritis:** Cicero says that if he is provoked to do so, even though he is extremely busy, he will master the practice of the law in three days. He had of course studied under the jurist, Q. Mucius Scaevola, in his youth and was said to have written a legal treatise.

l. 16. **de scripto:** Legal formulae.

l. 17. **scripta sunt omnia:** They are all written down in text-books.

l. 17. **tam anguste:** ' so precisely '. The written formulae are all so much alike that a lawyer has only to select one at random and add the words ' Qua de re agitur '.

l. 19. **quae consuluntur:** i.e. requests for verbal advice.

l. 21. **videare:** Potential subjunctive. ' you would seem '.

l. 22. **controversum ius:** ' a disputed point of view '.

l. 22. **nosse et tractare:** ' to have detected and be dealing with '.

Section 29

29. line 2. **formulis:** The legal forms used by jurists.

l. 2. **actionibus:** Legal processes.

l. 3. **dicendi:** Cicero continues to distinguish between the pettifogging details of the law and the court appearance in the grand manner. This is not, as has been pointed out, an entirely just distinction since the two are often found together, but this line of approach is a good example of Cicero's skill as an advocate, and of course then as now few jurists had the talent to make them great advocates and that way lay political success.

l. 3. **vestrae exercitationi:** ' your profession '.

l. 4. **honorem:** Political advancement.

l. 5. **plerique:** Times do not change greatly. Many jurists were statesmen *manqués*. This is also a sly dig at Sulpicius of whom he says elsewhere that he preferred to be first in a second-rate profession than second in a first-rate. In the *Brutus* Cicero is very much more complimentary. See Introduction, p. xxxii.

l. 5. **multo:** Ablative of the measure of difference in conjunction with the comparative idea implied in *maluisse*.

l. 5. **hoc ... id:** Oratory. **istuc:** To the legal profession.

l. 7. **artificibus:** ' artistes '.

l. 7. **eos ... qui ... qui ... eos:** A good example of chiasmic (a : b, b : a) order. So called from the Greek letter *chi* and the diagrammatic representation of the figure.

l. 7. **auloedos:** Performers who sing to the accompaniment of the *aule*. Similarly *citharoedi*.

l. 10. **res:** ' task '.

l. 11. **salubritas ... salus:** The former is a weaker and vaguer word. ' general well-being ' as opposed to ' safety ' i.e. a matter of life and death.

l. 11. **eis qui dicunt:** Orators.

l. 12. **responsa atque decreta:** ' legal opinions and decisions '.

l. 14. **In qua ... profecissem:** A nice touch of self-depreciation to forestall any suggestion that he was an interested party in this praise of orators.

l. 15. **nunc:** ' but, as it is '.

Section 30

XIV. 30. line 1. **artes:** ' professions '.

l. 2. **dignitatis:** ' office '.

l. 3. **pacis ornamenta:** A phrase found elsewhere in Cicero which means the outward signs of the prosperity and rise in the community's standard of living brought about by a time of peace.

l. 4. **retinentur:** ' are maintained '.

l. 4. **Ceterae tamen:** Cicero grants that other virtues have their power, but says that they are irrelevant to the present discussion about professions appropriate to men seeking public office.

l. 6. **Servi:** It is useful to be able to compliment your opponent upon the possession of qualities which you are saying are irrelevant to the point at issue.

l. 7. **appositis:** ' suited ', ' appropriate '.

l. 10. **motus:** Any disturbance, whether war or revolution.

l. 10. **bellicum canere:** ' to give the signal for war '.

l. 11. **poeta:** Q. Ennius (239–169), ' the father of Roman poetry ', wrote an epic in eighteen books of hexameters – the *Annales* – recounting Roman history down to 171. These quotations are drawn from *Annales*, VIII. 2 ff:

> Pellitur e medio sapientia, vi geritur res,
> Spernitur orator bonus, horridus miles amatur.
> Haut doctis dictis certantes nec maledictis
> Miscent inter sese inimicitiam agitantes
> Non ex iure manum consertum sed mage ferro
> Rem repetunt regnumque petunt vadunt solida vi.

l. 11. **auctor valde bonus:** ' completely trustworthy authority '. The word *auctor* means ' teacher ', ' authority ' rather than merely ' author '. ' **proeliis promulgatis**': ' upon the declaration of war '. Printed by editors as a loose quotation from Ennius, although the words do not scan as they stand, because the use of the verb *promulgare* with a noun such as *proelium* is not found in Cicero. Argument from negative evidence is notoriously fallible, but the phrase is probably closely based on what Ennius wrote.

l. 14. ' **sapientia** ': Widely held to mean ' eloquence ' but without sufficient reason. Rather ' good sense '. There are two contrasts in this passage: Between **simulatio prudentiae** and **sapientia,** and between **sapientia** and **vis;** between a pretence of knowledge or good sense and good sense itself, and between war and diplomacy seen as the sensible way of solving disputes rather than as a solution by words. This passage certainly does not demand that **sapientia** mean ' eloquence ', and indeed the contrast between ' good sense ' and ' force ' or ' violence ' makes better sense in the context. There is no need to equate **sapientia** so closely with **orator bonus** as to require the translation ' eloquence '.

l. 15. **odiosus:** ' tiresome '.

l. 15. **bonus:** An epithet of approval in contrast with **horridus.**

l. 17. **manum consertum:** cf. 26, l. 6. p. 14. There is here a *double entendre* from both legal and military usage.

l. 18. **rem repetunt:** The technical legal term for the recovery of goods improperly acquired, particularly by extortion in the provinces.

l. 19. **forum castris:** In contrast with the famous line from Cicero's epic poem *de temporibus suis* fr. 1. ' Cedant arma togae, concedat laurea laudi '.

l. 19. **otium:** ' peace within the community '.

l. 19. **stilus:** ' the pen '.

l. 20. **umbra soli:** A difficult concept for us northerners. The contrast is between a life of retirement in the coolness of the shade and an active one in the heat of the sun; the life that requires energy and endurance. This distinction is equated with that between the lawyer and the soldier.

l. 20. **sit denique:** Let that quality through which Rome herself has become *princeps* be *primus* in the city.

Sections 31–34

31. line 3. **mulierculis:** A contemptuous diminutive applied to Asiatics ' feeble women '. Murena's conduct of affairs in the East may have been open to reproach but in this ridicule of his enemy Cato is on weak ground. Mithridates was as formidable an opponent as ever confronted Rome.

l. 4. **Quod . . . existimo:** The following sentence substantiates this view.

l. 4. **pauca:** Cicero is not going to spend much time in dealing with this reproach because it is not vital to the case – **neque enim ... continetur.**

l. 7. **Pyrrho:** M'. Curius Dentatus, the consul of 295, celebrated a triumph over Pyrrhus and the Samnites after the final defeat of the king near Malventum.

l. 8. **Philippo:** T. Quinctius Flamininus, the consul of 198, was assigned Macedonia and as proconsul had his *imperium* prorogued until the Senate should send a successor. In 197 he won the Battle of Cynoscephalae and returned with his army in 194 to celebrate a triumph over Macedonia and Philip.

l. 8. **Aetolis:** M. Fulvius Nobilior, the consul of 189, was assigned the Aetolian War, had his *imperium* prorogued for a year and returned in 187 to celebrate a triumph over the Aetolians and Cephallenians.

l. 9. **Perse:** L. Aemilius Paulus, the consul of 168, was given charge of the war against Perseus of Macedonia whom he defeated at Pydna and later captured. In the following year he was proconsul and *imperator* in Macedonia and after re-organising Macedonia and Greece returned to celebrate a magnificent triumph over King Perseus and the Macedonians.

l. 9. **Pseudophilippo:** Q. Caecilius Metellus Macedonicus, the praetor of 148, recaptured Macedonia from the pretender Andriscus. He was propraetor for the following two years and returned in 146 to celebrate a triumph over the Macedonians and Andriscus.

l. 10. **Corinthiis:** L. Mummius, the consul of 146, was allotted the province of Achaea and sacked Corinth and reduced the other Achaean cities. He organised Achaea with the help of a senatorial commission and returned in the following year to celebrate his triumph over the Achaeans and Corinthians.

l. 11. **cur ... contemnitur:** A pertinent question. Note that Cicero draws no distinction between the inhabitants of Greece and Macedonia on the one hand and those of Asia Minor on the other. They had after all both been part of the empire of Alexander the Great and the distinction between

Greek and Asiatic would not be so strong in Roman as in Greek minds. **ille ... hostis:** Mithridates.

l. 13. **monumentis:** ' records '.

l. 14. **cum Antiocho:** Antiochus III, the Great, was born in 241 and in 223 succeeded to the Kingdom of Syria. In 196 he aroused the Senate's alarm by invading Europe. After three years of negotiations with Rome he invaded Greece but was defeated by the Romans in two land battles, at Thermopylae in 191 and at Magnesia in 189, and lost a naval campaign. The Peace of Apamea (188) ended the Seleucid Kingdom as a Mediterranean power.

l. 15. **L. Scipio:** L. Cornelius Scipio Asiaticus was with M'. Acilius Glabrio at Thermopylae and succeeded him as consul in the following year. His brother accompanied him to the East and in that year Lucius crossed to Asia Minor where in the New Year he defeated Antiochus. He returned home to celebrate a triumph in 188 but appears to have been a much lesser figure than his brother.

l. 15. **P. fratre:** P. Cornelius Scipio Africanus Maior (236–184), the conqueror of Hannibal at Zama in 202, was an ardent philhellene and urged against the Roman evacuation of Greece for fear that Antiochus might invade it. When his brother was given the command against Antiochus, since he had been consul in 194, he could not again hold office constitutionally and so became his brother's *legatus*. He fell ill, however, and took no part in the Battle of Magnesia.

l. 16. **ille:** Publius, the better known of the two; **hic** is in contrast.

l. 16. **cognomine:** *Africanus* and *Asiaticus*. The Roman system of nomenclature is as follows. Romans had regularly at least two names: (i) The *praenomen* or personal name. (ii) The *nomen* indicating the *gens* or clan to which an individual belonged. Frequently, but not always, there was a third name, the *cognomen*, originally a personal title or nickname which would often pass to a man's descendants and so become a family name. A man could have more than one *cognomen*. See H. J. Rose, *A Handbook of Latin Literature* (Methuen 1936) p. 19, and A. E. Douglas, *Greece and Rome*, V (N.S.) pp. 62–6.

32. line 19. **M. Catonis**: M. Porcius Cato Censorius (234–149) served with distinction under M'. Acilius Glabrio at Thermopylae in 191.

l. 19. **quo**: To be taken with *esset profectus*.

l. 20. **ut . . . statuo**: ' as I judge '.

l. 22. **arbitraretur**: The imperfect subjunctive was commonly used in past unreal conditions to represent the past point of view of someone looking forward; similarly **putaretur** below.

l. 23. **egisset**: This account conflicts with that given by Livy who makes Scipio offer his services. Unless Livy can be shown to be wrong for other reasons his version is on the face of it more likely to be correct, since Cicero has good reason to present the proposal as coming from the Senate. Livy's account would not give so convincing a picture of a Senate moved by the seriousness of the impending war and taking the initiative in overcoming the constitutional difficulties to having the leading general of the time at the scene of action.

XV. line 28. **qui**: ' what sort of '.

l. 31. **L. Sulla**: By the Peace of Dardanus in August 85 after sacking Athens and defeating the forces of Mithridates at Chaeronea and Orchomenus during the course of the First Mithridatic War.

l. 31. **maximo . . . imperator**: These qualities of the general and his army are included to make the point that it was the stature of the enemy and not any Roman deficiencies which led to peace. **rudis**: ' inexperienced ', ' unskilled '. He had served as quaestor in 107 under Marius against Jugurtha and played a distinguished part in the Social War.

l. 32. **ut . . . dicam**: ' to say no more ', ' to put it no higher '.

l. 33. **cum pace dimisit**: In contrast with *cum bello*. This phrase means that Mithridates was only driven from the territory which he had invaded and that the war was not carried into his own kingdom of Pontus. Cicero omits all mention of the political situation at Rome which had much to do with Sulla's readiness to come to terms.

l. 33. **L. Murena**: Left by Sulla in 84 as propraetor in

Asia he disobeyed his instructions and provoked the Second Mithridatic War (83–81) in which he was worsted. Cf. note on *patre suo* 11, l. 10. p. 67.

l. 34. **vehementissime ... reliquit:** Contains both alliteration and a play on the meaning of the compounds of *premo*.

l. 36. **aliquot annis:** Freed from Murena's attacks, Mithridates spent the years between the end of the Second Mithridatic War and 75 in strengthening his position.

l. 38. **Oceanum:** The Atlantic. **Ponto:** The Black Sea.

l. 38. **Sertori:** In the winter of 76/5 negotiations were conducted between Mithridates and Sertorius who was at this time holding Spain against the government at Rome. Mithridates offered Sertorius ships and money in return for the recognition of his claims in Asia Minor.

33. line 39. **duobus consulibus:** The consuls of 74, L. Licinius Lucullus and M. Aurelius Cotta.

l. 40. **ita ... ut:** ' with orders that '. Lucullus was to pursue Mithridates while Cotta covered Bithynia.

l. 41. **alterius:** Cotta. He had received command of a fleet to protect his province of Bithynia and the Propontis but was defeated by land and sea and blockaded in Chalcedon until Lucullus relieved him.

l. 43. **L. Luculli:** He checked the forces of Mithridates in a battle at the River Rhyndacus and in the winter of 74/3 trapped him into a disastrous defeat while he was besieging Cyzicus, a city of Mysia, and compelled him to raise the siege.

l. 48. **provincia:** The Roman province of Asia which contained Mysia, Lydia, Caria, and Phrygia.

l. 49. **haec:** ' this campaign '.

l. 51. **pugnam navalem:** After his retreat from Cyzicus in 73 Mithridates embarked ten thousand men in a fleet of fifty ships led by M. Marius who had been sent by Sertorius to join him. Lucullus met and destroyed this force when on its way to Italy in two battles off Tenedos and Lemnos.

l. 52. **contento cursu:** ' in full sail '.

l. 52. **acerrimis ducibus:** Sent by Sertorius.

l. 53. **Italiam:** To relieve the pressure on Mithridates by renewing the fighting in Italy.

l. 53. **spe atque animis inflata:** ' with high hope and spirits '.

l. 55. **Mitto:** ' I pass over '.

l. 56. **expulsus regno:** Lucullus in the summer of 73 advanced into Pontus and, crossing the River Halys, marched on Amisus. A number of engagements were fought and in the last Mithridates was nearly killed and his army cut to pieces. He abandoned his kingdom to take refuge with Tigranes. The conquest of Pontus was completed by 70. The participle is concessive in force as is made clear by the following **tamen.**

l. 56. **tandem aliquando:** ' at long last '.

XVI. line 61. **proelia:** In 69 Lucullus marched on Armenia, took Tigranes by surprise, and captured Tigranocerta. In the following year he put the army of Mithridates to flight in a battle at Artaxata.

34. line 62. **Hoc:** ' only this '.

l. 62. **ille:** Because Mithridates had died this year.

l. 65. **L. Lucullus:** A critical audience might wonder why, when Lucullus had conducted the campaign with such distinction, the people should have been so eager to entrust its completion to Pompey. The facts are that Lucullus had his limitations as a leader of men and had by his firm settlement of the economic crisis in Asia earned the hatred of the *Equites* at Rome. See also note on *legatus, L. Lucullo* 20, l. 12 p. 79. He was, however, a good strategist and administrator, and Cicero finds it politically prudent to speak well of him with the adroit skill he had used in his speech *pro lege Manilia* which supported the bill proposing that Pompey be given his command. This proposal, offensive naturally to Lucullus himself and bitterly opposed by the Optimates – hence **populus Romanus** alone – was eagerly supported by the people. Cicero, as he had to be, was adept at complimenting opponents. See also Introduction, p. xi.

l. 68. **acerrima ... illa:** A battle at Nicopolis in Pontus in 66.

l. 70. **Qua:** Watch the word-order when translating.

l. 71. **Bosphorum:** The Cimmerian Bosporus, now the Crimea. The preposition we might expect is occasionally omitted with the name of a country, particularly when Greek.

l. 72. **nomen . . . regium:** ' the title of king '. *Sc.* even though an exile.

l. 73. **regno possesso:** ' although he held Pontus '.

l. 75. **tantum . . . posuit:** ' rated the life of a single man so highly '.

l. 75. **cum ipse . . . possideret:** ' although he (Pompey) . . . held '. The subject of **tenuerat, adierat, sperarat** is Mithridates. The first refers to his own kingdom of Pontus, the second to the Roman province of Asia, and the third to his further designs.

l. 77. **vita:** This is contrasted with **sedibus.** The resilience of Mithridates' record against Rome justified Pompey's appreciation.

l. 78. **Hunc tu . . . Cato:** As he nears the end of this section Cicero brings his audience back to Cato whose depreciation of the importance of this war has caused it to be included.

l. 81. **denique:** ' only then '.

l. 82. **arbitrarentur:** This reading (MSS *arbitraretur* from *arbitro*) must have **tot imperatores** as the subject.

l. 83. **animi . . . consili . . . laboris:** Genitives of Description. Three vital qualities.

l. 84. **defendimus:** ' I maintain '. Cicero does not state directly that Murena's qualities as a general should lead to his acquittal, but with rather more subtlety takes the opportunity given him by the prosecution of parading them in front of the court and then later in the speech (83, l. 5 f. p. 45.) showing that these are the qualities that the times demand.

Sections 35–36

XVII. 35. line 1. **At enim:** The regular formula for introducing an opponent's objection – real or imagined.

l. 1. **prior renuntiatus est:** See note on ' *Quaesturam . . . prior.*' 18, l. 1. p. 76.

l. 2. **ex syngrapha:** written agreement ', ' promissory note '. The tone is a mixture of incredulity and contempt at the idea that the hands of the people should be tied in this way; that because a man was elected first on one occasion he should always be so elected. Yet to have been increased elected first must have increased a man's *auctoritas*.

l. 3. **agere cum populo:** ' to propose to the people '.

l. 5. **Euripum:** The strait between the coast of Attica and Euboea. Here of straits in general, as we might say ' Channel '. It was notorious for its difficult currents.

l. 8. **ratio comitiorum:** ' the way of elections '. This comparison was a commonplace of ancient oratory, both Greek and Latin.

l. 10. **aura:** Nominative.

l. 11. **sine ulla:** ' without any apparent cause your expectation is so belied that '.

l. 13. **quasi vero:** An ironical phrase implying that of course the people were the cause.

36. line 16. **L. Philippum:** In 93 he was unexpectedly defeated in the consular elections by M. Herennius, a *novus homo*, but he was a successful candidate two years later.

l. 16. **ingenio:** Note the qualities with which the man whom people expected to be elected was endowed: natural ability, high regard among others, an active life in the Forum (**opera** sc. *forensi*), and the right family background.

l. 17. **Q. Catulum:** A leader of the Optimates, he was defeated three times in consular elections owing to the alliance of *Equites* and people: by C. Atilius Serranus in 106, Cn. Mallius in 105, and C. Flavius Fimbria in 104, He was finally elected consul for 102.

l. 18. **humanitate:** He was a highly educated man and closely connected with the Scipionic circle. He succeeded Laelius as a centre of cultured life and combined military, political and literary prestige.

l. 19. **Cn. Mallio:** A *novus homo*.

l. 19. M. Scaurum: Defeated by Q. Fabius Maximus Eburnus in the consular elections for 116, he was elected consul for the following year. He eventually became *princeps Senatus* and Cicero regards him as the Optimate *par excellence*.

l. 21. Non modo: Not only were these electoral defeats unexpected, but when they had occurred, could not be explained.

l. 23. Nam: The exact meaning of this sentence is not immediately apparent though the general drift is clear. Just as storms usually have their accompanying signs, but can break unexpectedly without them on occasion, so it is often possible to see the signs of impending electoral surprises, yet at times these signs which may explain them are missing. **certo ... signo:** ' with some clear waring in the sky '. **saepe improviso:** Adversative in sense. ' but often '. So also **saepe ita. in hac ... populari:** ' in this storm of popular elections '. **intellegas:** This use of the potential subjunctive is very common with the generalising second person. In it the writer represents the action denoted by the verb as something which he has thought of as being possible, likely, or certain. **quo signo ... sit:** *Lit.* ' to the accompaniment of what sign it has arisen '. i.e. ' the signs of its outbreak '.

Section 37

XVIII. 37. line 1. **Sed tamen:** Resumes after a digression. After his musings upon the fickleness of popular elections Cicero returns to the theme raised in 35.

l. 1. ratio: sc. why Murena's name came after that of Sulpicius in the election of praetors.

l. 2. vehementer ... desideratae sunt: ' were badly misesd '.

l. 2. in praetura: Sc. *petenda.* ' when a candidate for the praetorship '. Similarly **consulatu** below.

l. 3. una ... creverat: This passage has caused considerable difficulty. The most satisfactory explanation is that there was no *exspectatio muneris* when Murena was a candidate for the praetorship since he had not been aedile and the public therefore did not know how good a show he would be likely to provide. When, however, he was a consular candidate he had behind him the *ludi Apollinares* over which he had had control as *praetor urbanus* and the *exspectatio* that was now widely entertained was inflated by the political campaign of his competitors who were joined by Murena in an electoral auction of public shows to Murena's advantage since he had the credit of a *munus amplissimum* behind him. **muneris:** ' public show '. **et rumore ... competitorum:** ' with the general opinion and the politically inspired (**studiis**) talk of his fellow candidates '.

l. 5. **ei:** The soldiers of the army of Lucullus whose command had been removed from him in 66 but who did not celebrate his triumph until 63 as a result of popular opposition. See also, 69, l. 21. p. 38.

l. 6. **legatione omni:** ' the whole of his time as a *legatus* '.

l. 7. **decesserant:** The regular word for leaving a province.

l. 10. **comitiis:** ' at the elections '.

l. 10. **L. Murenae:** Dative with *praesto fuit*.

Sections 38–40

38. line 2. **voluntas militum:** The arrangement of the subject-matter is similar to that found in chiasmus. In 37. l. 4 f. firstly the *munus* then the *milites*; here the *milites* and then the *munus* in 38, l. 17 f.

l. 2. **cum ... cum ... tum:** ' both ... and ... and '.

l. 3. **multitudine:** Plutarch in his *Life of Lucullus* says that Pompey left him only sixteen hundred men and they went with him unwillingly.

l. 3. **apud suos gratia:** ' by their influence with their friends '.

l. 4. **multum ... auctoritatis:** The weight of this *auctoritas* must be in doubt unless it be taken to include the type of strong-arm methods employed by Pompey's returned soldiers to influence political decisions a few years later. Yet the loyal troops of a successful general seen *en masse* might be a powerful influence.

l. 5. **suffragatio militaris:** ' the soldiers' support '. In the emphatic position at the end of the sentence, but adding little in sense to **voluntas militum.**

l. 7. **verborum interpretes:** i.e. Lawyers. A dig at Sulpicius.

l. 8. ' **Me saucium . . .':** A picture of the popular general. One of the problems which assisted the fall of the Republic was the personal loyalty of the rank and file of an army to their successful general rather than to the state. Any good leader of men will win the esteem of his troops but the state of affairs in Rome at this time ensured that the ties between a general and his army could become too strong for the good of Rome herself. Armies were recruited as required for campaigns and wars which kept them for many years away from their homes and families, and at the end of the war they were demobilised without the state making any provision for their future. This security they sought from their general; he could only obtain allotments of land for them by political pressure at Rome; they, therefore, supported him in his political aspirations.

The picture painted here gives the more personal side of soldiers' attachment to their general during their service under him. The subsequent political link as this section shows was no less close and important.

l. 11. **fortis . . . felix:** Two of the most important character-istics of the successful general: personal valour and good fortune. Luck is perhaps rather out of fashion today as a factor of such importance, but it was considered to be an essential ingredient of success in the ancient world, as the next two sentences show. Cf. note on 12, l. 28. p. 69.

l. 11. **Hoc . . . voluntatem:** ' what weight do you think this carries in winning a reputation with men and their goodwill? ' The implication is that it is considerable.

l. 13. **religio:** Regard for due religious observances.

l. 13. **omen . . . praerogativum:** In the election the centuries voted in an order decided by lot. The century to vote first was called *centuria praerogativa* and its vote was regarded as most important in deciding the final result, which rarely differed from the way in which its vote had gone. Hence its vote is looked upon as an *omen* or heavenly indication of the result.

l. 14. **in hoc ... valuisse:** ' if in this case the reputation and talk of his good fortune has had a great effect '. Politics and religion were closely connected at Rome and the conduct of *comitia* was certainly hedged about by *religio*. The thought behind this sentence is that if the first tribe's vote can be regarded as an omen then a reputation for *felicitas* will have a similar effect upon the outcome.

XIX. line 16. **ducis:** ' you regard '.

l. 17. **hanc urbanam suffragationem:** ' the support of civilians '.

l. 20. **volgus imperitorum:** ' the ignorant herd '. For some time the mass of the citizen body had been becoming increasingly impervious to rational argument in politics. The rather cynical view that Cicero takes here of Roman elections was not unjustified. The *faex Romuli* had come a long way from the days of the Hannibalic War.

l. 22. **Quamquam:** ' And yet that is sufficient for my case '. **id** refers to the fact that the common people delights in shows. If this is the case, there is no cause for surprise in Murena's victory.

l. 22. **sunt enim:** ' an election is a question of the common people and of mere numbers '.

39. line 29. **de multitudine indocta:** Not ' at the ignorant crowd ' but ' at the fact that the ignorant crowd delights in them '.

40. line 30. **L. Otho:** L. Roscius Otho, a tribune in 67 – a year notable for the volume of tribunician legislation – carried a law to reserve for the *Equites* the front fourteen rows in the theatre, immediately behind the orchestra where the senators sat. Cf. introduction p. xvi.

l. 30. **vir .... necessarius:** Stock phrases.

l. 31. **restituit:** By a *lex Cornelia* of 81 Sulla had transferred the juries from the *Equites* to the Senate and we may assume that other honours were taken from them at this time, so that ' restored ' is probably appropriate. **dignitatem:** Their rightpoful sition in the front as required by their status. **voluptatem:** Because they would obtain a better view. It was not a popular measure and Roscius was hissed in the theatre for it.

l. 33. **gratissima:** The law was a highly partisan piece of legislation aimed at influencing the *Equites* during the political struggle over Gabinius' proposal that Pompey be given sole command over the pirates. Cicero had spoken for it in a speech now lost.

l. 33. **honestissimo ... splendore:** Words regularly used of the Equestrian Order.

l. 34. **fructus ... iucunditatis:** ' the enjoyment of pleasure '.

l. 36. **dissimulant:** ' pretend that they do not '.

l. 37. **petitione:** sc. ' for the consulship '.

l. 38. **Quod si ego:** If Cicero who as aedile had given three lots of games was disturbed by Antonius' display, has not Sulpicius good cause to give Murena credit for the electoral effect of his lavish spectacle?

l. 38. **trinos ludos:** ' three sets of public games '. Note **trinos** not *ternos*. The distributive is used because the meaning of *ludi* in the sense of ' public games ' has no singular. These games were dedicated to Ceres, Liber and Libera, and to Flora.

l. 39. **aedilis:** In 69, probably as plebeian aedile.

l. 39. **Antoni:** C. Antonius gave some magnificent games when *praetor urbanus* in 66, and was the other successful consular candidate in 64.

l. 39. **commovebar:** ' felt anxiety '.

l. 40. **casu:** He had not been either aedile or *praetor urbanus*.

l. 40. **nihil ... adversatam:** ' did you no damage '.

l. 40. **huius:** Murena.

l. 41. **argenteam scaenam:** We do not know how exactly the silver was used, but the point – an extremely lavish spectacle – is clear.

Sections 41–42

41. line 1. **sane:** ' for the sake of argument '.

l. 5. **sortem:** There had since the reforms of Sulla been eight praetors. Two – *urbanus* and *peregrinus* – had *iuris dictio* in

civil cases and six had charge of the criminal courts, the
quaestiones perpetuae. Murena had the good fortune to draw
the lot for the *praetura urbana* while the *quaestio de peculatu*
fell to Sulpicius. The two ' home ' praetors (the additional
praetors had originally been appointed to serve in the provinces)
ranked higher than their colleagues, and the *praetor urbanus*
was thought to hold the more distinguished position.

XX. line 7. **magnitudo negoti:** ' the importance of the
business '.

l. 7. **gratiam:** ' influence '.   Conferred by the praetor's
freedom to exercise discretion.

l. 7. **aequitatis largitio:** ' the bestowal of justice '. i.e. the
power to give judgements in the spirit rather than according
to the letter of the law.

l. 9. **aequabilitate decernendi:** ' the impartiality of his
decisions '.

l. 10. **lenitate:** ' courtesy '.

l. 11. **provincia:** ' sphere of administration ', ' office '.
Here used in its original sense. See note on *provinciam* 18, l. 8.
p. 77.

l. 12. **ad extremum ... concluditur:** ' is rounded off by '.
i.e. the celebration of the *ludi Apollinares* gives the finishing
touch. Not ' at the end ' because the games were held early in
July.

42. line 13. **sors:** The *provinciae* of the six praetors presiding
over the criminal courts were possibly decided by the Senate, but
it is certain that they were distributed among the magistrates
concerned by lot.

l. 13. **peculatus:** The embezzlement of public funds.

l. 14. **squaloris:** Defendants sought to excite pity by wearing
the poorest possible clothes – *vestem mutare*.

l. 15. **indicum:** ' informers '.   One of the curses of a society
which had not developed a system of criminal investigation
with agents paid by the authorities to discover the truth, but
which relied upon information laid by individuals for private
gain.

l. 16. **scriba damnatus:** A *scriba* was a magistrate's secretary. Nothing more is known of this case which brought the wrath of the whole *ordo* down on Sulpicius' head. They were influential men and Sulpicius could not afford their ill-will in the consular elections.

l. 17. **Sullana gratificatio:** Those who had received state property from Sulla were now worried by the prospect of actions for *peculatus*. **reprehensa:** Presumably in some judgement. Nothing is known of this case either. **multi viri fortes:** Sulla's veterans were a group to be reckoned with. This is made clear by their inclusion in Cicero's list of Catiline's supporters where he refers to them in similar terms.

l. 18. **pars:** ' a considerable part '.

l. 18. **lites:** ' the fine ', ' retribution '. The *litis aestimatio* was the assessment of damages which followed conviction on the main charge. See Introduction, p. xxvii.

l. 19. **cui placet . . . cui dolet:** The prosecution and defendant respectively.

l. 22. **provincia:** ' the government of provinces '. *Gallia Transalpina* and *Gallia Cisalpina*.

l. 24. **proficiscens:** ' on his journey '.

l. 24. **dilectum:** Northern Italy was one of the chief recruiting-grounds for Roman armies.

l. 24. **res publica:** ' the condition of the state '.

l. 25. **liberalitatis:** ' generosity '.

l. 25. **tribus:** Consuls were elected by the *comitia centuriata*, so strictly speaking, tribes are irrelevant. But Cicero would have it in mind that the inhabitants of these Umbrian *municipia* which received Roman citizenship under the *lex Iulia* of 90 were confined to certain tribes in order to check their importance in the *comitia*.

l. 27. **Gallia:** Transalpine and Cisalpine in 64.

l. 27. **nostri homines:** The *publicani* and their employees.

l. 27. **desperatas iam pecunias:** ' sums already written off '. We frequently hear of debt settlements in the provinces, evidence of the importance to Rome of her provincial revenues and the unsatisfactory method of collection.

l. 28. **exigerent:** ' collect '.

l. 29. **scilicet:** Heavily ironical. ' of course '.

l. 30. **non nullorum:** i.e. those who hope for an appointment on your staff.

l. 30. **studia:** ' enthusiasm '.

Sections 43–46

XXI. 43. line 3. **provincialium:** ' official '.

l. 5. **amisso iam tempore:** i.e. the election has taken place.

l. 6. **re integra:** ' when the matter was still undecided '.

l. 7. **nescire:** ' did not know how to '.

l. 7. **in eis rebus ipsis:** His preparations for the prosecution of a successful rival.

l. 11. **terrores:** ' intimidation '.

l. 12. **a spe adipiscendi:** They make people think that he abandoned all hope of success.

l. 14. **hoc fit:** This looks forward to **ut** coming after the parenthesis. As soon as a candidate starts making accusations against his opponent, he appears to have despaired of office.

44. line 17. **Quid ergo:** This is followed by a question which receives a negative answer.

l. 17. **acceptam ... placet:** ' ought you not prosecute a wrong you have had done to you? Sulpicius is represented as missing the point of what Cicero has just said and as asking whether it is not perfectly reasonable to try by instituting a prosecution to right a wrong done to him.

l. 18. **Immo:** ' Yes, of course '.

l. 19. **sed aliud:** 'But you should not start a prosecution at election time if you want to win the election '.

l. 21. **magnis copiis:** This is part of the Roman client system. The larger the crowd of clients and supporters that he could get to accompany him to the Forum where canvassing (*prensatio*) took place and to the Campus Martius where the

voting took place and the more distinguished its members, the
more likely, it was held, was a candidate to be elected.

l. 21. **deduci:** ' to be escorted '. The normal word for showing a candidate your regard and support by accompanying him

l. 22. **inquisitio candidati:** This is more likely to be a
subjective genitive in view of the following *praenuntia repulsae.*
' a collection of evidence on the part of the candidate '. It is
the *repulsa* of the man initiating the *inquisitio* about which we
are talking here, and were it an objective genitive *competitor*
(See 45, l. 31. below) would have been the more natural word.

l. 24. **comparatio:** ' organisation '.

l. 25. **denuntiatio:** Directed at your rivals. Cf. *in istam
accusandi denuntiationem* 46, l. 56. below.

l. 25. **persalutatio:** The act of greeting everyone you meet
to solicit his vote.

l. 25. **praesertim cum:** In view of the modern tendency to
judge a candidate's chance of success from his demeanour.

l. 26. **omnium:** sc. *candidatorum.*

l. 28. **animi et facultatis:** ' confidence and chance of success '.

45. line 29. **iacet:** ' he's down '.

l. 30. **abiecit hastas:** ' he has thrown in the sponge '.

l. 32. **Alium fac iam:** ' I'll get another candidate elected ',
' I'll vote for another candidate '. For this meaning of *facio,*
cf. 18, l. 1. *sum ego factus prior.*

l. 34. **debilitantur:** ' lose their confidence '. i.e. in the
candidate.

l. 34. **studia deponunt:** ' lose their enthusiasm '.

l. 34. **certam:** ' as already decided '. They either abandon
all political activity or transfer their energies from the election
to the trial.

XXII. line 36. **Accedit eodem:** Lit. ' Besides this, it
happens to the same purpose that '. ' A further result is that '.

l. 40. **sed nimirum omnium maxima:** Originally a consideration subsidiary to his candidature, the prosecution has grown
in the candidate's mind until it is his main concern.

l. 41. **e civitate:** The *lex Tullia de ambitu* of this year extended the penalties established by the *lex Calpurnia* of 67 and made provision for a sentence of ten years' exile.

l. 42. **non inopem neque infirmum:** Or he would not have been a consular candidate.

l. 44. **Omnes ... concurrimus:** For the less disinterested motives involved in this haste to help anyone who was not a downright enemy, see note on *consuetudini* 6, l. 13. p. 59. Cicero had started his political career with his defence of Roscius of Ameria in 80 and had subsequently proved adept in his choice of case.

46. line 52. **adornet:** ' equip ' and so ' prepare '.

l. 52. **instruat:** ' draw up ', ' marshal ' and so ' organise '.

l. 53. **curriculo:** ' course '. The metaphor has changed from a military scene to chariot-racing. It should not be pressed home in too great detail.

l. 58. **in ista ratione:** ' in effecting that plan '. **sc.** of prosecuting your opponent.

Sections 46–47

XXIII. line 1. **Legem ambitus:** The *lex Tullia.*

l. 2. **erat enim:** ' for there already existed '.

l. 2. **Calpurnia:** See Introduction, p. xxiv.

l. 2. **Gestus est mos ... tuae:** ' Your wish was gratified and your position recognised '. *morem alicui gerere* = to do the will of somebody.

l. 5. **refragata est:** ' thwarted '. Since Murena was innocent Sulpicius' demand for harsher legislation harmed his own election campaign for the reasons given in the following section.

47. line 6. **in plebem:** For this provision and what follows, see introduction p. xxiv.

l. 6. **efflagitata est:** ' was secured '.

l. 7. **tenuiorum:** The poorer citizens who would be indignant because deprived of the chance of turning a dishonest penny in electoral corruption.

l. 7. **nostrum ordinem:** The Senate.

l. 8. **concessit:** ' gave way to ', ' yielded to '. An intransitive use.

l. 9. **fortunae communi:** The common lot to which all senators would be liable. It was of course open to the senators to refrain from bribery but they were notably reluctant to do so.

l. 10. **Morbi excusationi:** Defendants sometimes failed to appear before a court on the grounds of illness and if they could maintain this plea until they entered office, they evaded prosecution. Before the *lex Tullia* illness was a legitimate ground for absence, This law either did not admit it or only under severe conditions. See Introduction, p. xxvi.

l. 11. **contra valetudinis commodum:** ' to the detriment of their health '.

l. 12. **laborandum est:** i.e. in court.

l. 12. **incommodo morbi:** An Ablative of Attendant Circumstances. ' together with the disability of ill-health '

l. 14. **Is qui:** Cicero is trying to shift responsibility for the measure onto Sulpicius.

l. 15. **cui minime proderant:** Having attained the consulship he cannot under Sulla's *lex Cornelia annalis* be a candidate for office for ten years, and will therefore not benefit from these measures against *ambitus*.

l. 16. **frequens:** ' crowded '.

l. 18. **Confusionem suffragiorum:** Voting by heads rather than by tribes or centuries to prevent any particular set of voters having undue influence and to stop bribery. It was not acceptable to the leading men of Italian towns who expected to gain influence when their candidate was successful.

l. 18. **perrogationem legis Maniliae:** Mommsen's emendation for the meaningless *praerogationum* of the manucripts.

l. 23. **editicios iudices:** The panel of jurymen presented by the accuser and modified by the challenge of the defendant.

l. 23. **odia occulta:** Because the accuser might select *iudices* who were personal enemies of the accused.

l. 24. **quae ... continentur:** 'which are now limited to silent disagreements'.

l. 25. **optimi cuiusque:** The political supporters of the Optimates.

Sections 48–53

48. line 1. **muniebant:** 'paved your way'. The normal word for building roads.

l. 2. **adipiscendi:** sc. *consulatum*.

l. 3. **ex omnibus:** To be taken with *maxima*.

l. 3. **illa plaga:** The blow is *cum populum Romanum ... adduxisti* l. 13 below.

l. 4. **non tacente me:** cf. 43, l. 6, where Cicero says that he had often warned him.

l. 6. **Quo:** Ablative of Comparison.

l. 6. **durior:** 'more difficult'.

l. 7. **ut:** 'namely that', 'in view of the fact that'.

l. 9. **in extremo:** sc. *loco*. Senior counsel spoke last, a position conceded to Cicero by Hortensius.

l. 10. **de tota re:** Hortensius presumably dealt with the specific points raised by the accusation while Cicero dealt with the political desirability of Murena's acquittal. See Introduction, p. xxxviii.

l. 11. **occurro:** 'meet' in the sense of 'meet half way', meaning that he will try to avoid wearying them too much.

XXIV. line 12. **Sed tamen:** Resumes from **Atque ... maxima,** regarding what follows as a digression.

l. 13. **cum ... adduxisti:** Indicative because the *cum*-clause 'identifies' the time at which the action of the main verb took place.

49. line 17. **inquirere:** Cf. 45, l. 31.

l. 18. **observationes:** Keeping a watch on your rival candidates for breaches of the law.

l. 18. **testificationes:** The collection of depositions from witnesses for subsequent use in court.

l. 18. **seductiones:** Taking witnesses on one side for confidential discussions.

l. 18. **secessiones:** Private conferences with the leading counsel's juniors.

l. 20. **obscuriores:** If this reading is to be accepted, the word must mean ' less familiar ' sc. ' to the voters '. ' the very features of the candidates usually fade from the public eye ' because interest is transferred to the subject of the impending prosecution.

l. 21. **Catilinam:** For the historical background see introduction p. xix.

l. 23. **conlegae:** C. Antonius Hibrida.

l. 24. **circumfluentem ... exercitu:** ' with the ample support of an army of '. **colonorum Arretinorum et Faesulanorum:** Sulla's veterans whom he had settled at Arretium and Faesulae and who had been reduced to poverty by their extravagant way of life. It is hard to settle down to a farmer's life after the free-booting ways of an army.

l. 26. **dissimillimo ex genere:** To be taken with *homines.*

l. 26. **distinguebant:** ' gave variety to '.

l. 27. **perculsi ... calamitate:** Supporters of Marius who had lost everything in Sulla's reign of terror but who joined his veterans in support of Catiline, led on by their common poverty and readiness to solve their difficulties by violence.

l. 29. **exploratus:** ' assured ', ' certain '.

l. 29. **domi conditus:** ' stored at his home ', i.e. there ready for the asking.

l. 31. **numerabat:** ' reckoned as '.

XXV. 50. line 32. **Quibus rebus:** Note word order.

l. 34. **factus esset:** Sc. *consul.*

l. 34. **nolite ... velle:** A type of periphrasis not uncommon in Cicero.

l. 36. **gladiatoris:** Here a term of reproach.

l. 37. **contione domestica:** The private meeting at which Catiline gave his instructions. See Introduction, p. xx.

l. 40. **integrorum:** In contrast with *saucios.*

l. 41. **qui consumpta replere:** Sulla's veterans.   **erepta reciperare:** The followers of Marius.

l. 42. **quid ipse deberet:** ' the extent of his debts '.

51. line 45. **Tum igitur ... meministis:** Resuming from 50, l. 36.

l. 46. **senatus consultum:** See introduction, p. xx.

l. 47. **ut ... possemus:** It was not constitutional for an election and meeting of the Senate to be held on the same day.

l. 51. **apertissimus:** In a bad sense, ' unabashed '.

l. 52. **indicavit:** ' openly confessed '. *Indico* is of a confession willingly given, *confiteor* unwillingly.

l. 52. **induit:** Sc. *in laqueos.* ' entangled himself in the snare '.

l. 53. **alterum:** Thóse whom Catiline sought to lead.

l. 54. **ita:** i.e. so long as it remained *firmum.*

l. 56. **neque tamen ... decrevit:** We have no record of any decree passed at this stage.

l. 58. **quia nihil timebant:** They thought that the danger was exaggerated and so there was nothing to fear.

l. 58. **Erupit:** Cf. the famous passage in *Cat.* II. 1,' Abiit, excessit, evasit, erupit.'

l. 60. **in eodem ordine:** The Senate.

l. 63. **in suas fortunas:** The candidature for the consulship.

l. 63. **non aqua sed ruina:** A threat to destroy the whole fabric of the constitution. Razing a whole area was a much commoner method of fire-fighting in the ancient world with its tightly-packed cities and less developed system of hydrants and pumps. It was just this readiness to pull down the whole state that distinguished Catiline from other ambitious and violent politicians and that united against him individuals and factions which had little in common.

XXVI. 52. line 66. **cum gladiis:** ' with swords in their hands ' not ' with swords ' which would be expressed by the simple ablative.

l. 68. **insigni:** ' conspicuous '.

l. 70. **petere:** ' to thrust at '.

l. 72. **id quod est factum:** These words refer to what follows.

53. line 77. **Magna est:** ' is of great importance '. **Magna** is predicative.

l. 79. **incubuit:** ' has supported '.

l. 79. **multis ... petitionis:** ' many other aids to his campaign '. i.e. in addition to his being *bonus*. They are briefly listed in the next sentence.

l. 80. **Qui cum:** ' And since he '. The ablative denotes attendant circumstance.

l. 80. **honestissimo ... maioribus:** See 15, l. 11 f.

l. 81. **clarissima legatione:** See 34.

l. 82. **praetura ... iure:** See 41.

l. 82. **grata ... munere:** See 37 and 38.

l. 82. **ornata in provincia:** Cisalpine and Transalpine Gaul; see 42,. l. 22 f. **ornata:** This word qualifies *praetura* not *provincia*.

l. 83. **petisset ... et ita petisset:** This sentence structure is found quite frequently in Cicero. The consecutive clause is used to limit the first statement.

l. 84. **minanti:** Sulpicius, by his prosecution.

l. 84. **huic ... fuisse:** A predicative dative accompanied as usual by another dative, that of the person concerned. Catiline's sudden hope of obtaining the consulship was of great assistance to Murena, because men would see how necessary it was for the safety of the state that a man with Murena's background should be consul.

Sections 54–56

54. line 1. **locus:** ' heading ', ' part ', ' division '.

l. 2. **ab eis:** Hortensius and Crassus; **a me:** Not the usual dative, probably under the influence of the previous phrase.

l. 4. **C. Postumo:** Nothing is known about him.

l. 5. **de divisorum indiciis:** ' the discosures of the bribery-agents '.

l. 6. **de equitum centuriis:** See 73, l. 78 ff. for the allegation. It would be important for Murena to obtain these votes.

l. 8. **de senatus consulto:** See 67, l. 9 ff.

l. 8. **de re publica:** ' the condition of the state '. See 74 ff.

XXVII. 55. line 11. **cum ... iudicarem ... tum:** In this correlative use where *cum* introduces a universal statement and *tum* follows with a particular, both the subjunctive and the indicative (See 56, l. 24) are regularly used in the *cum*-clause. It is best translated as a concessive.

l. 14. **otium ac tranquillitatem vitae:** Here, although Cicero is making a calculated point on Murena's behalf, his personal feelings about the pressures upon the *novus homo*, if he were to succeed, and about the needs of the Republic, if it were to survive, cannot lie deep beneath the surface.

l. 16. **non queam:** Cicero always uses *non queo* rather than *nequeo* in the first person.

l. 17. **omnium nostrum:** ' all us statesmen '.

l. 18. **eventum:** The outcome of his political career.

l. 18. **primum ... deinde:** There is no real distinction between the material contained under these two headings.

l. 19. **honoribus:** For the family background and offices held, see 15, l. 11 ff.

l. 20. **unum ... gradum dignitatis:** The consulship.

l. 21. **ea ... relicta:** His praetorian and senatorial rank.

l. 21. **ab ipso parta:** His distinguished military career in the East.

l. 22. **studium novae laudis:** His candidature for the consulship.

l. 23. **discrimen:** Because he would lose his senatorial rank.

56. line 25. **odio inimicitiarum:** ' hatred based on personal hostility '. The singular *inimicitia* is only used in good prose with abstract meaning. Personal enmity is apparently a

justifiable reason for prosecution. Cicero is deploring the fact that an accusation, desired for another reason, leads to *inimicitiae* and then goes on to show that the three accusers all had good reason to be friends of Murena rather than his enemies.

l. 27. **descenderint:** ' have sunk '.

l. 28. **iniuria L. Murenae:** ' wrong done to him by Murena '.

l. 28. **honoris contentione:** ' contest for office '.

l. 29. **paternus amicus:** ' his father's friend '.

l. 33. **sodalis:** Either ' close companion ' or ' fellow-member of a *sodalitas* (political club) '. A son would be expected to follow his father in such allegiances.

l. 37. **praesidio . . . exitio:** Predicative datives.

Section 57

57. line 1. **Postumo primum:** Note the pun.

l. 3. **desultorius:** A rider in a circus-act who rode two horses tied together and jumped from one to another. He was regarded as the inferior of the driver of a team of four horses. Cicero is saying that it is intolerable for Postumus, a candidate for the praetorship, to concern himself with the affairs of consular candidates. Their office is as much superior to the praetorship as the driver of a *quadrigae* is to be classed above the *desultor*.

l. 5. **concessit:** He admitted their superior worth by withdrawing.

l. 5. **sin autem:** An unexpected ironical twist. If one of his fellow-candidates did commit bribery, he had found a friend indeed in Postumus who had not avenged a wrong done to himself (*suam iniuriam*) by prosecuting him but tackled instead the alleged injury suffered by Murena's fellow-candidate, Sulpicius (*alienam*).

l. 8. **DE . . . ADUIESCENTIS:** Cicero dealt with these charges when he delivered the speech but left them out in the published version.

Sections 58-59

XXVIII. 58. line 1. **quod:** The ' rule ' that the relative agrees with its antecedent in gender and number, but not in case, is highly suspect. Such examples of a ' breach of the rule ' as we appear to have here are usually explained by ' attraction ' which, as was pointed out long ago, merely means ' agreement with the wrong noun '. This ' attraction ' is regular in Cicero and most other writers of this period.

If the traditional rule is abandoned and the relative treated as an adjective agreeing with a noun in the clause which may be, as here, expressed or, as more frequently, understood from the antecedent, and following the normal rules of agreement, many of the difficulties found by those who believe in this ' rule ' will disappear. See J. W. Haime in *Greece and Rome*, VII, pp. 115-7

l. 2. **fundamentum ac robur:** ' the root and core '.

l. 3. **ita ... ut:** An example of a consecutive clause used to express a concession. **ita**, therefore, must not be taken with **gravis** but translated ' although ', and **ut** taken as introducing the main clause. The sense is that while he is an energetic prosecutor who carries great weight, yet I am more afraid of his personal influence than his charges. **gravis** refers to **auctoritatem** and **vehemens** to **criminationem.**

l. 6. **exspectatio tribunatus:** Cato was tribune-elect and would enter office on 10 December.

l. 8. **bona:** ' resources '. Cicero hopes that Cato's distinguished career in the service of the state will not harm Murena. He then goes on to cite precedents of distinguished statesmen of the past who have failed in their prosecution because the Roman people was unwilling to see their prestige used in court against an individual. Again Cicero finds a way of complimenting the prosecution and then turning the compliment to his own advantage.

l. 10. **P. Africanus:** P. Cornelius Scipio Aemilianus Africanus Numantinus (185/4-129) was consul in 147 and 134. As proconsul in 146 he destroyed Carthage and in 133 Numantia.

l. 12. **L. Cottam:** L. Aurelius Cotta, consul in 144, was in 138 accused *de repetundis* and was defended by Q. Metellus Macedonicus. After several adjournments he was acquitted by a bribed jury.

l. 12. **fides:** 'trustworthiness'.

l. 14. **tenebatur:** 'maintained', 'upheld' (= *sustinebatur*). Cf. 83, l. 7.

l. 18. **cadere in iudicio:** 'to lose his case'.

l. 19. **abiectus:** 'overwhelmed', 'crushed'.

59. line 19. **Ser. Galbam:** Servius Sulpicius Galba was praetor in Further Spain in 151. He continued his command in the following year as propraetor and with L. Licinius Lucullus, who had the previous year been consul, invaded Lusitania where he treacherously slew eight thousand members of three tribes whom he had induced to surrender and sold the rest into slavery. In 149 the tribune, L. Scribonius Libo, proposed to condemn Galba but in spite of the support of the aged M. Porcius Cato Censorius failed to prevent his acquittal which Galba secured by playing upon the people's feelings.

l. 20. **nam ... est:** Cato wrote his speech down and included it in his *Origines*.

l. 21. **incumbenti ad:** 'doing his utmost to'.

l. 24. **multum ... prospicientes:** 'far-sighted'.

l. 25. **Nolo ... non ... non ... non:** The subsequent negatives continue the negative force in **Nolo.**

l. 26. **vim maiorem aliquam:** 'some excessive force'.

l. 29. **impotentium:** 'the weak'.

Sections 60–66

60. line 3. **legem ... condicionem:** 'principle ... situation'.

l. 4. **periculis hominum:** Defendants against whom charges involving them in *periculum* have been brought.

l. 4. **iudicium accusatoris:** The prosecutor is only bringing the case before the court because he has already decided that the defendant is guilty.

l. 5. **pro aliquo praeiudicio:** 'as a sort of prejudged verdict'.

XXIX. line 8. **conformare:** To give *forma* or ' right shape ' to something which lacks it.

l. 9. ' **Non multa . . .':** Printed as a quotation and said to be from a tragedy of L. Attius, the *Myrmidones*. Phoenix or Chiron (**senior magister**) is speaking to Achilles (**fortissimo viro**) and using a vocabulary which would seem to be particularly appropriate for the Stoic Cato. A *peccatum* (**peccas**) was (in Stoic terminology) a wrong or sinful deed and *rectum* (**regere**) a good or virtuous action. See Appendix, p. 140. **regere:** ' correct '.

l. 11. **verissime dixerim:** A potential subjunctive. ' I could perhaps most truly say '.

l. 13. **corrigendus . . . inflectendus:** *Corrigere* is to straighten out what is crooked, a strong word; *inflectere* to bend back what is only slightly out of true.

l. 16. **ad omnis . . . virtutes:** ad is to be taken with **magnum.** ' great . . . in respect of '.

l. 17. **istuc:** To the list of qualities just recited.

l. 17. **doctrina:** The teaching of a philosophical school – here the Stoics.

l. 19. **veritas:** The way in which the world in fact works.

l. 19. **natura:** Our natural feelings.

61. line 20. **non . . . in imperita multitudine:** Flattery of the jury. For Cicero's true opinion of them, see *de finibus bonorum et malorum* 4, 74. ' Apud imperitos tum (in this trial) illa dicta sunt '.

l. 22. **de studiis humanitatis:** ' cultural pursuits '. *Humanitas* is a ' liberal education '.

l. 25. **requirimus:** ' miss ', i.e. feel the lack of something which we think should be present but which we cannot find. The absence of these good qualities for which we vainly look in Cato is caused not by his nature but by his master. Some would translate ' deplore ', ' deprecate ' on the grounds that ea must in the context refer to faults. It is preferable, however, to accept a quite natural looseness of expression. There is no evidence that *requiro* can mean ' deplore '.

l. 26. **Fuit enim:** ' For there was '.

l. 27. **Zeno:** Zeno (335–263) of Citium in Cyprus was the founder of the Stoic school of philosophy. For an account of its ethical system which needs to be known for this passage to be fully understood, see Appendix p. 140.

l. 27. **inventorum:** ' tenets ', ' teaching '.

l. 28. **aemuli:** ' followers ', ' disciples '.

l. 28. **Stoici:** So-called after the Stoa Poikile or Painted Colonnade at Athens in which they met.

l. 28. **sententiae:** ' maxims ', ' dogmas '.

l. 29. **praecepta:** ' teaching '.

l. 29. **Sapientem:** The ideal wise man of the Stoics. For this sentence, see p. 140.

l. 31. **viri:** ' a true man '.

l. 34. **servitutem serviant:** An archaic legal expression. ' are in a state of slavery '.

XXX. 62. line 42. **auctoribus eruditissimis:** ' by the authority of very learned men '. Hence we have an ablative of the instrument rather than *a* with an ablative of the agent as might have been expected with the personal *auctoribus*.

l. 42. **inductus:** ' led on ' and so ' misled '.

l. 42. **adripuit:** ' caught up ' – too hastily and eagerly.

l. 43. **ut magna pars:** ' as most men do '.

l. 43. **ita vivendi:** ' of living by them '.

l. 43. **Petunt ... publicani:** The rest of this section consists of a number of situations in which the rigidity of the Stoics' application of their rules is ridiculed. Each statement receives Cato's Stoic reply. The conversational form of the passage makes the ridicule more vivid. **publicani:** The equestrian tax-farmers who might be seeking an alteration in the terms of the contract as we know they did at the end of the decade when they met Cato's stern opposition.

l. 44. **cave:** The Stoic wise man is not permitted to be influenced by considerations of personal friendship.

l. 45. **Supplices:** This word is the predicate. Take **aliqui** (an adjective) with **miseri** and **calamitosi** (used as nouns).

l. 49. **At**: ' But, you may say, it is '.

l. 50. **Dixisti quippiam**: ' You made some casual remark '.

l. 50. ' **fixum . . . est** ': Once said it is settled once and for all and cannot be altered, because the Wise Man is never wrong.

l. 52. **male dici putat**: This is inserted by Cicero as a remark of his own, not as the Stoic's reply.

l. 52. **Hac ex disciplina**: ' We owe the following arguments to this teaching '. **nobis**: Ethic Dative.

l. 53. **Dixi in senatu**: Once Cato has said that he is going to impeach a consular candidate, he cannot as a Stoic abandon his plan. The implication is that he is only accusing Murena because Stoic principles insist that he accuse someone.

l. 53. **nomen . . . delaturum**: A technical term. *Nomen deferre* is to bring the name of the accused before the praetor. See Introduction, p. xxvi.

l. 55. **At temporis causa**: ' Well, then, you said it to suit the occasion '. Not, in the light of the next sentence ' in view of the present circumstances (i.e. a crisis) ', supplying *nomen detulisti*.

l. 57. **scelus . . . flagitium**: The degree of moral guilt is greater in the first word.

63. line 58. **Nostri . . . illi**: sc. *magistri*.

l. 59. **adiumenta doctrinae**: ' the support given by education '.

l. 60. **illi . . . Aristotele**: The construction is in imitation of the Greek. Plato, the Athenian philosopher who lived *c.* 429–327, founded *c.* 385 the Academy which survived as a philosophical school until its dissolution by Justinian together with the other pagan schools in A.D. 529. His pupil, Aristotle of Stagirus (384–322) in 335 founded the Peripatetic School, so named from the covered court (peripatos) at Athens in which he worked.

l. 62. **viri boni esse**: ' it *is* the mark of a good man '.

l. 63. **et**: ' and consequently '.

l. 64. **locum**: ' place ', ' room '.

l. 65. **nesciat:** ' does not know for certain '.

l. 66. **eundem:** ' he too '.

l. 68. **mediocritate quadam: quadam** shows that the word **mediocritate** is used in a technical sense – to translate a Greek philosophical term ' a " mean " ' i.e. that which lies midway between two extremes.

l. 69. **moderatas:** ' tempered '.

XXXI. 64. line 69. **Hos ad magistros:** ' If some happy chance, Cato, had carried you with your character off to these masters, you would certainly not be a better man ... but ...'

l. 74. **pudentissimum:** ' most honourable '.

l. 76. **te:** Cato was tribune designate.

l. 77. **aliquo ... coniunctum:** ' that you had been linked with him in some bond to the state '.

l. 79. **mitiorem ... interpretarere:** ' you would voice it in a milder fashion '.

65. line 82. **elatum:** ' carried away '.

l. 83. **flagrantem:** ' fired '.

l. 83. **iam:** ' soon ', ' presently '.

l. 83. **usus ... dies:** ' experience ' ... ' time '.

l. 84. **Etenim ... consisteremus: Etenim ... praeceptores:** ' Indeed those very teachers of yours '. **finis officiorum ..· protulisse:** ' to have extended the bounds of moral duty '. **ut:** After *vellet.* **cum ... consisteremus:** ' since we had in intent pressed on to the limit (perfection), we should yet stop where we ought '. The meaning of this sentence is that the Stoics have been right to insist upon an ideal higher than that of which men are capable (**paulo longius quam natura vellet**), because then men may achieve what duty demands (**ut ... ubi oporteret, consisteremus**).

There then follow examples of circumstances in which rigid Stoic doctrine may be modified.

l. 88. **ignoveris ... feceris ... commotus sis:** The perfect subjunctive is regularly used to express a negative order or prohibition with *ne* or negative words formed from *ně*, e.g. *nihil.*

l. 88. **Immo:** Correcting the previous statement. ' No; something, but not everything '.

l. 90. **resistito:** The ' future ' imperative is regularly found in the text of laws and in general precepts or proverbs. The style is thus made more pompous. Similarly *permaneto* l. 93 below.

l. 91. **Etiam:** A strong affirmative. ' Yes, certainly '.

l. 91. **in dissolvenda severitate:** ' in an excessive relaxation of severity '.

l. 92. **humanitatis:** ' sympathy '.

l. 93. **Vero, nisi:** ' Yes, of course, unless '.

l. 93. **sententiam:** Your original opinion.

66. line 94. **Scipio:** Scipio Africanus Minor (185-129), a man of liberal culture, literary interests, and Stoic convictions. He was the centre of the brilliant circle which flourished at Rome during his lifetime.

l. 95. **non paenitebat:** ' enjoyed '.

l. 95. **idem quod tu:** Cato had apparently got Athenodorus Cordylium, a Stoic contemporary, to come to live with him in Rome.

l. 96. **Panaetium:** The Stoic philosopher of Rhodes (*c.* 185-109). He joined the Scipionic circle in about 144, accompanied him to the East in 141, and thereafter divided his time between Rhodes and Rome. He became head of the Stoa in 129 and held this position until his death.

l. 97. **oratione:** ' conversation '.

l. 97. **eadem ista:** Stoic teaching.

l. 98. **ut accepi:** *Accipio* normally means in Cicero ' learn from tradition ', but Cicero was born in 106, twenty-three years after Scipio's death, so could have in his youth met men who had known Scipio.

l. 99. **lenissimus:** Panaetius' contribution to the development of Stoicism was his attempt to adapt Stoic ethics to the needs of Roman public life. This he did by laying more emphasis on the positive virtues of magnanimity, benevolence, and liberality than on the negatively interpreted virtues of fortitude (*not* being alarmed in times of danger) and justice (*not* doing wrong).

l. 99. **C. Laelio:** C. Laelius Minor, consul in 140 and named *Sapiens* for his Stoic learning. He was a cultured and eloquent man, the close friend of Scipio, and a leading member of his circle.

l. 100. **iucundior:** ' more amiable ', ' more agreeable '.

l. 100. **eodem ex studio isto:** With concessive force ' although he was a member of that same school ' (as yourself).

l. 101. **L. Philo:** L. Furius Philus, another friend and member of the Scipionic circle. He was consul in 136.

l. 101. **C. Gallo:** C. Sulpicius Gallus, consul in 166, was famous for his knowledge of astronomy.

l. 102. **sed . . . tuam:** ' but now I will bring you to your own family '.

l. 103. **Catone, proavo tuo:** M. Porcius Cato Censorius (234–149). A surprising description follows for a man who was notorious for rustic bluntness and ill manners. It is interesting to speculate how deeply Cicero has his tongue in his cheek and how far the grandson's sense of humour, betrayed in his wry remark about our witty consul, appreciated this sentence.

l. 104. **commodiorem:** ' more affable '.

l. 104. **ad omnem . . . humanitatis:** ' in every type of social contact '.

l. 106. **domesticum:** ' in your family '.

l. 107. **Est illud quidem . . . sed tamen . . . vero:** ' You certainly have . . . but . . . yet '. There are two threads of thought in this sentence: ' You have a pattern in him, but so do I ' and ' Your character is more like his than is ours, since you are descended from him '. **naturae similitudo illius:** ' a character like his '.

l. 112. **comitatem et facilitatem:** ' courtesy and affability '.

l. 113. **asperseris . . . condita:** A metaphor introducing words used in cookery.

l. 113. **ista:** Your qualities.

Sections 67–68

XXXII. 67. line 2. **nomen Catonis:** A Genitive of Definition instead of a noun in apposition. Cf. *voluptatis nomen* 13, l. 17

l. 4. **congredere:** ' join battle '.

l. 6. **non defendo:** I offer no defence if Murena can be shown to be guilty. I do not defend bribery.

l. 7. **idem ... quod:** Bribery.

l. 8. **ambitum ... ipsum:** ' true bribery '. i.e. not a trumped -up accusation of it.

l. 9. **senatus consultum:** This decree preceded the *lex Tullia*. See introduction, p. xxiv. A *senatus consultum* was the advice of the Senate to the magistrates and under the Republic, although it had no legislative force, it was regarded as binding.

l. 10. **mercede:** Ablative of Price. ' if men were paid to meet the candidates '.

l. 11. **si conducti sectarentur:** ' if their companions were hired '.

l. 11. **gladiatoribus:** ' at the gladiatorial games '.

l. 12. **volgo:** ' indiscriminately '.

l. 12. **locus:** sc. *datus esset*.

l. 12. **tributim:** It was illegal to provide free seats for a whole tribe which might thereby be induced to vote as a whole for the candidate providing them.

l. 13. **contra legem ... videri:** An accusative and infinitive of indirect speech introduced by *senatus consultum*. ' it was deemed a contravention of the *lex Calpurnia* '. **videri:** Used in official announcements to express an opinion rather than a decision.

l. 15. **decernit:** ' its decree, while it satisfies the candidates, is pointless '. This decree, which was passed because the candidates had asked for it (See 68. l. 20 below), is pointless since it only lists what is illegal under the *lex Calpurnia* and that is not in doubt. The point at issue is ' Has anything illegal been done? '.

68. line 18. **Est igitur ridiculum:** sc. on the part of the Senate.

l. 18. **quod est dubium:** Whether anything illegal has been done.

l. 19. **quod . . . esse:** That if these deeds have been committed the law has been broken.

l. 20. **iudicare:** ' to give a decision '.

l. 20. **Atque:** ' And moreover '. The senatorial decree does not show that Murena is guilty of any of these malpractices.

l. 22. **Qua re:** Show that Murena has in fact done what is alleged of him and then I shall agree that the law has been broken.

Sections 68–73

XXXIII. line 2. **decedenti:** The word regularly used of leaving one's province at the end of a term of office.

l. 4. **istam rationem:** i.e. *istius rei rationem* ' an explanation of it '.

l. 5. **quid habet admirationis:** ' what cause is there for surprise '.

69. line 8. **quod . . . abhorret:** This refers to the accusative and infinitive which follows.

l. 10. **filios:** When a young man assumed the *toga virilis*, part of the ceremony involved a journey to the Forum escorted by his family and close friends.

l. 11. **deductum:** sc. *in forum.* A supine of purpose after the verb of motion.

l. 12. **hora tertia:** i.e. at a much more convenient time than **prope de nocte** ' before dawn '.

l. 13. **in campum Martium:** Where officials were greeted on their return from their province.

l. 13. **talis viri nomine:** ' on account of so important a man '.

l. 14. **societates:** The *societates publicanorum*, companies of tax-farmers, would bid for the contracts to collect the taxes in the provinces. The leading figures in these *societates* were equestrians. By the *lex Aurelia* of 70 the juries were drawn from three *decuriae* or panels: of senators, of *Equites*, and of *tribuni aerarii*. The last two were members of the *ordo equester*, hence **quarum ... iudices.** See Introduction, p. xxv.

l. 16. **nostri ordinis:** Senatorial.

l. 17. **non honeste:** 'without proper respect'.

l. 18. **natio:** Here, as often, contemptuous. They would come to secure the electoral support of so eminent a man.

l. 19. **bene magna:** 'a very big'.

l. 21. **exercitum Luculli:** cf. 37. l. 9 f., p. 22.

l. 23. **frequentiam ... defuisse:** A crowd (**frequentiam:** Abstract for concrete) has always voluntarily and freely (not **mercede** 'for reward') performed this duty of attendance upon a man, not only if his *dignitas* merited it, but even if it did not but he wished it.

XXXIV. 70. line 26. **Hoc ... remoto:** 'This apart'.

l. 29. **tenues:** cf. 47. l. 7, p. 26.

l. 29. **unum ... locum:** 'one opportunity only'.

l. 30. **promerendi ... benefici:** 'of deserving or repaying a favour'. See note on *benefici collocandi* 28, l. 6. p. 88.

l. 31. **operam atque adsectationem:** 'the effort of constant attendance'. The handbook *Commentariolum Petitionis*, 34 lists three kinds: salutatorum, cum domum veniunt, altera deductorum, altera adsectatorum.

l. 35. **celebratur:** 'is frequented', 'is crowded'.

l. 36. **si uno ... honestamur:** 'if we are honoured by a single turn in a basilica'. Basilicas were covered halls, often divided by rows of columns, and they formed a sort of extension to the Forum. They were used for public and, in particular, legal business.

71. line 40. **inferiori generi:** The dative is used of the person deprived, not, as might be expected, an Ablative of Separation. It denotes the person to whose disadvantage the act is performed. See Woodcock, 61, p. 44.

l. 40. **fructum:** The profit of their *officium* or service done in repayment of their obligation.

l. 42. **Si ... gratia:** If the only repayment that the poorer classes can make is their vote, then they are without influence, even if they support us, since their vote is unimportant. This was because group-voting was a characteristic of the *comitia* and the groups were arranged in such a way that the wealthier citizens exercised a disproportionate influence.

l. 44. **loqui ... dicere:** 'say ... speak'.

l. 47. **quae ... consequuntur:** The subject of *compensari ... posse*.

l. 48. **legi Fabiae:** Nothing is known about this law. It was possibly a tribunician measure of the previous year.

l. 50. **L. Caesare consule:** We know nothing more about this decree of 64. In view of *quod est ... factum* it can hardly be the measure increasing the penalty for bribery mentioned by Asconius (83, 85–6, 88 C) since this was vetoed by the tribune, Q. Mucius Orestinus.

l. 50. **restiterunt:** 'ignored', 'paid no attention to'.

l. 52. **vetere instituto efficiorum:** 'their old practice of fulfilling their obligations'.

72. line 52. **spectacula:** 'grand-stands'.

l. 53. **volgo:** cf. 67, l. 12, p. 37.

l. 55. **modo:** 'in moderation'.

l. 57. **punctorum:** 'votes'. In the voting a mark – *punctum* – was made on a wax tablet.

l. 57. **nobis:** You, the candidate, and I, your supporter.

l. 59. **ambitio:** Canvassing or the soliciting of votes which was legal as opposed to the illegal *ambitus*.

l. 59. **liberalitas:** cf. 67, l. 11. f., p. 37.

l. 60. **in foro:** Gladiatorial games took place in the Forum before the days of the amphitheatres.

l. 61. **tribulibus:** But the charge against Murena was that he gave free seats to a *whole* tribe.

XXXV. 73. line 65. **Praefectum fabrum:** 'aide-de-camp'. *Fabri* were smiths rather than military engineers as we understand the term and were commanded by *praefecti*. By this time, however, the *praefectus fabrum* was more of a general's aide-de-camp whose duties bore no relation to his title. See article ' fabri ' by H. M. D. Parker in *The Oxford Classical Dictionary*, p. 355. The preceding *lacuna* makes it impossible for us to be certain, but if this is Murena himself it must have been before 74.

l. 67. **totas tabernas:** ' whole booths ' or ' whole blocks of seats '.

l. 67. **compararunt:** ' have provided '.

l. 69. **in tuam ... coniecta sunt:** ' have been attributed to your excessive industry ', sc. in making accusations against others.

l. 71. **auctoritate:** ' decree '. *Senatus auctoritas* means either ' the will of the senate ' or, more frequently, ' a decree of the senate ' i.e. its expressed will. A distinction is sometimes drawn between a *senatus consultum* and a *senatus auctoritas*, the former being a senatorial decree passed without opposition, the latter one invalidated by a tribune of the people. In this passage Murena must have been protected by the terms of a senatorial decree rather than their unexpressed ' will '.

l. 73. **Convince:** Prove that those who met Murena *were* hired. Similarly **Doce.**

l. 76. **L. Natta:** L. Pinarius Natta was a stepson of Murena and brother-in-law of Clodius. When Pontifex in 58 he helped in the destruction of Cicero's house and officiated at the dedication of a shrine of Libertas on its site.

l. 78. **hoc officium necessitudinis:** His duty as a stepson of Murena of helping him in his candidature for the consulship by obtaining the support of the *Equites*.

l. 79. **ad reliquum tempus:** Presumably with an eye to his own advantage in the future.

l. 80. **fraudi:** ' injury ', ' harm '.

l. 81. **locum suum:** The Vestals had, with their other privileges, special seats at shows. The charge is that one had given her seat to Murena for him to offer it to someone else in return for political support.

Sections 74–77

74. line 1. **At enim:** Not here in its usual role of introducing an objection.

l. 2. **verum:** ' right ', ' fair ' not ' true '.

l. 3. **corrumpi:** ' be spoiled ', ' be injured '.

l. 5. **condemnetur:** Deliberative subjunctive.

l. 5. **' Quippe ':** ' Yes, certainly ' with ironical force.

l. 5. **mihi:** Ethic Dative.

l. 7. **petas:** ' are you (to be allowed) to seek '.

l. 9. **grege:** ' crew ', ' gang '.

l. 13. **istius vitae atque orationis:** Your Stoic way of life and Laconic speech.

l. 14. **cotidianis epulis:** The common meals in which Spartan citizens joined daily without distinction of age or rank.

l. 14. **in robore:** ' on bare benches '. i.e. without cushions.

l. 14. **Cretes:** The Cretans also had common messes and sat at table.

l. 18. **alteri:** The Cretans were conquered by the consul of 69, Q. Caecilius Metellus Creticus, in 68/7 with three legions. The island then became a Roman province.

l. 18. **deleti:** ' conquered '.

l. 18. **alteri:** Sparta had been incorporated as a *civitas foederata* in the province of Achaea, retaining her own laws and institutions.

XXXVI. 75. line 21. **comprobat:** ' vindicates '

l. 23. **eodem ex studio:** The Stoic school.

l. 24. **Q. Tubero:** A grandson of L. Aemilius Paulus and pupil of the Stoic philosopher, Panaetius of Rhodes. The family tree is as follows:—

L. Aemilius Paulus Macedonicus (ob. 160) = 1. Papiria = 2. ?

Son adopted by the Fabii Maximi and became Q. Fabius Maximus Aemilianus	Son adopted by P. Cornelius Scipio and became P. Cornelius Scipio Africanus Minor (in whose honour the banquet was held)	Aemilia Prima = Q. Aelius Tubero
Q. Fabius Maximus (the giver of the banquet)		Q. Aelius Tubero (approached by Fabius)

l. 24. **epulum**: ' a funeral banquet '. This word is used in the singular of official or religious banquets as opposed to *epulae*, which are social occasions.

l. 25. **Q. Maximus**: Q. Fabius Maximus Allobrogicus, consul in 121 and conqueror of the Allobroges.

l. 25. **P. Africani**: P. Cornelius Scipio Aemilianus Africanus Numantinus (185/4–129), destroyer of Carthage and Numantia.

l. 25. **nomine**: ' in honour of '.

l. 26. **triclinium sterneret**: He was asked to provide the trappings for the tables and couches which were themselves provided by Fabius.

l. 28. **homo eruditissimus**: Concessive in force. He should have known better.

l. 28. **Stoicus**: Causal. This is the reason for his behaviour.

l. 29. **pelliculis haedinis**: ' shabby goat skins '. The diminutive is contemptuous. There should have been elaborate and expensive coverings.

l. 29. **lectulos Punicanos**: ' Punic couches '. So called because they were introduced to Rome from Carthage. They were small, low benches made of wood.

l. 29. **exposuit**: ' set out ', ' put on the table '.

l. 29. **vasa Samia**: Earthenware; not, as they should have been, metal.

l. 30. **Diogenes:** Diogenes of Sinope, the Cynic philosopher. Part of the Cynic philosophy was a contempt for all the refinements of civilised life. In their moral beliefs they were the forerunners of the Stoics.

l. 32. **supremo eius die:** 'on the day of his funeral'. *Supremus dies* can be either the day of death or the day of burial.

l. 32. **laudaret:** In the funeral oration (*laudatio*) delivered from the Rostra in the Forum by a relative or colleague of the dead man.

l. 36. **sapientiam:** 'philosophy'.

76. line 38. **cum:** 'although'.

l. 39. **praetura deiectus est:** The people were so disgusted by his behaviour that they did not elect him praetor.

l. 42. **inhumanitatem:** 'boorishness'.

l. 42. **distinguit . . . voluptatis:** The Roman people recognises that one type of occasion requires one sort of behaviour and another something different. Both work and pleasure have their place.

l. 44. **Nam quod ais:** The argument runs thus: You say that voters should be influenced only by the candidate's merits. If so, why do you who have such merits seek the support of others? You ask me to support you in order that you, when a magistrate, may protect me. Would it not be more appropriate for me to ask you for your protection than for you to offer it?

l. 48. **Rogas:** ut . . . praesis is final after ut . . . tibi which is itself an indirect command after **Rogas. praesis:** As a magistrate.

l. 49. **Quid tandem:** 'What can I say to that?'.

77. line 52. **nomenclatorem:** A slave whose duty it was to accompany a candidate and to whisper to his master the names of those citizens whom he met while out canvassing. It was held to create a better impression with the voters whom he greeted in this way. The practice had in earlier times been illegal.

l. 52. fallis et decipis: It is sometimes maintained that there is a difference in meaning between these two words. **fallis** is negative in emphasis – ' fail ' rather than ' deceive ' and looks forward to **Nam . . . tibi.** while **decipis** indicates a positive effort and looks forward to **Sin . . . salutas.** But this distinction should not be pressed too hard in view of the Roman practice of using a pair of synonyms or near-synonyms to increase the emphasis ' you are utterly deceitful '. Cf. *despexit atque contempsit* 78, l. 10. and many other examples.

l. 52. Nam, si: The use of a *nomenclator* is undesirable because, if it is *honestum* or honourable to greet fellow-citizens by name, it is *turpe* or shameful to have your slave better informed than yourself. These terms are drawn from the vocabulary of moral philosophy as are other words in what follows, e.g. *recta, pravissima.*

It is also deceitful in two ways:

1. **Sin . . . incertus sis:** It is deceitful when you do know a name to pretend that you do not and still use your *monitor* (=*nomenclator*).

2. **Quid . . . salutas:** It is deceitful when you have been given a name, to greet a man as if you had yourself known it.

l. 58. ad rationem . . . derigas: ' judge by the practice of the community '. i.e. the way in which things are normally conducted between citizens. The argument is that you must not judge the realities of civic life by the tenets of Stoicism.

l. 59. disciplinae: Stoicism.

l. 61. plebi Romanae: A dative with a verb of depriving indicating the person to whose disadvantage the action of the verb is directed.

l. 61. fructus: ' enjoyment '.

l. 63. comparaverunt: ' established '.

Sections 78–83

XXXVII. 78. line 1. **res publica:** ' the interests of the state '.

l. 3. imprudentia: The failure to realise that the real interests of the state require the acquittal of Murena.

l. 5. **pacis . . . vitae:** Threatened by the Catilinarian conspiracy. For the words used see note on *otium concordiamque* 1, l. 10. p. 52.

l. 8. **tantum:** ' only this much '.

l. 10. **despexit atque contempsit:** ' looked down upon and set little value on ' or ' despised with his whole heart '.

l. 11. **copia:** ' forces '. Usually plural in this sense (cf. 79, l. 17.). The use of the singular may be deliberate to show that he believes that Catiline's force outside the city is not as numerous or dangerous as his forces inside.

l. 13. **Intus, intus:** cf. Audite, audite l. 7. above and the Second Catilinarian Oration. Cicero's style becomes highly rhetorical when he comes to the peril of Catiline – the crux of his argument on Murena's behalf. Repetition adds weight to the individual words.

79. line 17. **quas hic video:** The conspirators in the city have not yet been arrested.

l. 20. **dicuntur:** Desertion is their cover-story.

l. 21. **in:** ' as a threat to '.

l. 22. **restiterunt:** ' have remained behind '.

l. 23. **natura:** ' character '.

l. 23. **fortuna:** ' circumstances ', ' position '. His own solid financial position makes it unlikely that he will be a revolutionary either in politics or economics.

l. 25. **vestris sententiis:** ' your verdict '.

l. 26. **in campo:** cf. 52, l. 66. See also introduction, p. xix.

l. 26. **in foro:** Particularly in the Second Catilinarian Oration.

l. 27. **domi meae:** The attempt by C. Cornelius and L. Vargunteius to enter his house and assassinate him. See Introduction, p. xx. There had been other similar attempts. **saepe** should be treated with caution. He is out to frighten the jury into acquitting Murena and may well be exaggerating.

l. 27. **his vos si:** *Hi, si vos iis.*

l. 30. **egi atque perfeci:** ' have worked hard to bring about '.

80. line 32. **mediocribus consiliis:** ' any ordinary plans '.

l. 35. **quaeritur:** ' is their [the conspirators] aim '.

l. 41. **In exitu:** The consuls went out of office on 31 December whether successors had been elected or not.

l. 42. **vicarium:** My successor, the man to whom I am going to hand over my task.

XXXVIII. 81. line 46. **non ... nonne:** In a series of questions it is usual for the particle *nonne* to be used in the first only.

l. 48. **contione:** In which he had presumably attacked Cicero's measures against the conspirators.

l. 48. **intonuit:** Continuing and extending the metaphor from *tempestatem*.

l. 48. **designati tribuni:** Q. Caecilius Metellus Nepos attacked Cicero for his execution of the conspirators and vetoed his final speech at the end of the year. In the following year he continued his attack upon Cicero and tried to carry two bills, one of which proposed to appoint Pompey to take command against Catiline, the other that he should be elected consul *in absentia*. His colleague, Cato, vetoed his proposals, martial law was declared, and Nepos left Rome to join Pompey. See Introduction, p. xxix.

l. 49. **tua mens ... vocaverunt:** At first he had not allowed himself to be persuaded by his friends to stand for the tribunate but after hearing that Nepos was a candidate changed his mind.

l. 52. **ab eo tempore:** Of the so-called First Catilinarian Conspiracy in 65. See Introduction, p. xviii.

82. line 58. **meo nomine:** ' on my own account '.

l. 61. **agunt et moliuntur:** A pair of words of which Cicero seems to be fond.

l. 68. **fore:** i.e. *ne sufficiatur consul*. The tribune could by his veto prevent elections from being held.

l. 68. **D. Silanum:** Decius Iunius Silanus, the other consul-designate.

83. line 1. **tuum:** ' your duty '.

l. 4. **cupidum:** Because he regards his office merely as a path to personal honour or wealth.

l. 5. **fortuna:** See note on *fortuna* 79. l. 23. p. 134.

l. 6. **scientia:** In the light of his campaign in the East.

l. 7. **animo et usu:** ' spirit and experience '.

l. 7. **quod velis:** *Quodvis.*

Sections 83–86

XXXIX. line 8. **Quamquam:** ' And still ', ' And yet '.

l. 10. **tenetis:** ' are sustaining '. Cf. 58, l. 14, p. 32.

l. 11. **consilio:** Those who deliberate and hence a council of war or a court of justice. Catiline and his fellow-conspirators are represented as sitting in judgement on Murena.

l. 13. **rationes:** ' plans '.

l. 14. **auxilio:** sc. from the consuls.

l. 15. **tribunis plebis:** He has Nepos in mind.

l. 17. **ex amplissimis ordinibus:** Senatorial and equestrian. For the composition of the court, see Introduction, p. xxv.

l. 19. **importunissimus:** ' utterly ruthless '.

l. 19. **gladiator:** cf. 50. l. 36, p. 28.

l. 19. **hostis:** Almost a technical term – ' enemy of the state '.

84. line 24. **resistamus:** ' regain our footing '.

l. 26. **apud Anienem:** ' at the Anio '. In 211 Hannibal advanced to the Anio, some three miles from Rome, in the hope of forcing the Romans to raise the siege of Capua.

l. 28. **non nemo:** ' one or two ' i.e. senators involved in the conspiracy.

l. 29. **sacrario:** ' shrine ', ' sanctuary '.

l. 30. **faxint:** The archaic form adds weight and solemnity to the prayer.

l. 30. **meus conlega:** C. Antonius Hibrida, the uncle of the Triumvir. He had been expelled from the Senate in 70 and had stood for the consulship of 63 in association with Catiline. Cicero won him over from this association by handing over to him the province of Macedonia. After Catiline had fled to northern Italy Antonius assumed command of the troops in Etruria but took no part in the final battle.

l. 31. **latrocinium:** Abstract for concrete. 'band of gangsters'.

l. 32. **togatus:** Wearing the *toga* – as a civilian – in contrast with *armatus*.

l. 34. **discutiam et comprimam:** 'rend and crush'.

85. line 35. **haec:** Dangers.

l. 36. **redundarint:** 'overflow'.

l. 37. **in sufficiendo conlega:** The one consul will be concerned with the arrangements for electing Murena's successor rather than in fighting the war against Catiline, and his efforts will be obstructed by tribunes like Nepos who are sympathisers of Catiline.

l. 41. **in urbe ... vastitas:** In this vivid picture Cicero depicts the passion of revolution in the city itself, panic in the Senate, conspiracy in the place where men meet and talk, the armed force of rebellion on the city's own parade ground, and the devastation of the surrounding countryside.

l. 44. **ornata suis praesidiis:** 'equipped with the necessary means of protection'.

l. 46. **privatorum:** Men who do not hold any public office.

XL. 86. line 49. **pro:** 'in accordance with', 'by virtue of', 'in proportion to'. Each of the three times that this word is used in this sentence it requires a slightly different translation.

l. 50. **moneo ... hortor ... obtestor:** Note the climax.

l. 52. **consulatis:** With dative 'consult the interest of', 'pay heed to'.

l. 53. **oro atque obsecro:** Another common pair. Pairs of words are frequent in this highly rhetorical end to the speech.

l. 54. **ut ne:** Instead of the more usual *ne*.

l. 55. **morbo:** cf. 47. l. 12, p. 27.

l. 56. **gratulationem:** On his recent electoral success.

l. 57. **beneficio:** The consulship. cf. 2, l. 21. and 90, l. 3. below.

l. 58. **in familiam veterem**: cf. 17. l. 40, p. 9.

l. 59. **municipium**: Lanuvium. An ancient Latin town in the Alban Hills which had received the Roman citizenship when Rome dissolved the Latin League in 338. At the same time it officially adopted its famous cult of Juno Sospes (See 90, l. 7. below).

l. 60. **in squalore et sordibus**: See note in *squaloris* 42, l. 14. p. 105.

l. 61. **perditus**: ' made hopeless ', ' desperate '.

l. 63. **intuetur**: ' looks to '.

Sections 87–89

87. line 1. **hac ... re**: The consulship.

l. 3. **honestatibus**: *Honestas* is the quality conferred by *honores* – ' distinction '. The plural is not elsewhere used in this meaning.

l. 4. **ita**: As I have just described him.

l. 5. **neminem ... nullius ... nemini**: A convenient example of Latin usage in the oblique cases of *nemo*.

l. 6. **ut ... dicam**: ' to say the least ', ' to put it very mildly '.

l. 9. **pudori**: cf. 30, l. 6. and 64, l. 74.

l. 9. **spoliatio**: Passive in meaning. ' the being deprived of '.

l. 10. **habere**: ' to contain ', ' to cause '. cf. l. 11. below and 89, l. 32.

l. 12. **obicitur**: ' is exposed to '.

l. 15. **opponitur**: ' is set to face '.

88. line 16. **praeclaro**: ' fine ', ' glorious '. Ironically.

l. 17. **miseranda**: Remember that the function of the Roman advocate is not merely to prove, but to bend (*flectere*). The introduction of an appeal to irrelevant considerations was a proper part of his task.

XLI. line 19. **omen**: The use of the unlucky word **adflixeritis** ' cast down ', ' ruin '.

l. 21. **imaginem:** A Roman noble kept in the *atrium* of his house the busts of those of his ancestors who had held curule. office. On special occasions they were crowned with laurel (Cf. **laureatam**); in this case when Murena became consul designate **in sua gratulatione** ' in his honour '.

l. 23. **ignominia:** Strictly of any punishment which affected a man's civil or military position.

89. line 27. **appello:** ' name '.

l. 28. **nova poena:** Of exile under the new provisions of the *lex Tullia.*

l. 35. **summo cum imperio:** As proconsul in 64 and 63 until he returned for the consular elections, leaving his brother in command as Legate.

l. 39. **perturbatio:** ' a turning upside down '. ' disorganisation '.

l. 40. **sermonis:** Because in his changed circumstances what was appropriate is now no longer so.

l. 42. **celebrassent:** ' had spread the news '.

Section 90

90. line 6. **in hac tota causa:** ' throughout this case '.

l. 6. **frequens:** ' in crowds '. The people of Lanuvium had come to Rome to support him.

l. 8. **facere:** ' to sacrifice '.

l. 9. **suum:** Because Murena was a native of Lanuvium in which the cult had originated.

l. 10. **momenti:** ' weight '. i.e. to turn the scales sufficiently to get a favourable verdict.

l. 12. **bonorum:** Masculine.

APPENDIX

Stoic Ethics

A man's whole object in life is to live in absolute con-
formity with his own reason which is itself a part of the
Divine Reason. He cannot in fact escape obedience to
what is decreed by the Divine Reason, but he can choose
how he will obey it. The duty of a man, therefore, is
to agree willingly and joyfully with what is ordained by
the Divine Reason. This is reason and virtue. Acting
reasonably and virtuously are one and the same thing,
and this is the only and absolute good. All passions,
emotions, and desires are perverted reason. They are
wrong judgements about what is good and bad for us,
just as virtue is right judgement by our reason about
what is universally good or bad. And so all passions
and emotions must be eliminated. The ideal is freedom
from all passions and emotions.

These views produced the repellent figure of the
Stoic Wise Man, their ideal, who is completely in-
different to all external considerations – riches, health,
power –, who is completely without irrational affection
for family or friends, whose every thought and action
is pure reason and virtue. Such a man alone is truly
rich, truly healthy, truly king. Virtue is the only thing
worth having and in it he who possesses it has everything and is impervious to the chances of life and changes
of fortune. There is no intermediate position between
good and bad. You are either a Wise Man living a

perfect life according to the reason within you or you are utterly depraved and foolish. No degree of moral worth short of perfection has any value.

SELECT BIBLIOGRAPHY

1. HISTORICAL BACKGROUND

Cambridge Ancient History, ed. S. A. Cook, F. E. Adcock and M. P. Charlesworth, vol. IX (Cambridge University Press, 1932).

Marsh, F. B., *A History of the Roman World from 146 to 30 B.C.*, (2nd ed., Methuen, 1952).

Cary, M., *A History of Rome* (2nd ed., Macmillan, 1954).

Scullard, H. H., *From the Gracchi to Nero* (Methuen, 1959).

2. CICERO

Haskell, H. J. *This was Cicero* (Alfred A. Knopf, New York, 1942).

Cowell, F. R. *Cicero and the Roman Republic* (Pitman, 1948).

Dorey, T. A., ed. *Cicero* (Studies in Latin Literature and its Influence; Routledge, 1965).

Smith, R. E., *Cicero the Statesman* (Cambridge University Press, 1966).

3. MISCELLANEOUS

Broughton, T. R. S., *The Magistrates of the Roman Republic* (American Philological Association, Vol. I, 1951; Vol. II, 1952).

Greenidge, A. H. J., *The Legal Procedure of Cicero's Time* (Frowde, 1901).

Woodcock, E. C., *A New Latin Syntax* (Methuen, 1959).

The Oxford Classical Dictionary (Oxford University Press, 1949).

INDEX OF PROPER NAMES

143

VOCABULARY

The perfects and supines of all verbs of the third conjugation and of all irregular verbs of other conjugations are given. Otherwise the figure following a verb denotes that it is a regular example of that conjugation. The omission of a perfect or supine indicates that it is not in normal use.

The comparatives and superlatives of adjectives and adverbs are not listed separately unless formed irregularly.

a, ab, abs, *prep. with abl.*, from, by.

abdo, -didi, -ditum (3), *tr.*, hide.

abeo, -ire, -ii, -itum, *intr.*, go away.

abicio, -ieci, -iectum (3), *tr.*, throw away, give up, abandon.

abiectus, -a, -um, crushed, overwhelmed.

abrogo (1), *tr.*, annul, repeal.

absum, abesse, afui, *intr.*, am away, am absent.

absurdus, -a, -um, absurd.

ac, *conj.*, and, and furthermore.

accedo, -cessi, -cessum (3), *intr.*, am added, happen in addition.

accido, -cidi (3), *intr.*, happen.

accipio, -cepi, -ceptum (3), *tr.*, receive, hear, inherit.

accumbo, -cubui, -cubitum (3), *intr.*, recline at table.

accusatio, -onis, *f.*, accusation, prosecution.

accusator, -oris, *m.*, accuser.

accusatorius, -a, -um, of an accuser.

accuso (1), *tr.*, accuse.

acer, acris, acre, active, eager, brave, fierce; bitter.

acerbe, *adv.*, bitterly.

acerbus, -a, -um, bitter.

acerrimus, -a, -um, *superl. of* **acer.**

acies, -ei, *f.*, line of battle.

actio, -onis, *f.*, (legal) action.

ad, *prep. with acc.*, to, for; according to; near, off.

adclamo (1), *tr.*, greet with groans.

addo, -didi, -ditum (3), *tr.*, add.

adduco, -duxi, -ductum (3), *tr.*, lead on.

adeo, -ire, -ii, -itum, *tr. and intr.*, approach.

adfero, -ferre, attuli, -latum, *tr.*, bring, bring to, bring about.

adficio, -feci, -fectum (3), *tr.*, treat, provide with, honour.

adfligo, -flixi, -flictum (3), *tr.*, dash down.

adgredior, -gressus (3), *dep.*, approach.

adgrego (1), *tr.*, add to, reckon among.

adhibeo (2), *tr.*, summon, employ.

adhuc, *adv.*, hitherto.

adimo, -emi, -emptum (3), *tr.*, take away, remove.

adipiscor, adeptus (3), *dep.*, attain.

aditus, -us, *m.*, approach.

adiumentum, -i, *n.*, help, support.

adiungo, -iunxi, -iunctum (3), *tr.*, join to.

adiutor, -oris, *m.*, helper, supporter.

adiuvo, -iuvi, -iutum (1), *tr.*, help.

adlicio, -lexi, -lectum (3), *tr.*, attract.

administro (1), *tr.*, organise, conduct.

admirabilis, -e, admirable, wonderful.

admiratio, -onis, *f.*, surprise, wonder, awe.

admiror (1), *dep.*, wonder at, am surprised.

admodum, *adv.*, much, very, greatly.

admoneo (2), *tr.*, inform, advise, warn.

adorno (1), *tr.*, equip.

adripio, -ripui, -reptum (3), *tr.*, seize, snatch.

adrogans, -ntis, presumptuous, arrogant.

adrogantia, -ae, *f.*, presumption, arrogance.

adsectatio, -onis, *f.*, accompaniment.

adsector (1), *dep.*, accompany.

adsequor, -secutus (3), *dep.*, attain, achieve, master.

adsiduitas, -atis, *f.*, constant attendance.

adsum, -esse, -fui, *intr.*, am at hand, support.

adsumo, -sumpsi, -sumptum (3), *tr.*, receive, take.

adulescens, -ntis, young; *as subst.*, young person.

adulescentia, -ae, *f.*, youth.

advenio, -veni, -ventum (4), *intr.*, arrive.

adventus, -us, *m.*, arrival.

adversarius, -i, *m.*, opponent, enemy, rival.

adversor (1), *dep.*, resist, oppose.

advocatus, -i, *m.*, legal helper (as witness or counsel).

advolo (1), *intr.*, fly to.

aedilis, -is, *m.*, aedile.

aemulus, -i, *m.*, disciple.

aequabilitas, -atis, *f.*, impartiality.

aequatio, -onis, *f.*, equal distribution.

aeque, *adv.*, equally.

aequitas, -atis, *f.*, equity, fairness.

aequus, -a, -um, equal; favourable, advantageous.

aestimo (1), *tr.*, value, judge.

aestus, -us, *m.*, tide; ferment, commotion.

aeternus, -a, -um, everlasting.

ager, agri, *m.*, territory.

agitatio, -onis, *f.*, movement, disturbance.

agito (1), *tr.*, do, accomplish; deride, ridicule.

ago, egi, actum (3), *tr.*, do, conduct, bring about; **partes ago**, play a part; *with abl.*, negotiate, treat with; **causam ago**, plead a case; **de aliquo ago**, deal with something; **gratias ago**, thank.

agrestis, -is, *m.*, rustic.

aio, *defect. intr.*, say.

alacer, -cris, -cre, active, cheerful.

alienus, -a, -um, of another, alien; *as subst.*, stranger.

aliquamdiu, *adv.*, for some time.

aliquando, *adv.*, once, formerly; sometimes; at last.

aliqui, -qua, -quod, some.

aliquis, -quid, *indef. pron.*, some one, some thing.

aliquot, *indecl. adj.*, some, several, a few.

aliter, *adv.*, differently, otherwise.

alius, -a, -um, other, different.

alter, -era, -erum, one of two, the other, second.

altum, -i, *n.*, the high sea, the deep.

ambitio, -onis, *f.*, canvassing; ambition.

ambitiosus, -a, -um, fond of honour, ambitious.

ambitus, -us, *m.*, bribery, corruption.

ambo, -ae, -o, both.

amicitia, -ae, *f.*, friendship.

amicus, -i, *m.*, friend.

amitto, -misi, -missum (3), *tr.*, lose.

amo (1), *tr.*, love.

amoenus, -a, um, pleasant, delightful.

amor, -oris, *m.*, love, lust.

amplector, -plexus (3), *dep.*, embrace.

amplitudo, -inis, *f.*, distinction.

amplus, -a, -um, distinguished, elaborate.

an, *conj.*, or; *after* utrum *or* -ne; *also used elliptically to ask single questions.*

anguste, *adv.*, narrowly, closely, exactly.

anima, -ae, *f.*, life.

animadverto, -verti, -versum (3), *tr.*, notice.

animus, -i, *m.*, mind, state of mind, spirit.

annales, -ium, *m. pl.*, (sc. *libri*), chronicle, annals.

annus, -i, *m.*, year.

ante, *adv.*, before; *prep. with acc.*, before; ante quam, *conj.*, before.

antea, *adv.*, before, formerly.

antecello (3), *intr.*, surpass, excel.

antepono, -posui, -positum (3), *tr.*, place before, prefer.

antiquus, -a, -um, of old, living long ago; old.

aperte, *adv.*, openly.

apertus, -a, -um, clear, obvious; frank, open, unabashed.

appello (1), *tr.*, call, address, call upon.

appeto, -petivi, -petitum (3), *tr.*, seek, strive after.

appono, -posui, -positum (3), *tr.*, put by the side of.

appositus, -a, -um, fit, suitable.

aptus, -a, -um, suitable.

apud, *prep. with acc.*, among, with; in the time of; at.

aqua, -ae, *f.*, water.

arbiter, -tri, *m.*, witness; umpire, arbiter, judge.

arbitrium, -i, *n.*, will.

arbitror (1), *dep.*, consider.

arceo, arcui, arctum (2), *tr.*, ward off.

argenteus, -a, -um, of silver.

arguo, argui, argutum (3), *tr.*, show, prove.

armo (1), *tr.*, arm.

ars, artis, *f.*, skill.

artifex, -icis, *m.*, artiste.

artificium, -i, *n.*, skill, craft.

ascendo, -scendi, -scensum (3), *intr.*, ascend, climb.

asper, -era, -erum, rough, harsh.

aspergo, -spersi, -spersum (3), *tr.*, sprinkle.

aspicio, -spexi, -spectum (3), *tr.*, see, look upon.

astutus, -a, -um, cunning.

at, *conj.*, but.

atque, *see* **ac.**

atqui, *conj.*, but yet, and yet.

atrociter, *adv.*, cruelly, bitterly.

atrox, -ocis, cruel.

attingo, -tigi, -tactum (3), *tr.*, touch, take in hand.

auctor, -oris, *m.*, leader, supporter; guarantor; author, authority, teacher.

auctoritas, -atis, *f.*, authority.

audacia, -ae, *f.*, boldness, audacity, effrontery.

audax, -acis, bold, audacious.

audeo, ausus (2), *semi-dep.* dare.

audio (4), *tr.*, hear.

augeo, auxi, auctum (2), *tr.*, increase.

auguror (1), *dep.*, prophesy, divine.

auloedus, -i, *m.*, one who sings to the accompaniment of the *aule.*

aura, -ae, *f.*, breeze, wind.

auris, -is, *f.*, ear.

auspicium, -i, *n.*, augury from birds, auspice.

auspico (1), *intr.*, take the auspices.

austere, *adv.*, austerely.

aut, *conj.*, or; **aut ... aut,** either ... or.

autem, *conj.*, but, moreover.

auxilium, -i, *n.*, help.

avaritia, -ae, *f.*, greed, avarice.

avello, -velli *or* **-volsi, -volsum** (3), *tr.*, tear from, tear away.

averto, -verti, -versum (3), *tr.*, turn away, avert.

avus, -i, *m.*, grandfather.

barbatus, -a, -um, bearded.

basilica, -ae, *f.*, basilica, hall.

beatus, -a, -um, fine.

belle, *adv.*, well, finely, delightfully.

bellicum, -i, *n.*, signal for attack.

bellicus, -a, -um, of war.

bello (1), *intr.*, wage war.

bellum, -i, *n.*, war.

bene, *adv.*, well, very.

beneficium, -i, *n.*. benefit; office.

beneficus, -a, -um, generous, beneficent.

benevolentia, -ae, *f.*, good-will.

benignitas, -atis, *f.*, kindness, liberality.

bis, *adv.*, twice.

blanditia, -ae, *f.*, flattery (in good sense).

bucina, -ae, *f.*, trumpet.

cado, cecidi, casum (3), *intr.*, fall.

caelum, -i, *n.*, sky, heavens.

calamitas, -atis, *f.*, calamity, disaster, ruin.

calamitosus, -a, -um, disastrous; unfortunate, ruined, miserable.

campus, -i, *m.*, field; *esp.*, the Campus Martius.

candidatus, -i, *m.*, candidate.

cano, cecini, cantum (3), *tr.*, sound.

cantus, -us, *m.*, sound (of man, animal, or instrument).

capio, cepi, captum (3), *tr.*, take, undertake; make; capture.

caput, -itis, *n.*, head; civil rights, life.

carmen, -inis, *n.*, legal formula.

carus, -a, -um, dear.

castra, -orum, *n. pl.,* camp.

casus, -us, *m.,* chance, fortune.

caterva, -ae, *f.,* band.

causa, -ae, *f.,* case, cause; relation; *in abl. used with gen.,* for the sake of.

cautus, -a, - um, wary, cautious.

caveo, cavi, cautum (2), *tr. and intr.,* take care, take precautions, guard against.

cedo, *old imper. form,* here!, tell, say.

cēdo, cessi, cessum (3), *tr. and intr.,* yield.

celebro (1), *tr.,* crowd, fill; honour, praise, make famous; spread news.

cena, -ae, *f.,* dinner.

centuria, -ae, *f.,* century.

centurio (1), *tr.,* divide into centuries.

certamen, -inis, *n.,* struggle.

certe, *adv.,* surely, certainly, at least.

certus, -a, -um, fixed, certain, clear, particular.

cervix, -icis, *f.,* neck.

ceterus, -a, -um, the rest, remainder.

chorus, -i, *m.,* band.

cibus, -i, *m.,* food.

circumfluo, -fluxi (3), *intr.,* overflow with, have an abundance.

circumspicio, -spexi, -spectum (3), *tr. and intr.,* look around, be cautious; survey, consider.

circus, -i, *m.,* circus, arena.

citharoedus, -i, *m.,* one who sings to the accompaniment of the *cithara.*

civilis, -e, of a citizen, civil.

civis, -is, *c.,* citizen.

civitas, -atis, *f.,* state.

clamo (1), *tr. and intr.,* shout, assert.

clarus, -a, -um, distinguished, illustrious, famous.

classis, -is, *f.,* fleet.

claudo, clausi, clausum (3), *tr.,* shut.

claustra, -orum, *n. pl.,* barrier.

cliens, -ntis, *m.,* client.

coarguo, -argui (3), *tr.,* prove a crime.

coemptio, -onis, *f.,* marriage.

coepi, coeptum (3), *defect. intr.,* begin.

cogitatio, -onis, *f.,* consideration.

cogito (1), *tr.,* think, consider.

cognomen, -inis, *n.,* family name, epithet.

cognosco, -novi, -nitum (3), *tr.,* learn, recognise; *perf.,* know.

cogo, coegi, coactum (3), *tr.,* force, compel.

collum, -i, *n.,* neck.

colo, colui, cultum (3), *tr.,* look after, honour.

colonus, -i, *m.,* settler.

comes, -itis, *c.,* companion, accompaniment.

comis, -e, courteous, kindly, friendly.

comissatio, -onis, *f.,* revel, riot.

comitas, -atis, *f.,* courtesy.

comitia, -orum, *n. pl.,* assembly, election.

commemoro (1), *tr.,* call to mind, remember; mention, recount.

commendatio, -onis, *f.,* commendation.

commendo (1), *tr.,* commend, entrust.

commenticius, -a, -um, fabricated, false.

committo, -misi, -missum (3), *tr.*, do, commit, entrust; join (of battle).

commodum, -i, *n.*, advantage, profit.

commodus, -a, -um, affable.

commoneo (2), *tr.*, bring forcibly to mind, recall.

commoveo, -movi, -motum (2), *tr.*, move.

communico (1), *tr.*, communicate, impart, share.

communis, -e, common.

communiter, *adv.*, together.

commutatio, -onis, *f.*, changing, alteration.

commuto (1), *tr.*, change.

comparatio, -onis, *f.*, preparation, organisation, collection.

comparo (1), *tr.*, prepare, provide.

compenso (1), *tr.*, make good, compensate.

competitor, -oris, *m.*, fellowcandidate.

competitrix, -icis, *f.*, female competitor.

complures,-a,several, very many.

compono, -posui, -positum (3), *tr.*, compose, construct.

comprimo, -pressi, -pressum (3), *tr.*, restrain, crush.

comprobo (1), *tr.*, approve, vindicate.

conatus, -us, *m.*, effort.

concedo, -cessi, -cessum (3), *tr. and intr.*, grant, give up, concede; yield, retire.

concilio (1), *tr.*, win over, gain.

concipio, -cepi, -ceptum (3), *tr.*, conceive.

concito (1), *tr.*, stir up, arouse.

concludo, -clusi, -clusum (3), *tr.*, end, close, conclude.

concordia, -ae, *f.*, harmony, concord.

concurro, -curri, -cursum (3), *intr.*, run together.

concurso (1), *tr.*, visit, frequent.

condemno (1), *tr.*, condemn.

condicio, -onis, *f.*, condition, situation, circumstances.

condio (4), *tr.*, season.

condo, -didi, -ditum (3), *tr.*, put away, store.

conduco, -duxi, -ductum (3), *tr. and intr.*, hire; am advantageous to.

confero, -ferre, -tuli, -latum, *tr.*, bring together; **manum confero,** join issue, fight; **me confero,** take myself, go.

confessio, -onis, *f.*, confession.

conficio, -feci, -fectum (3), *tr.*, make from; finish, wear out.

configo, -fixi, -fixum (3), *tr.*, pierce, transfix.

confirmatio, -onis, *f.*, support.

confirmo (1), *tr.*, strengthen.

confiteor, -fessus (2), *dep.*, admit, confess.

conformo (1), *tr.*, put into good shape.

confugio, -fugi (3), *intr.*, flee for refuge.

confusio, -onis, *f.*, a mixing together.

congemo, -gemui (3), *intr.*, groan loudly.

congredior, -gressus (3), *dep.*, meet in battle.

conicio, -ieci, -iectum (3), *tr.*, attribute to.

coniectura, -ae, *f.*, inference.

coniunctus, -a, -um, closely joined, united.

coniungo, -iunxi, -iunctum (3), *tr.*, join.

coniuratus, -i, *m.*, conspirator.

conlega, -ae, *m.*, colleague.

conloco (1), *tr.*, invest.

conor (1), *dep.*, try.

conqueror, -questus (3), *dep.*, complain.

conquestio, -onis, *f.*, complaint.

consecro, (1), *tr.*, dedicate, consecrate.

consentio, -sensi, -sensum (4), *tr. and intr.*, agree.

consequor, -secutus (3), *dep.*, follow; attain, obtain.

consero, -serui, -sertum (3), *tr.*, join; **manum consero,** join issue, fight.

conservo (1), *tr.*, preserve.

considero (1), *tr.*, consider.

consido, -sedi, -sessum (3), *intr.*, lose force, subside, diminish, sink.

consilium, -i, *n.*, plan, policy, judgement, prudence; council.

consisto, -stiti, -stitum (3), *intr.*, stand, halt.

conspectus, -us, *m.*, sight.

conspicio, -spexi, -spectum (3), *tr.*, see.

constans, -ntis, stable, constant, steady, steadfast.

constituo, -stitui, -stitutum (3), *tr.*, appoint, decide, determine, establish.

consto, -stiti, -statum (1), *intr.*, consist of; *impers.*, is agreed.

consuetudo, -inis, *f.*, habit, custom, inclination, practice; close friendship.

consul, -is, *m.*, consul.

consularis, -e, of a consul, consular.

consulatus, -us, *m.*, consulate.

consulo, -sului, -sultum (3), *tr. and intr.*, consult; consult the interests of.

consultor, -oris, *m.*, client.

consultum, -i, *n.*, decree.

consultus, -i, *m.*, (iuris) lawyer.

consumo, -sumpsi, -sumptum (3), *tr.*, spend.

contagio, -onis, *f.*, contagion, disease.

contemno, -tempsi, -temptum (3), *tr.*, despise.

contendo, -tendi, -tentum (3), *intr.*, struggle, fight.

contentio, -onis, *f.*, fight, contest, struggle; comparison, contrast.

contentus, -a, -um, eager, intent; content.

conticisco, -ticui (3), *intr.*, become quiet, cease, stop.

continenter, *adv.*, temperately, moderately.

continentia, -ae, *f.*, self-control.

contineo, -tinui, -tentum (2), *tr.*, control, contain.

continuus, -a, -um, continual, repeated.

contio, -onis, *f.*, meeting, speech.

contra, *prep. with acc.*, against.

contrarius, -a, -um, opposite.

controversus, -a, -um, disputed.

convenio, -veni, -ventum (4), *intr.*, come together; *impers.*, it is fitting.

conventus, -us, *m.*, assembly.

conviciator, -oris, *m.*, reviler, slanderer.

convicium, -i, *n.*, wrangle, brawling; insult.

convinco, -vici, -victum (3), *tr.*, prove.

convivium, -i, *n.*, feast, banquet.

copia, ae, *f.*, plenty, abundance; *occas.*, force; *in plur.*, resources, wealth; numbers, forces, troops.

copiosus, -a, -um, fluent.

cornix, -icis, *f.*, crow.

corpus, -oris, *n.*, body.

corrigo, -rexi, -rectum (3) *tr.*, make straight, set right.

corrumpo, -rupi, -ruptum (3), *tr.* pervert.

cotidianus, -a, -um, daily.

cotidie, *adv.*, daily.

credo, credidi, creditum (3), *tr. and intr.*, believe; entrust, lend.

cresco, crevi, cretum (3), *intr.*, grow.

crimen, -inis, *n.*, charge, accusation.

criminatio, -onis, *f.*, accusation.

criminosus, -a, -um, worthy of accusation, criminal.

crucio (1), *tr.*, torture.

crudelis, -e, cruel.

crudelitas, -atis, *f.*, cruelty.

cubo, cubui, cubitum (1), *intr.*, recline at meals.

culpa, -ae, *f.*, blame, censure.

cum, *prep. with abl.*, with

cum, *conj.*, when, although, since; cum . . . tum, both . . . and.

cupiditas, -atis, *f.*, desire, cupidity.

cupidus, -a, -um, desirous of, greedy, ambitious.

cupio, cupivi, cupitum (3). *tr.*, desire, wish.

cur, *adv.*, why.

cura, -ae, *f.*, care, anxiety.

curia, -ae, *f.*, senate-house.

curo (1), *tr.*, care for, take care of.

curriculum, -i, *n.*, course.

curro, cucurri, cursum (3), *intr.*, run.

cursus, -us, *m.*, course, journey.

custodia, -ae, *f.*, guard, protection.

damno (1), *tr.*, condemn.

de, *prep. with abl.*, about, concerning.

debeo (2), *tr. and intr.*, owe, am indebted to; ought.

debilis, -e, weak, frail.

debilito (1), *tr.*, weaken.

decedo, -cessi, -cessum (3), *intr.*, go away, leave.

decerno, -crevi, -cretum (3), *tr. and intr.*, pass a decree, pronounce a decision, decree.

decipio, -cepi, -ceptum (3), *tr.*, deceive.

declaro (1), *tr.*, make clear, show, declare.

decoro (1), *tr.*, adorn.

decretum, -i, *n.*, legal decision, decree.

deduco, -duxi, -ductum (3), *tr.*, accompany, escort, bring.

defendo, -fendi, -fensum (3), *tr.*, defend, maintain.

defensio, -onis, *f.*, defence, protection.

defensor, -oris, *m.*, defender.

defero, -ferre, -tuli, -latum, *tr.*, carry off, confer upon; nomen defero, prosecute.

deflecto, -flexi, -flexum (3), *tr. and intr.*, turn aside.

deformo (1), *tr.*, disfigure, mar.

deicio, -ieci, -iectum (3), *tr.*, prevent from obtaining, deprive of.

deinde, *adv.*, next.

delabor, -lapsus (3), *dep.*, sink.

delectatio, -onis, *f.*, pleasure, amusement.

delecto (1), *tr.*, delight.

delenio (4), *tr.*, captivate, entice.

deleo, delevi, deletum (2), *tr.*, destroy, conquer.

delicatus, -a, -um, luxurious; addicted to pleasure, spoiled.

deliciae, -arum, *f. pl.*, delight, pleasure; beloved, darling.

delictum, -i, *n.*, fault, error, wrongdoing.

deligo, -legi, -lectum (3), *tr.*, choose, select.

delinquo, -liqui, -lictum (3), *tr. and intr.*, do wrong.

demitto, -misi, -missum (3), *tr.*, cast down.

demonstro (1), *tr.*, show.

demoveo, -movi, -motum (2), *tr.*, remove.

denique, *adv.*, finally, at last, in short.

denuntiatio, -onis, *f.*, announcement, warning, threat.

denuntio (1), *tr.*, announce, threaten.

depello, -puli, -pulsum (3), *tr.*, drive out, expel.

depono, -posui, -positum (3), *tr.*, give up, lay down.

deporto (1), *tr.*, carry home.

depravo (1), *tr.*, spoil.

deprecor (1), *dep.*, avert by prayer.

deprehendo, -prehendi, -prehensum (3), *tr.*, seize.

derideo, -risi, -risum (2), *tr.*, scoff at, deride.

derigo, -rexi, -rectum (3), *tr.*, direct, guide, arrange.

descendo, -scendi, -scensum (3), *intr.*, come down.

desero, -serui, -sertum (3), *tr.*, leave, desert.

desiderium, -i, *n.*, longing, desire, regret.

desidero (1), *tr.*, long for, wish for, desire, miss, lack.

desidia, -ae, *f.*, idleness, inactivity.

designatus, -a, -um, designate, elect.

desino, -sii, -situm (3), *tr. and intr.*, leave off, cease.

desisto, -stiti, -stitum (3), *intr.*, leave off, desist.

desperatio, -onis, *f.*, despair.

desperatus, -a, -um, given up.

despero (1), *tr.*, despair of.

despicio, -spexi, -spectum (3), *tr.*, look down on.

desultorius, -i, *m.*, vaulter, rider.

desum, -esse, -fui, *intr.*, am lacking, fail.

detraho, -traxi, -tractum (3), *tr.*, take away, withdraw.

deturbo (1), *tr.*, throw down, beat down.

deus, -i, *m.*, god.

devenio, -veni, -ventum (4), *intr.*, come down, sink, decline.

dico, dixi, dictum (3), *tr.*, say, speak, speak of, mean; **male dico,** insult; **ius dico,** hear a case, pronounce a legal decision.

dictum, -i, *n.*, remark, statement, utterance.

dies, -ei, *c.*, day; passage of time.

difficilis, -e, difficult.

difficultas, -atis, *f.*, captiousness.

diffido, -fisus (3), *semi-dep.*, despair; mistrust.

dignitas, -atis, *f.*, merit, worth, right, due.

dignus, -a, -um, worthy.

dilectus, -us, *m.*, levy.

diligenter, *adv.*, carefully.

diligentia, -ae, *f.*, care, industry.

diligo, -lexi, -lectum (3), *tr.*, love, like, approve.

dimicatio, -onis, *f.*, encounter, contest.

dimitto, -misi, -missum (3), *tr.*, send away.

disciplina, -ae, *f.*, discipline, profession; philosophical school; way of life.

disco, didici (3), *tr.*, learn.

discordia, -ae, *f.*, disagreement.

discrepo, -crepui (1), *intr.*, disagree, differ.

discrimen, -inis, *n.*, danger, peril, crisis.

discutio, -cussi, -cussum (3), *tr.*, dash to pieces, shatter.

dispar, -is, unequal.

dispertio (4), *tr.*, distribute, discuss, divide.

disputo (1), *tr. and intr.*, treat of, argue.

dissero, -serui, -sertum (3), *tr.*, speak, treat of.

dissimilis, -e, different.

dissimulo (1), *tr.*, pretend that something is not what it is, dissemble, conceal.

dissolvo, -solvi, -solutum (3), *tr.*, dissolve, destroy.

distinctus, -a, -um, different.

distinguo, -stinxi, -stinctum (3), *tr.*, distinguish, set off, mark.

distortus, -a, -um, misshapen, deformed.

diu, *adv.*, for a long time; **quam diu,** *adv.*, as long as.

diuturnitas, -atis, *f.*, length of time.

divinus, -a, -um, divine, exceptional.

divisor, -oris, *m.*, bribery-agent.

do, dedi, datum (1), *tr.*, give.

doceo (2), *tr.*, teach, show, prove.

doctrina, -ae, *f.*, teaching.

doleo (2), *tr. and intr.*, feel pain, grieve at.

dolor, -oris, *m.*, grief, pain, resentment.

domesticus, -a, -um, of a house, household; at home.

domina, -ae, *f.*, mistress.

domus, -us *and* **-i,** *f.*, house, home.

dono (1), *tr.*, present.

donum, -i, *n.*, gift, decoration.

dormio (4), *intr.*, sleep.

dubito (1), *tr. and intr.*, doubt.

dubius, -a, -um, doubtful.

duco, duxi, ductum (3), *tr.*, lead, command; consider.

dum, *conj.*, while; **dum modo** *conj.*, provided that.

duo, -ae, -o, two.

durus, -a, -um, hard, harsh, difficult.

dux, ducis, *m.*, leader, guide.

e, ex, *prep. with abl.*, from, out of, in accordance with.

ecquis, ecquid, *interrog pron.*, anyone, anything.

edisco, -didici (3), *tr.*, learn by heart.

editicius, -a, -um, chosen by the plaintiff.

educo, -duxi, -ductum (3), *tr.*, lead out.

effero, -ferre, extuli, elatum, *tr.*, praise, extol; **me effero,** rise.

efficio, -feci, -fectum (3), *tr.*, achieve, accomplish.

efflagito (1), *tr.*, demand.

effringo, -fregi, -fractum (3), *tr.*, break open, storm.

ego, mei, *pron.*, I.

egomet, *emphatic form of* **ego.**

egregius, -a, -um, outstanding, exceptional.

eicio, -ieci, -iectum (3), *tr.*, throw out.

elabor, -lapsus (3), *dep.*, slip from.

elaboro (1), *tr. and intr.*, take pains over, exert oneself.

elatus, -a, -um, carried away.

elegantia, -ae, *f.*, good taste.

eloquentia, -ae, *f.*, eloquence.

emendo (1), *tr.*, correct, improve.

enim, *conj.*, for.

eniteo, -nitui (2), *intr.*, shine out, am distinguished.

enuntio (1), *tr.*, publish.

eo, *adv.*, to that place, thither.

eo, ire, ii, itum, *intr.*, go.

eodem, *adv.*, to the same place, for the same purpose.

epulum, -i, *n. in s., f. in pl.*, meal, banquet.

eques, -itis, *m.*, member of the equestrian order.

equester, -tris, -tre, equestrian.

equus, -i, *m.*, horse.

ergo, *adv.*, consequently, therefore, then.

eripio, -ripui, -reptum (3), *tr.*, take away; **me eripio,** flee, escape.

erro (1), *intr.*, wander, err.

error, -oris, *m.*, mistake, error.

eruditus, -a, -um, learned.

erumpo, -rupi, -ruptum (3), *intr.*, burst out.

eruo, -rui, -rutum (3), *tr.*, dig out, bring out, elicit.

et, *conj.*, and; **et . . . et,** both . . . and.

etenim, *conj.*, and indeed.

etiam, *adv. and conj.*, even, also; yes.

evado, -vasi, -vasum (3), *intr.*, turn out, become.

evenio, -veni, -ventum (4), *intr.*, come to pass, happen to.

eventus, -us, *m.*, outcome.

everto, -verti, -versum (3), *tr.*, eject, overthrow.

evolo (1), *intr.*, fly away.

excello, -cellui, -celsum (3), *intr.*, eminent, surpass.

excelsus, -a, -um, distinguished, excellent.

excipio, -cepi, -ceptum (3), *tr.*, assume, incur.

excito (1), *tr.*, call forth, produce, start, make stand up.

excludo, -clusi, -clusum (3), *tr.*, shut out, cut off.

excurro, -cucurri, -cursum (3), *intr.*, spread out, display oneself.

excusatio, -onis, *f.*, plea.

excutio, -cussi, cussum (3), *tr.*, shake out, examine.

exemplar, -aris, *n.*, pattern.

exemplum, -i, *n.*, example, model, formula.

exeo, -ire, -ii, -itum, *intr.*, go out.

exercitatio, -onis, *f.*, profession.

exercitatus, -a, um, well-practised.

exercitus, -us, *m.*, army.

exigo, -egi, -actum (3), *tr.*, exact.

eximius, -a, -um, oustanding, exceptional.

existimatio, -onis, *f.,* thought, estimation, reputation.

existimo (1), *tr.,* value, estimate; suppose, think.

exitium, -i, *n.,* destruction.

exitus, -us, *m.,* end, fate.

exoro (1), *tr.,* persuade by entreaty.

expedio (4), *absol. and impers.,* is advantageous.

expello, -puli, -pulsum (3), *tr.,* drive out, expel, banish.

expertus, -a, -um, experienced.

expeto, -petivi, -petitum (3), *tr.,* seek out.

exploratus, -a, -um, certain, assured.

expono, -posui, -positum (3), *tr.,* set out

exsilium, -i, *n.,* exile.

exsisto, -stiti, -stitum (3), *intr.,* appear, become, exist.

exsorbeo, -sorbui (2), *tr.,* swallow.

exspectatio, -onis, *f.,* expectation.

exstinguo, -stinxi, -stinctum (3), *tr.,* destroy.

exsul, -is, *c.,* exile.

exsuscito (1), *tr.,* arouse, awake.

extra, *prep. with acc.,* outside.

extremus, -a, -um, last, final, extreme.

exturbo (1), *tr.,* drive out.

faber, -bri, *m.,* smith; **praefectus fabrum,** aide-de-camp.

facile, *adv.,* easily.

facilis, -e, easy.

facilitas, -atis, *f.,* good nature, affability.

facinus, -oris, *n.,* misdeed, crime.

facio, feci, factum (3), *tr.,* do, make; **certiorem facio,** inform.

factum, -i, *n.,* deed, action.

facultas, -atis, *f.,* ability, capacity, opportunity.

fallax, -acis, deceptive.

fallo, fefelli, falsum (3), *tr.,* deceive.

falso, *adv.,* falsely.

fama, -ae, *f.,* report, rumour, reputation.

familia, -ae, *f.,* family, household.

familiaris, -is, *m.,* friend.

familiaritas, -atis, *f.,* friendship, intimacy.

fas, *n. indecl.,* right.

fasti, -orum, *m. pl.,* court-days, calendar.

fastidium, -i, *n.,* loathing, aversion.

fateor, fassus (2), *dep.,* confess.

fauste, *adv.,* favourably.

faveo, favi, fautum (2), *intr.,* am well disposed to, favour.

felicitas, -atis, *f.,* good fortune.

feliciter, *adv.,* with good fortune.

felix, -icis, fortunate.

fere, *adv.,* nearly, generally.

fero, ferre, tuli, latum, *tr.,* carry, bear, endure; **legem fero,** propose a law; **graviter fero,** take amiss.

ferrum, -i, *n.,* iron, weapon, sword.

fidelis, -e, faithful.

fides, -ei, *f.,* faith, trust, honour, sense of honour; protection; pledge.

figo, fixi, fixum (3), *tr.,* fix.

filiola, -ae, *f.,* little daughter.

filius, -i, *m.,* son.

fingo, finxi, fictum (3), *tr.,* invent, feign; make, create.

finis, -is, *usually m.,* end; *in pl.,* boundary.

fio, fieri, factus sum, *intr.,* am made, am done, become, happen.

firmo (1), *tr.,* strengthen.

firmus, -a, -um, firm, strong, steadfast, incontrovertible.

flagitium, -i, *n.,* shame, disgrace.

flagito (1), *tr.,* demand.

flagro (1), *intr.,* burn.

flamma, -ae, *f.,* flame, fire.

flecto, flexi, flexum (3), *tr.,* bend, turn, prevail upon, appease.

floreo, florui (2), *intr.,* am eminent, distinguished.

fluctus, -us, *m.,* current, wave.

fons, fontis, *m.,* spring, fount, source, supply.

fore, *see* sum.

forensis, -e, of the forum.

formosus, -a, -um, handsome, beautiful.

formula, -ae, *f.,* formula, model.

forsitan, *adv.,* perhaps.

fortasse, *adv.,* perhaps.

forte, *adv.,* by chance, of course.

fortis, -e, strong, brave.

fortuna, -ae, *f.,* fortune, luck, misfortune.

fortunatus, -a, -um, fortunate.

forum, -i, *n.,* market-place, forum (especially the meeting-place for business at Rome).

foveo, fovi, fotum (2), *tr.,* pamper.

frater, -tris, *m.,* brother.

fraus, fraudis, *f.,* deceit; harm, injury.

frequens, -ntis, crowded, in crowds, in large numbers.

frequentia, -ae, *f.,* crowd.

fretum, -i, *n.,* strait.

fretus, -a, -um, relying on.

fructus, -us, *m.,* fruit, reward, enjoyment.

fuco (1), *tr.,* paint, colour.

fuga, -ae, *f.,* flight.

fugio, fugi (3), *tr. and intr.,* flee, escape.

fugitivus, -i, *m.,* fugitive.

fundo, fudi, fusum (3), *tr.,* rout.

fundus, -i, *m.,* farm, property.

furor, -oris, *m.,* madness, fury.

fundamentum, -i, *m.,* foundation.

gallinaceus, -a, -um, of domestic poultry.

gallus, -i, *m.,* cock (with **gallinaceus**).

gaudium, -i, *n.,* joy.

gemitus, -us, *m.,* groan.

genus, -eris, *n.,* descendants, posterity, family; kind.

gero, gessi, gestum (3), *tr.,* carry on, do, administer; **morem gero,** humour.

gladiator, -oris, *m.,* swordsman, fighter; gladiatorial show.

gladiatorius, -a, -um, for gladiatorial games.

gladius, -i, *m.,* sword.

gloria, -ae, *f.,* glory, distinction.

gradus, -us, *m.,* step, order.

gratia, -ae, *f.,* favour, goodwill, popularity; thanks, recompense; *in abl. used with gen.,* for the sake of.

gratificatio, -onis, *f.,* a showing kindness.

gratiosus, -a, -um, enjoying favour, agreeable, showing favour, advantageous.

gratuitus, -a, -um, without reward.

gratulatio, -onis, *f.,* cause for congratulation, congratulation.

gratulor (1). *dep.*, show joy, congratulate.

gratus, -a, um, pleasing, welcome, popular; grateful.

gravis, -e, heavy, serious, important; oppressive; dignified.

gravitas, -atis, *f.*, dignity, sternness.

graviter, *adv.*, with weight, deeply.

gravor (1), *dep.*, feel annoyed; do unwillingly.

grex, gregis, *m.*, flock, herd; crew, gang.

gubernaculum, -i, *n.*, guidance, government.

guberno (1), *tr.*, steer, control.

gusto (1), *tr.*, take a light meal, eat a little.

habeo (2), *tr.*, have, hold; think.

habito (1), *tr. and intr.,* live. inhabit.

hasta, -ae, *f.*, spear.

hesternus, -a, -um, of yesterday.

hic, haec, hoc, this.

hice, haece, hoce, *intens. form* of **hic.**

historicus, -a, -um, with antiquarian knowledge.

homo, -inis, *m.*, human being, man.

honestas, -atis, *f.*, distinction, position, good name.

honeste, *adv.*, honourably.

honesto (1), *tr.*, honour.

honestus, -a, -um, respectable, honourable.

honos, -oris, *m.*, honour, public office.

horribilis, -e, awful.

horridus, -a, -um, rough, uncouth.

hortor (1), *dep.*, exhort.

hospes, -itis, *m.*, host, guest.

hostis, -is, *m.*, enemy.

humanitas, -atis, *f.*, humanity, kindness, culture.

iaceo (2), *intr.*, lie, lie prostrate.

iacio, ieci, iactum (3), *tr.*, throw, lay (foundations).

iactatio, -onis, *f.*, a tossing to and fro, violent motion.

iacto (1), *tr.*, throw, toss to and fro.

iam, *adv.*, now, already.

ianua, -ae, *f.*, gateway.

ibi, *adv.*, there.

idcirco, *adv.*, for that reason, therefore.

idem, eadem, idem, same; **eodem,** to the same place.

ideo, *adv.*, so, for that reason.

igitur, *conj.*, therefore.

ignobilitas, -atis, *f.*, lack of nobility.

ignominia, -ae, *f.*, disgrace.

ignosco, -novi, -notum (3), *tr.*, pardon.

ilico, *adv.*, immediately.

ille, illa, illud, that.

illinc, *adv.*, thence.

imago, -inis, *f.*, bust.

imitor (1), *dep.*, copy.

immanis, -e, monstrous, savage.

immo, *part.*, no.

immortalis, -e, immortal.

impedio (4), *tr.*, hinder, prevent.

imperator, -oris, *m.*, general, commander.

imperitus, -a, -um, unskilled, ignorant.

imperium, -i, *n.*, authority, command, power, empire.

impertio (4), *tr.*, share with, bestow, impart.

impetus, -us, *m.*, attack; impetus, force, fury.

imploro (1), *tr.*, beg for.

impono, -posui, -positum (3), *tr.*, place upon, impose.

importunus, -a, -um, ruthless.

impotens, -ntis, weak.

improbe, *adv.*, wrongly, improperly.

improbitas, -atis, *f.*, depravity.

improbus, -a, -um, wicked, evil, abandoned, reprobate.

improviso, *adv.*, unexpectedly.

improvisus, -a, -um, unforeseen.

imprudentia, -ae, *f.*, lack of foresight, lack of knowledge.

in, *prep. with acc.*, into, to, against; *with abl.*, in, on, among.

inanis, -e, empty.

incendium, -i, *n.*, fire.

incertus, -a, -um, uncertain.

inclinatio, -onis, *f.*, tendency, bias, favour.

incolumis, -e, unharmed, safe.

incommodum, -i, *n.*, disadvantage.

increpo, -crepui, -crepitum (1), *intr.*, make a noise.

incumbo, -cubui, -cubitum (3), *intr.*, lean towards, turn to.

incurro, -curri *and* -cucurri, -cursum (3), *intr.*, run into.

inde, *adv.*, then, next, for that reason.

index, -icis, *c.*, informer.

indico (1), *tr.*, declare, reveal.

indico, -dixi, -dictum (3), *tr.*, declare, say truly.

indignitas, -atis, *f.*, unworthiness; insolence.

indoctus, -a, -um, untaught, ignorant.

induco, -duxi, -ductum (3), *tr.*, lead on; mislead.

induo, -dui, -dutum (3), *tr.*, entangle.

industria, -ae, *f.*, hard work, effort.

industrius, -a, -um, hard working.

ineo, -ire, -ii, -itum, *tr. and intr.*, enter, begin; **consilium ineo,** form a plan, resolve.

ineptiae, -arum, *f. pl.*, foolery, absurdities.

inermis, -e, unarmed.

inertia, -ae, *f.*, idleness.

infamia, -ae, *f.*, ill fame, disgrace.

inferior, -us, inferior, lower, lesser.

infimus, -a, -um, lowest, humblest.

infirmitas, -atis, *f.*, weakness.

infirmus, -a, -um, weak.

inflatus, -a, -um, puffed up, proud, exalted.

inflecto, -flexi, -flexum (3), *tr.*, bend, bend back.

ingeniosus, -a, -um, clever.

ingenium, -i, *n.*, nature, ability, cleverness.

ingratus, -a, -um, ungrateful.

ingredior, -gressus (3), *dep.*, enter.

inhumanitas, -atis, *f.*, unkindness, boorishness.

inicio, -ieci, -iectum (3), *tr.*, direct at.

inimicitia, -ae, *f., usually in pl.*, enmity, hostility.

inimicus, -a, -um, hostile; *as subst.*, enemy.

iniquus, -a, -um, unfair.

initium, -i, *n.*, beginning.

iniuria, -ae, *f.,* injury.

iniuste, *adv.,* unjustly.

iniustus, -a, -um, unfair, unjust.

inlustris, -e, notable, outstanding, distinguished.

innocens, -ntis, innocent.

innocentia, -ae, *f.,* innocence.

innumerabilis, -e, countless.

inops, -opis, poor, weak.

inquam, *defect. intr.,* say.

inquiro, -quisivi, -quisitum (3), *tr.,* search for grounds of accusation against.

inquisitio, -onis, *f.,* a hunting up of evidence.

inrideo, -risi, -risum (2), *tr. and intr.,* laugh, laugh at, mock.

inritus, -a, -um, invalid.

insanio (4), *intr.,* am mad.

insanus, -a, -um, mad.

insector (1), *dep.,* censure, blame, attack.

insidiae, -arum, *f. pl.,* ambush.

insignis, -e, conspicuous.

insitus, -a, -um, innate, natural.

instituo, -stitui, -stitutum (3), *tr.,* determine, establish, begin.

institutum, -i, *n.,* plan, practice, institution.

instruo, -struxi, -structum (3), *tr.,* draw up.

integer, -gra, -grum, upright, honourable; undecided; unharmed.

integritas, -atis, *f.,* integrity, honesty, honour.

intellego, -lexi, -lectum (3), *tr.,* learn, understand.

intendo, -tendi, -tentum *and* **-tensum** (3), *tr.,* direct one's course to.

inter, *prep. with acc.,* between, among.

interdum, *adv.,* sometimes.

interea, *adv.,* meanwhile.

intereo, -ire, -ii, -itum, *intr.,* perish, die out.

interficio, -feci, -fectum (3), *tr.,* kill.

interimo, -emi, -emptum (3), *tr.,* abolish, destroy.

intermitto, -misi, -missum (3), *tr.,* leave as an interval.

intermortuus, -a, -um, dead.

interpono, -posui, -positum (3), *tr.,* place between, interpose.

interpres, -etis, *c.,* interpreter.

interpretor (1), *dep.,* interpret, expound.

interpunctio, -onis, *f.,* punctuation between words.

intersum, -esse, -fui, *intr.,* take a part in; am different; *impers.,* is of interest, is important; **magni interest,** it is of great importance.

intervallum, -i, *n.,* interval.

intimus, -a, -um, closest.

intono, -tonui (1), *intr.,* thunder.

intra, *prep. with acc.,* inside.

introeo, -ire, -ii, -itum, *intr.,* enter.

intueor (2), *dep.,* look to.

intus, *adv.,* inside, within.

inuro, -ussi, -ustum (3), *tr.,* brand.

inveho, -vexi, -vectum (3), *tr.,* carry in.

invenio, -veni, ventum (4), *tr.,* find.

inventum, -i, *n.,* device, invention; teaching.

invidia, -ae, *f.,* envy, jealousy.

invidus, -a, -um, envious, jealous; *as subst.,* an envious person.

invito (1), *tr.,* invite.

ipse, -a, -um, self, in person.

irascor, iratus (3), *dep.*, am angry.

is, ea, id, that; eo, thither.

iste, ista, istud, that, that of yours.

istuc, *adv.*, thither.

ita, *adv.*, thus, so.

itaque, *conj.*, and so, accordingly.

item, *adv.*, in the same way, likewise.

iubeo, iussi, iussum (2), *tr.*, order.

iucunditas, -atis, *f.*, enjoyment.

iucundus, -a, -um, pleasing, pleasant.

iudex, -icis, *m.*, judge, juryman.

iudicium, -i, *n.*, judgement, trial.

iudico (1), *tr.*, judge.

ius, iuris, *n.*, right, justice, law.

iustitia, -ae, *f.*, justice.

iustus, -a, -um, just; regular, properly constituted.

iuventus, -utis, *f.*, youth; young men.

labefacto (1), *tr.*, overthrow, destroy.

labor, -oris, *m.*, work, labour, toil, effort.

labor, lapsus (3), *dep.*, slip, fall.

laboro (1), *intr.*, work hard, strive, toil.

lacesso, -ivi, -itum (3), *tr.*, incite, provoke.

lacrima, -ae, *f.*, tear.

laedo, laesi, laesum (3), *tr.*, harm, hurt.

laetus, -a, -um, happy.

lamentatio, -onis, *f.*, grief, lamentation.

large, *adv.*, abundantly, liberally.

largior (4), *dep.*, bribe.

largitio, -onis, *f.*, bestowal; bribery, corruption.

lateo (2), *intr.*, lie hid.

latio, -onis, *f.*, proposal of a new law, bill.

lator, -oris, *m.*, mover, proposer (of a law).

latrocinium, -i, *n.*, brigandage; band of robbers.

lātus, -a, -um, large, broad, wide.

latus, -eris, *n.*, flank.

laudo (1), *tr.*, praise.

laureatus, -a, -um, wreathed in laurel.

laus, laudis, *f.*, praise, glory.

lectulus, -i, *m.*, small couch, eating couch.

legatio, -onis, *f.*, appointment as legate, embassy.

legatus, -i, *m.*, legate, staff-officer.

lenio (4), *tr.*, soften, soothe, calm.

lenis, -e, gentle.

lenitas, -atis, *f.*, mildness, leniency.

lenocinium, -i, *n.*, the job of pander.

levis, -e, light, unimportant, trivial.

leviter, *adv.*, slightly, lightly.

lex, legis, *f.*, law.

libenter, *adv.*, gladly, willingly.

liber, -bri, *m.*, book.

liberalitas, -atis, *f.*, generosity.

libero (1), *tr.*, free.

libertas, -atis, *f.*, freedom.

libido, -inis, *f.*, self-indulgence, excess, lust.

licentia, -ae, *f.*, licence, permission.

licet (2), *intr. and impers.*, it is lawful, allowed, permitted.

lis, litis, *f.*, case.

litigiosus, -a, -um, contentious.

littera, -ae, *f.*, letter; *pl.*, despatches.

litteratus, -a, -um, cultured.

loco (1), *tr.*, place, put.

locus *and* **-um, -i,** *m. and n.,* place, region, locality; rank; room, space.

longe, *adv.,* far.

longus, -a, -um, long.

loquaciter, *adv.,* talkatively, long-windedly.

loquax, -acis, talkative, long-winded.

loquor, locutus (3), *dep.,* say, speak.

lorica, -ae, *f.,* breastplate.

luctuosus, -a, -um, causing sorrow; feeling sorrow.

ludi, -orum, *m. pl.,* games.

lugeo, luxi, luctum (2), *tr. and intr.,* mourn.

luxuria, -ae, *f.,* riotous living, luxury, excess.

maerens, -ntis, mourning.

maeror, -oris, *m.,* grief.

maestus, -a, -um, sad, downcast.

magis *or* **mage,** *comp. adv.,* more.

magister, -tri, *m.,* master.

magistratus, -us, *m.,* magistracy, magistrate.

magnificentia, -ae, *f.,* splendour, magnificence.

magnificentissimus, -a, -um, *superl. of* **magnificus.**

magnificus, -a, -um, magnificent.

magnitudo, -inis, *f.,* size, greatness.

magnus, -a, -um, great; **magni,** of great value, at a high price, dear.

maior, -us, greater; *subst. in pl.,* ancestors.

male, *adv.,* badly, ill; **male dico,** insult, abuse.

maledictum, -i, *n.,* abuse.

maledicus, -a, -um, abusive.

malo, malle, malui, *tr.,* prefer.

malum, -i, *n.,* evil, calamity.

mancipium, -i, *n.,* the formal purchase of an object.

mando (1), *tr.,* bestow, entrust.

mansuetudo, -inis, *f.,* gentleness, clemency.

manus, -us, *f.,* hand; band, force; **manum consero,** join hands, fight.

mare, maris, *n.,* sea.

mater, -tris, *f.,* mother.

mature, *adv.,* in good time, early.

maxime, *adv.,* very greatly.

maximus, -a, -um, *superl. of* **magnus.**

mediocris, -e, middling, moderate, not remarkable, ordinary.

mediocritas, -atis, *f.,* mean.

mediocriter, *adv.,* moderately.

meditor (1), *dep.,* consider.

medium, -i, *n.,* the middle.

melior, -us, better.

memini, *defect. intr.,* remember.

memoria, -ae, *f.,* memory, remembrance.

mendacium, -i, *n.,* lie, falsehood.

mendicus, -a, -um, beggarly, needy.

mens, -ntis, *f.,* mind, opinion.

mensis, -is, *m.,* month.

merces, -edis, *f.,* pay, reward, bribe.

mereo *and* **mereor** (2), *tr. and dep.,* deserve, merit; **stipendia mereo,** serve (in an army).

metuo, metui, metutum (3), *tr.,* fear.

metus, -us, *m.,* fear.

meus, -a, -um, my.

miles, -itis, *m.*, soldier.

militaris, -e, of soldiers, military.

militia, -ae, *f.*, service.

minae, -arum, *f. pl.*, threats.

minime, *adv.*, very little, least; no, not at all.

minimus, -a, -um, very little.

minitor (1), *dep.*, threaten.

minor, -us, less

minor (1), *dep.*, threaten.

minuo, minui, minutum (3), *tr. and intr.*, lessen.

minus, *adv.*, less.

miror (1), *dep.*, wonder, am surprised.

mirus, -a, -um, surprising, wonderful.

miser, -era, -erum, wretched, in distress.

misereor (2), *dep.*, feel pity.

miseria, -ae, *f.*, misfortune, misery.

misericordia, -ae, *f.*, pity, mercy.

misericors, -ordis, having pity, merciful; pitiful, wretched.

miseror (1), *dep.*, pity.

mitis, -e, mild, gentle.

mitto, misi, missum (3), *tr.*, send; pass over.

moderatus, -a, -um, within due bounds, moderate, reasonable.

moderor (1), *dep.*, regulate, direct.

modestia, -ae, *f.*, sense of shame.

modestus, -a, -um, honest, virtuous.

modo, *adv.*, only; just now.

modus, -i, *m.*, limit, way, manner, moderation; eius modi, of that sort.

moenia, -ium, *n. pl.*, walls.

molestia, -ae, *f.*, trouble.

molestus, -a, -um, annoying, troublesome.

molior (4), *dep.*, endeavour, struggle, toil; set in motion, work at, construct; undertake, attempt.

momentum, -i, *n.*, weight, importance.

moneo (2), *tr.*, warn.

monitor, -oris, *m.*, remembrancer.

monumentum, -i, *n.*, record.

morbus, -i, *m.*, illness, disease.

morior, mortuus (3), *dep.*, die.

mors, mortis, *f.*, death.

mortuus, -a, -um, dead.

mos, moris, *m.*, manner, custom; morem gero, humour.

motus, -us, *m.*, movement, disturbance; current.

moveo, movi, motum (2), *tr.*, move.

mucro, -onis, *m.*, sword.

mulier, -is, *f.*, woman.

muliercula, -ae, *f.*, weak little woman.

multitudo, -inis, *f.*, crowd numbers.

multo, *adv.*, by much, much

multum, *adv.*, much, very

multus, -a, um, much, many.

munia, *n. pl.*, (*nom. and acc. only*), duties, obligations.

municipium, -i, *n.*, town.

munio (4), *tr.*, build, fortify.

munitus, -a, -um, defended, protected, safe.

munus, -eris, *n.*, gift; public show, games; office, service, duty.

muto (1), *tr.*, change.

mysterium, -i, *n.*, secret, mystery.

nam, *conj.*, for.

nascor, natus (3), *dep.*, am born.

natio, -onis, *f.*, crowd, crew; nation.

natura, -ae, *f.*, nature.

natus, -us, *m.*, birth.

navalis, -e, naval.

ne, *conj.*, that not, lest; **ne ... quidem,** not ... even.

nec, *conj.*, and not, nor; **nec ... nec,** neither ... nor.

necessario, *adv.*, of necessity.

necessarius, -a, -um, necessary; *as subst.*, a friend.

necesse, *neut. adj.*, necessary.

necessitudo, -inis, *f.*, friendship, intimacy.

necne, *adv.*, or not.

nefarius, -a, -um, wicked, execrable, abominable.

neglectio, -onis, *f.*, neglect.

neglegenter, *adv.*, casually, carelessly.

neglego, -exi, -ectum (3), *tr.*, ignore, neglect.

nego (1), *tr.*, say not, deny.

negotiosus, -a, -um, troublesome.

negotium, -i, *n.*, business.

nemo, nullius, *c.*, no one; **non nemo,** some one.

nepos, -otis, *c.*, grandchild.

neque, *conj.*, *see* **nec; neque enim,** for ... not.

nescio (4), *tr.*, do not know, do not know how to, am ignorant.

nexus, -us, *m.*, legal obligation.

nihil, *indecl.*, nothing.

nimirum, *adv.*, without doubt, to be sure.

nimis, *adv.*, too.

nimium, *adv.*, too, too much.

nimius, -a, -um, too great, excessive.

nisi, *conj.*, if not, unless.

nobilis, -e, noble.

nobilitas, -atis, *f.*, nobility.

nocens, -ntis, guilty.

noceo (2), *intr.*, hurt, harm.

nolo, nolle, nolui, *intr.*, am unwilling.

nomen, -inis, *n.*, name, fame, repute; **nomen defero,** prosecute.

nomenclator, -oris, *m.*, a slave who attended his master while canvassing and told him the names of those he met.

nomino (1), *tr.*, name.

non, *adv.*, not.

nondum, *adv.*, not yet, still not.

nonne, *adv.*, surely.

nonnulli, -ae, -a, some.

norma, -ae, *f.*, rule, pattern.

nosco, novi, notum (3), *tr.*, discover.

noster, -tra, -trum, our.

notus, -a, -um, known, well known.

novitas, -atis, *f.*, newness, lack of nobility.

novus, -a, -um, new.

nox, noctis, *f.*, night; **de nocte,** at night.

nullus, -a, -um, no.

num, *adv.*, whether; surely not.

numero (1), *tr.*, reckon.

numerus, -i, *m.*, number.

numquam, *adv.*, never.

nunc, *adv.*, now.

nuntio (1), *tr.*, announce.

nuntius, -i, *m.*, messenger, news.

nuper, *adv.*, recently.

ob, *prep. with acc.*, on account of.

obeo, -ire, -ii, -itum, *tr.*, travel over, traverse.

obicio, -ieci, -iectum (3), *tr.*, throw out against one, taunt, reproach with, expose.

oblecto (1), *tr.*, give pleasure to.

obligo (1), *tr.*, bind, make liable.

obliviscor, oblitus (3), *dep.*, forget.

obruo, -rui, -rutum (3), *tr.*, overwhelm.

obsaepio, -saepsi, -saeptum (4), *tr.*, block up, close.

obscurus, -a, -um, unfamiliar, obscure, uncertain.

obsecro (1), *tr.*, beseech.

observantia, -ae, *f.*, attention, regard, respect.

observatio, -onis, *f.*, a keeping watch.

observo (1), *tr.*, pay attention to, honour.

obsessio, -onis, *f.*, siege.

obsidio, -onis, *f.*, siege.

obsum, -esse, -fui, *intr.*, hinder, hurt.

obtestor (1), *dep.*, beseech.

obtineo, -tinui, -tentum (2), *tr.*, hold, preserve, obtain.

obviam, *adv.*, to meet.

occido, -cidi, -cisum (3), *tr.*, kill.

occultus, -a, -um, hidden.

occupatio, -onis, *f.*, occupation, business.

occupo (1), *tr.*, occupy, sieze, take up, fill, anticipate.

occurro, -curri, -cursum (3), *intr.*, meet.

oculus, -i, *m.*, eye.

odi, *defect. and tr.*, hate.

odiosus, -a, -um, tiresome.

odium, -i, *n.*, hatred.

offendo, -fendi, -fensum (3), *tr. and intr.*, hit, dash against; commit an offence; displease; suffer misfortune.

offensio, -onis, *f.*, dislike, discredit.

officiosus, -a, -um, obliging, ready to help; officious.

officium, -i, *n.*, service, duty, responsibility.

omen, -inis, *n.*, omen.

omitto, -misi, -missum (3), *tr.*, pass over, say nothing of, omit.

omnino, *adv.*, at all, altogether.

omnis, -e, all, every.

opera, -ae, *f.*, work; *pl.*, a day's work.

opinio, -onis, *f.*, opinion, belief.

opinor (1), *dep.*, suppose, think, surmise.

oportet, -uit (2), *impers.*, it is necessary, becoming, reasonable, right.

oppidum, -i, *n.*, town.

oppono, -posui, -positum (3), *tr.*, set to face.

opprimo, -pressi, -pressum (3), *tr.*, subdue, conquer, overwhelm, destroy.

oppugnatio, -onis, *f.*, a storming.

[ops], opis, *f.*, power, might; *pl.*, means, wealth, resources, might.

optimus, -a, -um, very good, best.

opto (1), *tr.*, wish.

opus, -eris, *n.*, work; need; value; magno opere, greatly.

ora, -ae, *f.*, shore.

oratio, -onis, *f.*, speech, eloquence, conversation.

orator, -oris, *m.*, orator.

orbo (1), *tr.*, deprive.

orbis, -is, *m.*, (terrarum), the world.

ordo, -inis, *m.*, degree, rank, order; right order.

orior, ortus (4), *dep.*, rise, descend from.

ornamentum, -i, *n.*, honour, decoration, distinction, advantage, ornament.

ornatus, -a, -um, distinguished, illustrious.

orno (1), *tr.*, equip, array.

oro (1), *tr.*, beg.

osculor (1), *dep.*, fondle, caress, kiss.

ostendo, -di, -sum (3), *tr.*, show.

otium, -i, *n.*, quiet, peace.

pactum, -i, *n.*, contract, agreement; means; *in abl.*, way, manner.

paene, *adv.*, nearly, almost.

paeniteo (2), *tr.*, cause to be sorry; *impers.*, **me paenitet,** I am sorry, regret.

par, paris, equal, suitable, right.

parcius, *comp. adv.*, more sparingly, more briefly.

parens, -ntis, *c.*, parent.

pareo (2), *intr.*, obey.

pario, peperi, paritum *and* **partum** (3), *tr.*, produce, bring about, acquire.

pars, partis, *f.*, part, party, side; *pl.*, part, role.

partim, *adv.*, partly.

parturio (4), *tr.*, bring forth, produce.

parvus, -a, -um, small, little.

passim, *adv.*, everywhere, universally.

pateo (2), *intr.*, am open, lie open, am accessible, am available.

pater, -tris, *m.*, father; *as proper subst. in pl.*, the Senate.

paternus, -a, -um, of a father.

patior, passus (3), *dep.*, suffer, allow.

patria, -ae, *f.*, fatherland.

patricius, -a, -um, patrician.

patrius, -a, -um, of a father, hereditary.

patronus, -i, *m.*, advocate.

patruus, -i, *m.*, uncle.

pauci, -ae, -a, few.

paulo, *adv.*, a little.

pax, pacis, *f.*, peace.

peccatum, -i, *n.*, misdeed, wrong.

pecco (1), *intr.*, transgress, sin.

peculatus, -us, *m.*, embezzlement.

pecunia, -ae, *f.*, money, sum of money.

pellicula, -ae, *f.*, small hide.

pello, pepuli, pulsum (3), *tr.*, drive.

per, *prep. with acc.*, through, by means of.

peragro (1), *tr.*, travel through, traverse.

percello, -culi, -culsum (3), *tr.*, cast down, ruin.

percrebresco, -crebrui (3), *ints.*, am spread abroad.

perdo, -didi, -ditum (3), *tr.*, destroy, lose, waste.

perendinus, -a, -um, after tomorrow.

perfero, -ferre, -tuli, -latum, *tr.*, bear, endure.

perficio, -feci, -fectum (3), *tr.*, achieve, accomplish, complete.

perfidia, -ae, *f.*, treachery.

perfruor, -fructus (3), *dep.*, enjoy fully.

perfugium, -i, *n.*, refuge.

perfungor, -functus (3), *dep.*, undergo, endure.

pergo, perrexi, perrectum (3), *intr.*, go on, proceed.

pergratus, -a, -um, very popular.

periculum, -i, *n.*, danger.

peritus, -a, -um, skilled, learned.

permaneo, -mansi, -mansum (2), *intr.*, remain, persist, persevere.

permoveo, -movi, -motum (2), *tr.*, move, sway.

permultus, -a, -um, very much, very many.

pernicies, -ei, *f.*, destruction.

perniciosus, -a, -um, destructive, ruinous.

perpauci, -ae, -a, very few.

perpendo, -pendi, -pensum (3), *tr.*, weigh exactly.

perpetior, -pessus (3), *dep.*, suffer, endure patiently.

perpurgo (1), *tr.*, clear up, explain.

perrogatio, -onis, *f.*, passage of a bill.

persaepe, *adv.*, very often.

persalutatio, -onis, *f.*, assiduous greeting.

persequor, -secutus (3), *dep.*, pursue, prosecute.

persona, -ae, *f.*, mask, character, part, role.

persuadeo, -suasi, -suasum (2), *intr.*, persuade.

pertimesco, -timui (3), *tr. and intr.*, fear greatly.

pertineo, -tinui (2), *intr.*, concern, pertain to.

perturbatio, -onis, *f.*, political disturbance, disorder, violent change.

perturbo (1), *tr.*, upset, throw into confusion.

pervenio, -veni, -ventum (4), *intr.*, arrive at, reach.

perversus, -a, -um, perverse, illtimed, inappropriate.

pervolgo (1), *tr.*, make publicly known, publish.

pestis, -is, *f.*, plague.

petitio, -onis, *f.*, candidature for office.

petitor, -oris, *m.*, candidate.

peto, petivi, petitum (3), *tr.*, seek, am a candidate for office, make for, thrust at.

petulans, -ntis, wanton, improper.

pie, *adv.*, dutifully, with propriety.

pietas, -atis, *f.*, dutiful affection.

placeo (2), *intr.*, please.

placo (1), *tr.*, placate.

plebeius, -a, -um, plebeian.

plebs *or* **plebes, plebis** *or* **plebei,** *f.*, the Plebs.

plenus, -a, -um, full.

plerique, -aeque, -aque, very many, most.

plus, pluris, *n.*, *adj. in pl.*, **plures, -a,** more.

plurimum, *adv.*, very much.

plurimus, -a, -um, most, very much, very many.

pluvius, -a, -um, of rain.

poena, -ae, *f.*, punishment, penalty.

poeta, -ae, *m.*, poet.

pono, posui, positum (3), *tr.*, place, put.

popularis, -e, of the people, popular.

populus, -i, *m.*, people.

porro, *adv.*, moreover, besides.

portus, -us, *m.*, port, harbour.

possideo, -sedi, -sessum (2), *tr.*, possess.

possum, posse, potui, *intr.*, can, am able.

post, *prep. with acc. and adv.*, after.

postea, *adv.*, afterwards; **postea quam,** *conj.*, after.

posterus, -a, -um, the following, next; *as subst.; n.,* the future; *m. pl.,* descendants, posterity.

posthac, *adv.,* afterwards, hereafter.

postremo, *adv.,* at last, finally.

postremus, -a, -um, last.

postridie, *adv.,* on the following day.

postulatio, -onis, *f.,* demand.

postulo (1), *tr.,* demand.

potentia, -ae, *f.,* power.

potestas, -atis, *f.,* power.

potior, -us, better, preferable, more important.

potissimum, *adv.,* above all, chiefly, principally, especially.

potius, *adv.,* rather.

prae, *prep. with abl.,* before, in front of.

praeceptor, -oris, *m.,* teacher.

praeceptum, -i, *n.,* teaching.

praecipio, -cepi, -ceptum (3), *tr.,* advise, warn, inform.

praeclare, *adv.,* very clearly.

praeclarus, -a, -um, fine, glorious.

praeda, -ae, *f.,* booty.

praeditus, -a, -um, endowed with, provided with.

praedo, -onis, *m.,* pirate, bandit, robber.

praefectus, -i, *m.,* commander; **praefectus fabrum,** aide-decamp.

praeiudicium, -i, *n.,* preceding judgement.

praemium, -i, *n.,* reward.

praenuntia, -ae, *f.,* harbinger.

praerogativus, -a, -um, that votes first.

praesens, -ntis, present.

praesertim, *adv.,* principally, especially.

praesidium, -i, *n.,* guard, protection, garrison.

praesto, *adv.,* at hand, ready, present.

praesto, -steti, -statum *or* **-stitum** (1), *tr. and intr.,* am superior to; am liable to; fulfil, show, discharge, perform.

praesum, -esse, -fui, *intr.,* am set over.

praeter, *prep. with acc.,* except.

praeterea, *adv.,* besides.

praetereo, -ire, -ii, -itum, *tr.,* pass over.

praetermitto, -misi, -missum (3), *tr.,* pass over.

praetextatus, -a, -um, wearing the *toga praetexta.*

praetor, -oris, *m.,* praetor.

praetorius, -a, -um, praetorian.

praetura, -ae, *f.,* praetorship.

prandium, -i, *n.,* feast, banquet.

pravus, -a, -um, wrong, depraved.

precatio, -onis, *f.,* prayer.

precor (1), *dep.,* pray.

pridem, *adv.,* long ago, long since.

primarius, -a, -um, of the first rank.

primum, *adv.,* first.

primus, -a, -um, first.

princeps, -ipis, pre-eminent, chief, first.

prior, -us, first.

prius, *adv.,* previously, first.

privatus, -a, -um, private, personal; *as subst.,* private citizen.

privo (1), *tr.,* deprive.

pro, *prep. with abl.,* for, on behalf of, in place of, in accordance with, by virtue of.

proavus, -i, *m.,* great-grandfather.

probo (1), *tr.*, prove, approve.

prodeo, -ire, -ii, -itum, *intr.*, go forward.

proelium, -i, *n.*, battle.

profecto, *adv.*, assuredly.

profero, -ferre, -tuli, -latum, *tr.*, carry forward, bring forward, produce; suspend (of business).

proficio, -feci, -fectum (3), *intr.*, am successful.

proficiscor, -fectus (3), *dep.*, set out.

profiteor, -fessus (2), *dep.*, declare myself to be.

profusus, -a, -um, lavish.

promereo (2), *tr.*, acquire, gain.

promissum, -i, *n.*, promise.

promitto, -misi, -missum (3), *tr.*, promise.

promptus, -a, -um, at hand, available.

promulgo (1), *tr.*, announce, publish.

propago (1), *tr.*, extend.

prope, *adv.*, nearly, almost; **prope modum**, *adv.*, nearly, almost.

propensus, -a, -um, inclined.

propinqua, -ae, *f.*, relative, kinswoman.

propono, -posui, -positum (3), *tr.*, set out, lay before, publish.

proprius, -a, -um, characteristic, one's own.

propter, *prep. with acc.,* on account of.

propterea, *adv.*, for this reason.

propulso (1), *tr.*, ward off, repel.

prorumpo, -rupi, -ruptum (3), *intr.*, burst forth.

prospere, *adv.*, favourably, with good fortune.

prospicio, -spexi, -spectum (3), *intr.*, look forward, have foresight.

prosum, prodesse, profui, *intr.*, am of benefit to.

provideo, -vidi, -visum (2), *tr.*, foresee.

provincia, -ae, *f.*, province.

provincialis, -e, of a province, official.

prudentia, -ae, *f.*, good sense, knowledge.

publicanus, -i, *m.*, tax-farmer.

publice, *adv.*, publicly.

publicus, -a, -um, public, official; of, from the state.

pudens, -ntis, honourable.

pudor, -oris, *m.*, decency, feeling of shame.

pugna, -ae, *f.*, battle.

pugnax, -acis, fond of fighting, warlike.

pugno (1), *tr.*, fight.

pulcher, -chra, -chrum, fine.

punctum, -i, *n.*, vote.

punio (4), *tr.*, punish.

purgo (1), *tr.*, clear, show as innocent.

puto (1), *tr.*, think.

quadrigae, -arum, *f. pl.*, four-horse team.

quaero, quaesivi, quaesitum (3), *tr.*, seek.

quaestio, -onis, *f.*, court.

quaestor, -oris, *m.*, quaestor.

quaestura, -ae, *f.*, quaestorship.

qualis, -e, such as.

quam, *adv.*, how, than, as.

quamquam, *conj.*, although; and yet.

quando, *adv. and conj.*, when.

quantus, -a, -um, how great, how much; **tantus ... quantus,** as great ... as, as much ... as.

quapropter, *adv.*, wherefore.

quasi, *adv.*, as if.

-que, *conj.*, and.

queo, quivi, quitum, *intr.*, am able.

qui, quae, quod, *rel. pron.*, who, which.

qui, quae, quod, *interrog. and indef. adj.*, which, what, what sort of.

qui, *adv.*, how.

quia, *conj.*, because.

quidam, quaedam, quoddam, a certain.

quidem, *adv.*, indeed; **ne ... quidem,** not ... even.

quietus, -a, -um, peaceful.

quin, *conj.*, that not, but that, but, without *and verbal noun.*

quippe, *adv. and conj.*, certainly, to be sure, of course.

quis, quid, *interrog. and indef. pron.*, who, what; *n.*, why.

quispiam, quae-, quod- *and* **quip-,** *indef. pron.*, anyone, someone.

quisquam, quaequam, quicquam, *indef. pron.*, anyone, anything.

quisque, quae-, quod-, *indef. pron.*, each.

quo, *rel. and interrog. adv. and conj.*, whither, why, because, that.

quoad, *adv.*, as far as.

quod, *conj.*, because, that; **quod si,** but if.

quondam, *adv.*, formerly.

quoniam, *adv.*, since, because.

quoque, *adv.*, also.

ratio, -onis, *f.*, account, transaction, business, affair, concern, care, manner, list, plan, calculation, judgement, reason, situation.

recens, -ntis, fresh, recent.

recipero (1), *tr.*, recover.

recordor (1), *dep.*, recall.

recreo (1), *tr.*, heal.

recte, *adv.*, rightly.

rectus, -a, -um, right, upright.

reddo, -didi, -ditum (3), *tr.* assign, give.

redeo, -ire, -ii, -itum, *intr.*, return.

redundo (1), *intr.*, overflow.

refercio, -fersi, -fertum (4), *tr.*, fill up, stuff.

refero, referre, rettuli, relatum, *tr.*, bring back; bring before, propose, repay.

reficio, -feci, -fectum (3), *tr.*, refresh.

refragor (1), *dep.*, oppose, thwart.

refringo, -fregi, -fractum (3), *tr.*, break down.

regius, -a, -um, of a king, royal.

regnum, -i, *n.*, kingdom.

rego, rexi, rectum (3), *tr.*, define; correc.

reicio, -ieci, -iectum (3), *tr.*, drive back, repel.

religio, -onis, *f.*, piety, religion; conscience; sanctity.

relinquo, -liqui, -lictum (3), *tr.*, leave, leave out.

reliquus, -a, -um, subsequent, future; remaining, left.

remissus, -a, -um, slack.

removeo, -movi, -motum (2), *tr.*, remove.

renovo (1), *tr.*, renew.

renuntiatio, -onis, *f.*, official announcement.

renuntio (1), *tr.*, announce.

repello, reppuli, repulsum (3), *tr.*, drive back.

repente, *adv.*, suddenly.

repentinus, -a, -um, sudden.

reperio, repperi, repertum (4), *tr.*, find.

repeto, -petivi, -petitum (3), *tr.*, recover.

repleo, -plevi, -pletum (2), *tr.*, replenish.

reprehendo, -prehendi, -prehensum (3), *tr.*, blame, censure.

reprehensio, -onis, *f.*, criticism, censure.

reprendo, *see* reprehendo.

reprimo, -pressi, -pressum (3), *tr.*, check, restrain.

repudiatio, -onis, *f.*, rejection.

repudio (1), *tr.*, reject, refuse.

repugno (1), *intr.*, fight against, oppose.

repulsa, -ae, *f.*, defeat.

requiro, -quisivi, -quisitum (3), *tr.*, need, miss, feel the lack of.

res, rei, *f.*, thing, affair, event, case, task; **res publica**, the state; **qua re**, wherefore.

reservo (1), *tr.*, keep back.

resisto, -stiti (3), *intr.*, resist, stop; regain a footing.

respondeo, -spondi, -sponsum (2), *tr.*, answer, reply.

responsum, -i, *n.*, reply, legal opinion.

respuo, -spui (3), *tr.*, reject.

restinguo, -stinxi, -stinctum (3), *tr.*, extinguish.

restituo, -stitui, -stitutum (3), *tr.*, restore.

retineo, -tinui, -tentum (2), *tr.*, retain, maintain, preserve.

retracto (1), *tr.*, reconsider, re-examine.

reus, -i, *m.*, defendant.

revello, -velli, -volsum (3), *tr.*, tear away, remove.

reverto, -verti, -versum (3), *tr.*, return.

revoco (1), *tr.*, recall; call in turn.

rex, regis, *m.*, king.

ridiculus, -a, -um, laughable.

robur, -oris, *n.*, strength, heart; wood.

rogo (1), *tr.*, ask; **populum magistratum rogo**, offer a magistrate for election; **legem rogo**, introduce a law.

rudis, -e, inexperienced.

ruina, -ae, *f.*, ruin, destruction.

rumor, -oris, *m.*, rumour, popular opinion.

rursum *and* rursus, *adv.*, again.

sacra, -orum, *n. pl.*, sacred rites.

sacrarium, -i, *n.*, shrine, sanctuary.

saepe, *adv.*, often.

saltatio, -onis, *f.*, dance, dancing.

saltator, -oris, *m.*, dancer.

salto (1), *intr.*, dance.

salubritas, -atis, *f.*, health, means of safety.

salus, -utis, *f.*, safety, acquittal.

saluto (1), *tr.*, greet.

sane, *adv.*, doubtless, of course.

sapiens, -ntis, wise.

sapientia, -ae, *f.*, good sense, wisdom.

satietas, -atis, *f.*, weariness, loathing, disgust.

satis, *adv.*, enough, sufficiently; **satis facio**, satisfy.

saucius, -a, -um, wounded, hurt.

scaena, -ae, *f.*, spectacle.

sceleratus, -a, -um, wicked, abandoned.

scelus, -eris, *n.,* crime.

scientia, -ae, *f.,* knowledge, science, skill.

scilicet, *adv.,* of course.

scio (4), *tr.,* know.

scriba, -ae, *f.,* clerk, secretary.

scribo, scripsi, scriptum (3), *tr.,* write.

scurra, -ae, *f.,* dandy, parasite.

se *or* **sese, sui,** *third pers. reflex. pron.,* self.

secessio, -onis, *f.,* secret conference.

sectator, -oris, *m.,* follower, attendant.

sector (1), *dep.,* follow, attend, accompany.

securis, -is, *f.,* axe.

secus, *adv.,* otherwise, differently.

sed, *conj.,* but.

sedeo, sedi, sessum (2), *intr.,* sit.

sedes, -is, *f.,* abode, dwellingplace.

seditio, -onis, *f.,* insurrection, revolution.

seditiosus, -a, -um, seditious.

seductio, -onis, *f.,* a taking aside.

semel, *adv.,* once.

semper, *adv.,* always.

senator, -oris, *m.,* senator.

senatus, -us, *m.,* senate.

senex, senis, *m.,* old man.

senior, -oris, older.

sensus, -us, *m.,* sense, feeling.

sententia, -ae, *f.,* opinion, vote, decision.

sentio, sensi, sensum (4), *tr.,* feel.

sequor, secutus (3), *dep.,* follow.

sermo, -onis, *m.,* talk, conversation, discourse.

serpo, serpsi, serptum (3), *intr.,* creep.

servio (4), *intr.,* serve, am a slave to.

servitus, -utis, *f.,* slavery.

servo (1), *tr.,* preserve, maintain; observe.

servus, -i, *m.,* slave.

severe, *adv.,* severely.

severitas, -atis, *f.,* strictness, severity.

severus, -a, -um, severe, harsh.

sevoco (1), *tr.,* call away, separate, withdraw.

si, *conj.,* if.

sic, *adv.,* thus, so.

sicarius, -i, *m.,* murderer.

sicut, *adv.,* just as.

signifer, -feri, *m.,* standard-bearer.

significo (1), *tr.,* show, indicate.

signum, -i, *n.,* sign, standard; statue; **signa confero,** engage in close fight.

similitudo, -inis, *f.,* likeness, similarity.

simul, *adv.,* at the same time, together; **simul atque,** *conj.,* as soon as.

simulatio, -onis, *f.,* pretence.

simultas, -atis, *f.,* enmity.

sin, *conj.,* but if.

sine, *prep. with abl.,* without.

singularis, -e, exceptional.

singulus, -a, -um, single.

sino, sivi, situm (3), *tr.,* allow.

situs, -a, -um, placed, set, lying.

sive . . . sive, *conj.,* whether . . . or.

sobrius, -a, -um, sober.

societas, -atis, *f.,* company.

socius, -i, *m.,* ally.

sodalis, -is, *c.,* comrade, companion, member of a society.

sol, solis, *m.,* sun.

solacium, -i, n., comfort, consolation.

soleo, solitus (2), semi-dep., am accustomed.

solitudo, -inis, f., solitude.

sollemnis, -e, established.

sollicitudo, -inis, f., anxiety.

sollicitus, -a, -um, agitated, alarmed, anxious.

solum, adv., only.

solus, -a, -um, alone.

solvo, solvi, solutum (3), tr., free, release; set sail.

sordes, -is, f., squalor, rags.

soror, -oris, f., sister.

sors, sortis, f., lot.

sortior, (4), dep., draw lots; appoint by lot, allot.

spatium, -i, n., space, period; walk.

spectaculum, -i, n., seat.

specto (1), tr., look at, observe.

specula, -ae, f., look-out, watchtower; in speculis, on the look out.

sperno, sprevi, spretum (3), tr., despise.

spero (1), tr., hope, hope for.

spes, spei, f., hope.

splendor, -oris, m., splendour, brilliance, lustre; good repute.

spoliatio, -onis, f., a being deprived of.

spolio (1), tr., rob, plunder.

spondeo, spopondi, sponsum (2), tr., pledge myself, promise.

sponte, adv., willingly.

squalor, -oris, m., squalor.

statim, adv., immediately.

statuo, statui, statutum (3), tr., decide, settle.

status, -us, m., condition; stability; position.

sterno, stravi, stratum (3), tr., prepare, arrange.

stilus, -i, m., pen.

stipendium, -i, n., pay, military service, campaign.

stipo (1), tr., surround, accompany.

stomachus, -i, m., irritation, anger.

studeo, studui (2), intr., am eager, take pains over, strive after.

studiosus, -a, -um, eager, zealous, assiduous.

studium, -i, n., enthusiasm, eagerness, goodwill; profession, philosophy; party spirit.

stultitia, -ae, f., stupidity.

stultus, -a, -um, foolish.

subeo, -ire, -ii, -itum, tr., undergo, submit to.

subitus, -a, -um, sudden.

sublevo (1), tr., alleviate, mitigate, lessen.

subscriptor, -oris, m., junior counsel.

subsidium, -i, n., help, support.

subtraho, -traxi, -tractum (3), tr., take away.

suburbanus, -a, -um, surrounding the city.

sufficio, -feci, -fectum (3), tr., substitute, supply.

suffoco (1), tr., strangle, suffocate.

suffragatio, -onis, f., a voting for, support.

suffragator, -oris, m., voter, supporter, partisan.

suffragium, -i, n., vote.

suffragor (1), dep., vote for, support.

sum, esse, fui, am.

summus, -a, -um, highest, greatest, most distinguished.

sumo, sumpsi, sumptum (3), *tr.*, assume, spend.

sumptus, -us, *m.*, expense; extravagance.

superbia, -ae, *f.*, pride, arrogance.

superbus, -a, -um, proud, arrogant; severe.

supero (1), *tr.*, conquer, defeat.

superstes, -itis, *m.*, witness.

supplex, -icis, *m.*, petitioner, suppliant.

supplico (1), *tr.*, beseech; worship.

supremus, -a, -um, last.

susceptio, -onis, *f.*, undertaking.

suscipio, -cepi, -ceptum (3), *tr.*, undertake, assume, incur.

suspicio, -onis, *f.*, suggestion; suspicion.

sustento (1), *tr.*, uphold, maintain, preserve.

sustineo, -tinui, -tentum (2), *tr.*, uphold, maintain, preserve.

suus, -a, -um, one's own, his own *etc.*

syngrapha, -ae, *f.*, written agreement.

taberna, -ae, *f.*, booth, block.

taceo (2), *intr.*, am silent.

tacitus, -a, -um, quiet, silent.

talis, -e, such.

tam, *adv.*, so, so much.

tamen, *adv.*, nevertheless, yet, however.

tametsi, *conj.*, even if.

tamquam, *adv.*, just as.

tandem, *adv.*, at length; *with questions and commands*, I ask you.

tantum, *adv.*, so much, only; tantum modo, *adv.*, only.

tantus, -a, -um, so great, so much; tanti, at so great a value.

tego, texi, tectum (3), *tr.*, protect.

telum, -i, *n.*, weapon.

temere, *adv.*, at random, rashly.

temperans, -ntis, temperate.

temperantia, -ae, *f.*, self-control.

temperatus, -a, -um, temperate.

tempestas, -atis, *f.*, weather, storm.

tempestivus, -a, -um, early.

tempus, -oris, *n.*, time, occasion.

teneo, tenui, tentum (2), *tr.*, hold, keep, uphold; *sc.* mente, understand.

tenuis, -e, slender, slight, trivial, petty, poor.

terra, -ae, *f.*, land.

terror, -oris, *m.*, terror, intimidation.

tertius, -a, -um, third.

testificatio, -onis, *f.*, a taking of depositions.

testis, -is, *c.*, witness.

testor (1), *dep.*, call to witness, testify.

tibicen, -inis, *m.*, flute-player.

timeo (2), *tr. and intr.*, fear, am afraid.

timidus, -a, -um, fearful, timid.

timor, -oris, *m.*, fear.

togatus, -a, -um, wearing the *toga.*

tollo, sustuli, sublatum (3), *tr.*, remove.

tot, *indecl. adj.*, so many.

totus, -a, -um, whole.

tracto (1), *tr.*, handle, use, employ.

trado, tradidi, traditum (3), *tr.*, hand over, hand on.

tranquillitas, -atis, *f.*, calmness, quiet, tranquillity.

transeo, -ire, -ii, -itum, *tr. and intr.*, cross.

transfero, -ferre, -tuli, -latum, *tr.*, transfer.

tribulis, -is, *m.*, fellow-tribesman.

tribunatus, -us, *m.*, tribunate.

tribunicius, -a, -um, of a tribune.

tribunus, -i, *m.*, tribune.

tribuo, tribui, tributum (3), *tr.*, assign, grant, give, attribute.

tribus, -us, *f.*, tribe.

tributim, *adv.*, by tribes.

triclinium, -i, *n.*, eating-couch.

triduum, -i, *n.*, a period of three days.

triennium, -i, *n.*, a period of three years.

trinus, -a, -um, triple, three.

tris, tria, three.

tristis, -e, sad, unhappy.

triumpho (1), *intr.*, triumph, exult.

triumphus, -i, *m.*, triumph.

trivium, -i, *n.*, cross-road.

trucido (1), *tr.*, slaughter.

tu, tui, *pron.*, you.

tueor, (2), *dep.*, watch over, guard, protect.

tum, *adv.*, then; cum ... tum, both ... and.

tumet, *intens. form of* tu.

tumultus, -us, *m.*, disturbance, war.

turba, -ae, *f.*, crowd.

turpis, -e, disgraceful, shameful.

turpitudo, -inis, *f.*, disgrace, dishonour, vileness.

tute, *intens. form of* tu.

tutela, -ae, *f.*, defence, protection, guardianship.

tutor, -oris, *m.*, guardian.

tuus, -a, -um, your.

ubi, *adv.*, where.

ullus, -a, -um, any.

ultimum, -i, *n.*, end, limit.

ultimus,-a,-um, furthest; earliest.

umbra, -ae, *f.*, shadow, shade.

umquam, *adv.*, ever.

una, *adv.*, together.

unde, *adv.*, whence.

universus, -a, -um, whole, entire; *pl.*, all.

unus, -a, -um, one.

urbanus, -a, -um, of the city.

urbs, urbis, *f.*, city.

usitatus, -a, -um, customary, usual, ordinary.

usquam, *adv.*, anywhere.

usque, *adv.*, so far.

usus, -us, *m.*, experience.

ut, *conj. and adv.*, as, how, when, in order that, so that, that.

uterque, utra-, utrum-, each of two.

utilitas, -atis, *f.*, usefulness, service, advantage, interest.

utor, usus (3), *dep.*, use.

utrum, *interrog. adv.*, whether.

valde, *adv.*, extremely, excessively.

valeo (2), *intr.*, am strong, powerful, important.

valetudo, -inis, *f.*, health (good or bad).

vallo (1), *tr.*, protect, defend.

varius, -a, -um, different.

vas, vasis, *n.*, (*pl.*, vasa, -orum), dish, vessel.

vastitas, -atis, *f.*, a laying waste, state of devastation; devastator.

vehemens, -ntis, vehement, forcible, vigorous, violent.

vehementer, *adv.*, strongly, extremely.

vel, *adv. and conj.,* even, or; *with superl.,* the very . . . est; **vel** . . . **vel,** either . . . or.

venia, -ae, *f.,* pardon.

venio, veni, ventum (4), *intr.,* come.

venter, -tris, *m.,* belly.

verbose, *adv.,* with many words.

verbosus, -a, -um, long-winded.

verbum, -i, *n.,* word.

vere, *adv.,* truly, justly.

vereor (2), *dep.,* fear.

veritas, -atis, *f.,* truth.

vero, *adv.,* in truth, but.

versor (1), *dep.,* am occupied with, concern, am concerned in.

verto, verti, versum (3), *tr. and intr.,* turn.

verum, *part.,* but yet, but.

verus, -a, -um, true, right, fair.

vester, -tra, -trum, your.

vestigium, -i, *n.,* trace.

vetus, -eris, old.

vetustas, -atis, *f.,* old age, antiquity.

vexo (1), *tr.,* harass.

via, -ae, *f.,* road, way.

vicarius, -i, *m.,* substitute, deputy.

vicinitas, -atis, *f.,* neighbourhood.

vicinus, -i, *m.,* neighbour.

vicissitudo, -inis, *f.,* alternation.

victor, -oris, *m.,* victor.

victoria, -ae, *f.,* victory.

video, vidi, visum (2), *tr.,* see; *pass.,* seem, seem right.

vigilanter, *adv.,* watchfully.

vigilo (1), *intr.,* keep awake, watch.

vinco, vici, victum (3), *tr.,* overcome, conquer.

vinculum, -i, *n.,* chain, bond, link.

vindico (1), *tr.,* lay legal claim to.

violo (1), *tr.,* injure, outrage, violate.

vir, viri, *m.,* man.

virgo, -inis, *f.,* virgin, girl.

virtus, -utis, *f.,* strength, vigour, goodness, merit, bravery, virtue.

vis, *acc.,* **vim,** *abl.,* **vi,** *pl.,* **vires,** *f.,* force, power; quantity; **vi,** by storm.

vita, -ae, *f.,* life, way of life.

vitiosus, -a, -um, bad, corrupt, vicious.

vitium, -i, *n.,* fault, vice.

vito (1), *tr.,* avoid.

vitricus, -i, *m.,* step-father.

vitupero (1), *tr.,* blame, censure.

vivo, vixi, victum (3), *intr.,* live.

vivus, -a, -um, alive.

vix, *adv.,* scarcely, hardly.

voco (1), *tr.,* call.

volgo, *adv.,* openly, publicly, indiscriminately.

volgus, -i, *m.,* the people, public.

volo, velle, volui, *tr.,* wish, wish for, am willing.

voltus, -us, *m.,* looks, expression, aspect.

voluntas, -atis, *f.,* will, wish, goodwill.

voluptas, -atis, *f.,* pleasure.

vox, vocis, *f.,* voice, speech, spoken word.